Centrality Metrics for Complex Network Analysis:

Emerging Research and Opportunities

Natarajan Meghanathan
Jackson State University, USA

A volume in the Advances in
Wireless Technologies and
Telecommunication (AWTT) Book
Series

Published in the United States of America by
    IGI Global
    Information Science Reference (an imprint of IGI Global)
    701 E. Chocolate Avenue
    Hershey PA, USA 17033
    Tel: 717-533-8845
    Fax: 717-533-8661
    E-mail: cust@igi-global.com
    Web site: http://www.igi-global.com

Library of Congress Cataloging-in-Publication Data

Names: Meghanathan, Natarajan, 1977- author.
Title: Centrality metrics for complex network analysis : emerging research
  and opportunities / by Natarajan Meghanathan.
Description: Hershey, PA : Information Science Reference, [2018]
Identifiers: LCCN 2017022538l ISBN 9781522538028 (hardcover) l ISBN
  9781522538035 (ebook)
Subjects: LCSH: Telecommunication systems--Mathematical models. l System
  analysis--Graphic methods. l Centrality (Mathematics)
Classification: LCC TK5102.83 .M44 2018 l DDC 511/.5--dc23 LC record available at https://lccn.
loc.gov/2017022538

This book is published in the IGI Global book series Advances in Wireless Technologies and Telecommunication (AWTT) (ISSN: 2327-3305; eISSN: 2327-3313)

British Cataloguing in Publication Data
A Cataloguing in Publication record for this book is available from the British Library.

All work contributed to this book is new, previously-unpublished material.
The views expressed in this book are those of the authors, but not necessarily of the publisher.

For electronic access to this publication, please contact: eresources@igi-global.com.

Advances in Wireless Technologies and Telecommunication (AWTT) Book Series

ISSN:2327-3305
EISSN:2327-3313

Editor-in-Chief: Xiaoge Xu, Xiamen University Malaysia, Malaysia

MISSION

The wireless computing industry is constantly evolving, redesigning the ways in which individuals share information. Wireless technology and telecommunication remain one of the most important technologies in business organizations. The utilization of these technologies has enhanced business efficiency by enabling dynamic resources in all aspects of society.

The **Advances in Wireless Technologies and Telecommunication Book Series** aims to provide researchers and academic communities with quality research on the concepts and developments in the wireless technology fields. Developers, engineers, students, research strategists, and IT managers will find this series useful to gain insight into next generation wireless technologies and telecommunication.

COVERAGE

- Virtual Network Operations
- Wireless Technologies
- Broadcasting
- Digital Communication
- Mobile Web Services
- Wireless Broadband
- Mobile Technology
- Cellular Networks
- Mobile Communications
- Global Telecommunications

IGI Global is currently accepting manuscripts for publication within this series. To submit a proposal for a volume in this series, please contact our Acquisition Editors at Acquisitions@igi-global.com or visit: http://www.igi-global.com/publish/.

Titles in this Series

For a list of additional titles in this series, please visit:
https://www.igi-global.com/book-series/advances-wireless-technologies-telecommunication/73684

Affordability Issues Surrounding the Use of ICT for Development and Poverty Reduction
Sam Takavarasha Jr. (University of Fort Hare, South Africa & University of Zimbabwe, Zimbabwe) and Carl Adams (University of Portsmuth, UK)
Information Science Reference • ©2018 • 319pp • H/C (ISBN: 9781522531791) • US $195.00

Handbook of Research on Environmental Policies for Emergency Management and ...
Augustine Nduka Eneanya (University of Lagos, Nigeria)
Engineering Science Reference • ©2018 • 393pp • H/C (ISBN: 9781522531944) • US $295.00

Positioning and Navigation in Complex Environments
Kegen Yu (Wuhan University, China)
Information Science Reference • ©2018 • 577pp • H/C (ISBN: 9781522535287) • US $195.00

Examining Cloud Computing Technologies Through the Internet of Things
Pradeep Tomar (Gautam Buddha University, India) and Gurjit Kaur (Gautam Buddha University, India)
Information Science Reference • ©2018 • 311pp • H/C (ISBN: 9781522534457) • US $215.00

Advanced Mobile Technologies for Secure Transaction Processing Emerging Research ...
Raghvendra Kumar (LNCT Group of Colleges, India) Preeta Sharan (The Oxford College of Engineering, India) and Aruna Devi (Surabhi Software, India)
Information Science Reference • ©2018 • 177pp • H/C (ISBN: 9781522527596) • US $130.00

Examining Developments and Applications of Wearable Devices in Modern Society
Saul Emanuel Delabrida Silva (Federal University of Ouro Preto, Brazil) Ricardo Augusto Rabelo Oliveira (Federal University of Ouro Preto, Brazil) and Antonio Alfredo Ferreira Loureiro (Federal University of Minas Gerais (UFMG), Brazil)
Information Science Reference • ©2018 • 330pp • H/C (ISBN: 9781522532903) • US $195.00

For an entire list of titles in this series, please visit:
https://www.igi-global.com/book-series/advances-wireless-technologies-telecommunication/73684

701 East Chocolate Avenue, Hershey, PA 17033, USA
Tel: 717-533-8845 x100 • Fax: 717-533-8661
E-Mail: cust@igi-global.com • www.igi-global.com

Table of Contents

Preface

INTRODUCTION

Network Science is about analyzing complex networks from a graph theory perspective and is an emerging discipline within the realm of Data Science. We model a network as a graph with the vertices representing the nodes and the edges representing the links between the nodes. Throughout the book, we will be using the terms 'network' and 'graph', 'node' and 'vertex' as well as 'link' and 'edge' interchangeably. They mean the same unless explicitly differentiated. The centrality of a node (or an edge) is a quantitative measure of the importance of the node (or the edge) with respect to its position in the topological structure of the network. Centrality is the most commonly and widely used metric for complex network analysis. The four commonly used node centrality metrics are the degree (DEG), eigenvector (EVC), betweenness (BWC) and closeness centrality (CLC) metrics; the two commonly studied edge centrality metrics are edge betweenness centrality (EBWC) and neighborhood overlap (NOVER). In this book, we will analyze the above node and edge centrality metrics in greater detail.

This is one of the very few books to comprehensively discuss both node and edge centrality metrics as well as their diverse applications. Most of the research in the literature revolves around the node centrality metrics that are computed based on the global knowledge of the network. There has been very limited work on centrality metrics that can be locally computed (with just the one hop or two hop neighborhood information) at both the node and edge levels. In this book, we will motivate the need to start focusing on computationally light localized centrality metrics that could be used to rank the vertices and edges in lieu of the computationally heavy global centrality metrics. In this pursuit, we make use of the notions of the egocentric network of a node and the egocentric network of an edge, both of which have been hitherto not explored to their fullest potential.

Some of the emerging opportunities based on the research advances presented in this book are as follows: With the identification of computationally-light localized alternatives for the computationally-heavy global knowledge-based centrality metrics, we could now adapt several of the existing communication network protocols and algorithms that are based on the latter. With the notion of egocentric network of an edge, a suite of edge centrality metrics (in addition to the ones discussed in this book) could be developed in order to fill the void in this category (a majority of the centrality metrics in the literature are at the node level and very few exist at the edge level). We also opine the book to be useful for developers and administrators of social networks as several characteristics of social networks (e.g., recommendation for new contacts/ friends, receiving and sharing of information through friends/followers, friends of friends, and etc) are dependent on the notions of localized computationally-light centrality metrics such as neighborhood overlap and local clustering coefficient complement-based degree centrality.

ORGANIZATION OF THE BOOK

The book has a total of seven chapters. The first chapter gives a detailed description of a suite of node and edge centrality metrics and their computation procedures; the chapter also explains the procedures to compute three different levels of correlation measures as well as introduces the 50 real-world networks analyzed in the rest of the chapters. Chapters 2-3 focus on the correlation study of the centrality metrics: Chapter 2 identifies the most appropriate computationally-light centrality metric for each of the computationally-heavy centrality metrics with respect to the three levels of correlation. Chapter 3 analyzes the assortativity of the real-world networks with respect to the four common node-based centrality metrics. Chapter 4 explores the temporal variation of the four centrality metrics (DEG, BWC, EVC and CLC) during the evolution of a scale-free network under the well-known Barabasi-Albert model. Chapters 5-7 present case studies that illustrate the diverse applications of centrality metrics spanning domains such as sensor networks, cyber security and curriculum networks. Chapter 5 introduces the notion of egocentric network of an edge and adapts graph theoretic metrics such as bipartivity index and algebraic connectivity (computed on the egocentric network of an edge) to quantify the stability of the links in a mobile sensor network without knowing the location and mobility information of the nodes. Chapter 6 presents an application of the eigenvector centrality metric in the area of cyber security to trace the trajectory of a mobile radioactive dispersal device in a region deployed with sensor nodes. Chapter 7 presents the application of the betweenness centrality metric along with other network measures and the topological sort algorithm to quantify the relative contribution of the courses in a curriculum network graph (a directed acyclic graph). We now briefly describe the contributions of each of the chapters.

Contributions of the Chapters

Chapter 1, "Node and Edge Centrality Metrics, Correlation Measures, and Real-World Network Graphs," presents a detailed description of the commonly studied node cand edge centrality metrics: DEG, EVC, BWC, CLC, EBWC and NOVER. In addition, the chapter presents a hybrid node centrality metric called local clustering coefficient complement-based degree centrality (LCC'DC) that incorporates the features of node betweenness and degree. For each of these centrality metrics, we present their underlying purpose, computation algorithm and its time-complexity as well as illustrate the computation using a running example graph. The Pearson's correlation measure is the most commonly used correlation measure to evaluate the correlation between centrality metrics. The Pearson's correlation coefficient for two centrality metrics X and Y is a measure of how well we could predict (using linear regression) the values for centrality metric Y using the values for centrality metric X. However, one of the emerging research trends in the literature is to explore the correlation between centrality metrics at different levels (in addition to the linear regression-based prediction). The two correlation levels that are of interest are: network-wide ranking and pair-wise comparison. The Spearman's correlation measure is a measure of the similarity in the network-wide ranking of the vertices with respect to two different centrality metrics. The Kendall's correlation measure is a measure of the similarity in the pair-wise ranking (a.k.a. concordance) of the vertices. Chapter 1 presents a detailed discussion of the Spearman's, Kendall's and Pearson's correlation measures and illustrates their computation procedures along with a running example. Finally, Chapter 1 presents a brief overview of the 50 real-world networks of diverse degree distribution and characteristics (spanning different domains such as friendship networks, collaboration networks, biological networks, etc.) that are analyzed in some of the chapters of this book.

A majority of the centrality metrics are computationally-heavy (i.e., take a significant amount of time, especially for networks with a larger number of nodes and/or edges) and also require the global network knowledge for their computation. One of the emerging research trends is to develop centrality metrics that are computationally-light and would not require the global knowledge of the network for their computation. The LCC'DC node centrality metric is one such latest development in the literature. The degree centrality metric has been hitherto considered the only computationally-light centrality metric that could be used in lieu of the computationally-heavy BWC, EVC and CLC metrics. In Chapter 2, "Correlation Analysis Between Computationally Light and Computationally Heavy Centrality Metrics," we revisit the correlation analysis involving the computationally-light metrics (DEG and LCC'DC) vs. the computationally-heavy node centrality metrics (BWC, EVC and CLC) at the three different levels of correlation (network-wide ranking, pair-wise concordance and linear regression-based predictoin) computed on the suite of 50 real-world network graphs. Contrary to the current perception, we observe the LCC'DC metric to be very strongly correlated (even stronger than DEG) with BWC with respect to all the three levels of correlation. We also observe the Kendall's correlation coefficient to serve as the lower bound for correlation coefficient for correlation study involving computationally-light vs. heavy node centrality metrics. We also analyze the correlation between EBWC and NOVER (edge centrality metrics) and observe the computationally-light NOVER could be more appropriately used to rank the edges in lieu of the computationally-heavy EBWC; but NOVER might not be appropriate to be used as an alternative (for EBWC) for pair-wise concordance or linear regression-based prediction. The stronger rank-based correlation between EBWC and NOVER could be exploited by the community detection algorithms for complex networks to process the edges on the basis of their NOVER values in lieu of EBWC.

Assortativity of a complex network is a measure of the similarity between the end vertices of the edges with respect to a node-level metric. The centrality metric that has been traditionally used in the literature to analyze the assortativity of complex networks is the remaining degree (R-DEG) centrality metric, which is simply one less than the degree centrality metric. Until now, the assortativity of the edges has been simply computed as the Pearson's correlation coefficient (referred to as assortativity index) of the R-DEG values of the end vertices of the edges. In Chapter 3, "Centrality-Based Assortativity Analysis of Complex Network Graphs," we analyze the assortativity of the suite of 50 real-world network graphs with respect to four different centrality metrics: R-DEG, EVC, BWC and CLC. We observe real-world networks to be more likely to be neutral with respect to R-DEG and BWC, and more likely to be assortitative with respect to EVC and CLC.

Thus, EVC and CLC could be preferred as the node-level metrics for maximal assortative matching of the edges, whereas BWC and R-DEG could be preferred as the node-level metrics for maximal node matching of the edges. We also observe the ranking of the real-world networks with respect to R-DEG based assortativity index values to exhibit a strong similarity (larger values for the Spearman's correlation coefficient) to the BWC based assortativity index values. Likewise, we observe a strong correlation between the ranking of the real-world networks with respect to the CLC and EVC-based assortativity index values.

Scale-free networks follow a power-law pattern with respect to the degree distribution of the vertices. This could be attributed to the preferential attachment phenomenon during the evolution of these networks: a newly joining node is more likely to attach to few selected nodes compared to the rest of the nodes. The Barabasi-Albert (BA) model is one of the commonly studied synthetic model to simulate the evolution of scale-free networks. According to the BA model, nodes with larger degree are more likely to be the candidate nodes that are selected to be connected to a newly joining node. As a result, at the end of the network evolution, there are a few nodes with significantly larger degree and the rest of the nodes have a very low degree (thus contributing to the power-law nature of the degree distribution). The current status of the literature is that the temporal variation in the degree centrality of the vertices under the BA model has been studied and it has been observed to depict a "concave down" pattern of increase with time. In Chapter 4, "Temporal Variation of the Node Centrality Metrics for Scale-Free Networks," we study the temporal variation in the values for the other commonly studied centrality metrics (BWC, EVC and CLC) during the evolution of a scale-free network under the BA model. We do not observe these three centrality metrics to exhibit a similar pattern of increase as that of the DEG centrality metric. We observe the BWC metric to exhibit a "concave up" pattern of increase and the CLC metric to exhibit a "linear" increase with time. On the other hand, we observe the EVC metric to exhibit a "concave up" pattern of decrease with time. The results of this chapter (about the pattern and rate of increase/decrease of the prominent centrality measures with time) present opportunities for future research to decide the appropriate values for the parameters to be used in the various generation models for studying the evolution of scale-free networks and for designing scale-free networks that should exhibit a certain distribution of the centrality measures of the nodes.

Mobile sensor networks is a newly emerging paradigm of wireless sensor networks in which the sensor nodes are considered to move independent of each other. Wireless sensor networks (WSNs) have been traditionally considered to comprise of static sensor nodes (that are fixed to a particular location); the data sensed by these sensor nodes are aggregated with the aid of network-wide spanning communication topologies towards the sink node. The communication topology typically employed for data aggregation in WSNs is a data gathering tree owing to its energy efficiency (due to the involvement of the minimal number of links needed to connect all the nodes). However, such communication topologies may not exist for a long time in mobile sensor networks due to the dynamically changing positions of the sensor nodes. Two sensor nodes may not be within the transmission range of each other throughout the duration of the network session. To avoid frequent reconfiguration of the communication topology for data aggregation, it becomes imperative to quantify the stability of the links in a mobile sensor network and incorporate only stable links (that could exist for a longer time) as part of the communication topology. As the area of mobile sensor networks is still in its early stages of research and development, strategies from a related area called mobile ad hoc networks have been heavily borrowed for determining stable communication topologies. Among such strategies, the approach of predicting the link expiration time using the mobility and location information of the nodes has been observed to yield relatively stable links. However, it would be too much of an energy drain to expect the sensor nodes to be location and mobility aware. In Chapter 5, "Edge Centrality Metrics to Quantify the Stability of Links for Mobile Sensor Networks," we explore the use of graph theoretic metrics such as bipartivity index (BPI) and algebraic connectivity (ALGC) that are traditionally computed on an entire network to quantify the stability of links in a mobile sensor network. We propose to determine these metrics (as edge centrality metrics) on the so-called egocentric network of an edge (comprising of the end nodes of an edge and their neighbors as vertices and the links incident on the end nodes as edges) that could be independently and identically constructed by the end nodes of an edge without requiring the location and mobility information of the nodes. We also use the neighborhood overlap (NOVER) metric as the third edge centrality metric to quantify the stability of links. We observe the NOVER, BPI and ALGC-based data gathering trees to be relatively more stable than that of the LET-based data gathering trees. The idea of location and mobility independent edge centrality metrics to quantify the stability of links in mobile sensor networks could open new avenues of research for determining stable topologies in dynamically changing communication networks.

Mobile target tracking is a widely researched topic under the realm of intrusion detection/cyber security. In Chapter 6, "Use of Eigenvector Centrality for Mobile Target Tracking," we focus on tracking a mobile radioactive dispersal device (RDD) that is moving randomly in an open field deployed with wireless sensor nodes. These sensor nodes are assumed to be able to detect the radioactive signals and quantify their strength along with the other signals emanating from the background. The sensor nodes periodically report the cumulative strength of the sensed signals to a control center (sink). The sink is assumed to know the topology of the static wireless sensor network and quantifies the weight of a link at any time as the sum of the latest signal strengths reported by the end nodes of the link. The sink periodically predicts the location of a mobile RDD by computing the eigenvector centrality (EVC) of the adjacency matrix of the wireless sensor network (with the link weights quantified as mentioned above). The top 5 nodes that incur the largest EVC are considered to constitute the neighborhood around which the mobile RDD could be located. This is the first such approach in using EVC for mobile target tracking and we are confident that the research idea introduced in this chapter could open new research proposals towards using EVC and other centrality measures for intrusion detection.

Chapter 7, "Use of Centrality Metrics for Ranking of Courses Based on Their Relative Contribution in a Curriculum Network Graph," presents an application on the use of centrality metrics for directed acyclic graphs (DAG). The curriculum network graph (CNG) is a DAG in which the courses are the nodes and there exists an edge $u \rightarrow v$ if course u is a pre-requisite for course v. The overall assessment of the courses in a curriculum is a classical problem faced by academic institutions. In Chapter 8, we propose a novel approach of using centrality metrics along with the level number of the vertices in a topological sort of the CNG as the basis to quantify the relative contribution of the courses in the CNG. The relative contribution scores of the courses could be considered the weights of the courses (the weights add up to 1) so that the overall assessment score for the curriculum could be computed as the weighted average of the assessment scores of the individual courses. Ours is the first approach to quantify the contribution of the courses in a curriculum on the basis of the topological structure of the CNG. We observe the betweenness centrality metric to play a significant role in deciding the relative contribution scores of the courses in a CNG. The research strategy proposed in this chapter could be adopted for curriculum assessment as well as for many such academic requirements that should consider all the courses in a curriculum, but with weights proportional to their topological significance in the CNG.

CONCLUSION

The book could be useful for both students and faculty researchers. It could serve as a good research-oriented reference for graduate students in disciplines such as Computer/Computational Science, Computer/Computational Engineering, Data Science and etc. The book covers all the essential elements of a course in the Network Science track of a graduate curriculum and hence could be used as a prescribed book for any special topics course on centrality metrics for complex network analysis. To the best of our knowledge, we have not come across a research-oriented book that exclusively focuses on centrality metrics and at the same time illustrates their broader applications for different categories of networks (like wireless sensor networks, curriculum networks, cyber security and etc.). We are confident that the book will be a comprehensive reference for both beginners and experienced researchers to explore the emerging research opportunities involving centrality metrics for complex network analysis.

Natarajan Meghanathan
Jackson State University, USA

Acknowledgment

The author acknowledges the collaboration with the following researchers in the area of Network Science.

Andras Farago, *The University of Texas at Dallas, USA*

Bhadrachalam Chitturi, *Amrita University, India*

Danda Rawat, *Howard University, USA*

Krishnaiyan Thulasiraman, *University of Oklahoma, USA*

Madhave Marathe, *Virginia Tech, USA*

Mohammed S. Khan, *Texas A&M University – Kingsville, USA*

Saroja Kanchi, *Kettering University, USA*

Yenumula Reddy, *Grambling State University, USA*

Chapter 1

Centrality Metrics, Measures, and Real-World Network Graphs:
Node and Edge Centrality Metrics, Correlation Measures, and Real-World Network Graphs

ABSTRACT

This chapter provides an introduction to various node and edge centrality metrics that are studied throughout this book. The authors describe the procedure to compute these metrics and illustrate the same with an example. The node centrality metrics described are degree centrality (DEG), eigenvector centrality (EVC), betweenness centrality (BWC), closeness centrality (CLC), and the local clustering coefficient complement-based degree centrality (LCC'DC). The edge centrality metrics described are edge betweenness centrality (EBWC) and neighborhood overlap (NOVER). The authors then describe the three different correlation measures—Pearson's, Spearman's, and Kendall's measures—that are used in this book to analyze the correlation between any two centrality metrics. Finally, the authors provide a brief description of the 50 real-world network graphs that are studied in some of the chapters of this book.

DOI: 10.4018/978-1-5225-3802-8.ch001

1. INTRODUCTION

This book presents an exclusive discussion of the state-of-the-art research on centrality metrics for complexity analysis. Centrality metrics capture the topological significance of a node (a.k.a. vertex) or a link (a.k.a. edge) with respect to one or more criteria (Newman, 2010; Shavitt & Singer, 2007; Fletcher & Wennekers, 2018). The node centrality metrics that are considered in this book could be categorized as neighborhood-based and shortest path-based metrics. The neighborhood-based metrics considered are Degree Centrality (DEG) (Newman, 2010) and Eigenvector Centrality (EVC) (Bonacich, 1987); the shortest path-based metrics considered are Betweenness Centrality (BWC) (Freeman, 1977) and Closeness Centrality (CLC) (Freeman, 1979). In addition to the two categories of centrality metrics, we also have a hybrid centrality metric called localized clustering coefficient complement-based degree centrality (LCC'DC) (Meghanathan, 2017) that incorporates features of both the degree and shortest path-based centrality metrics. The edge centrality metrics that are considered in this book could be categorized as those computed based on the global network knowledge (edge betweenness centrality, EBWC) (Girvan & Newman, 2002) and those computed based on the local neighborhood knowledge (neighborhood overlap, NOVER) (Easley & Kleinberg, 2010).

Certain chapters in this book focus on the correlation analysis of the centrality metrics. Three different correlation measures (Triola, 2012) are used: the pair-wise Kendall's concordance-based measure, the network-wide Spearman's rank-based measure and the linear regression-based Pearson's correlation measure. Correlation analysis of the node and edge centrality metrics is conducted in Chapter 2 to identify the computationally-light metrics that could be used in lieu of the computationally-heavy metrics. For analysis purposes, we need network data on which the centrality metrics could be computed and the correlation could be studied. In this regard, we will use a suite of 50 real-world networks of diverse degree distributions.

The rest of the chapter is organized as follows: Sections 2 and 3 provide respectively a detailed discussion of the five node centrality metrics and the two edge centrality metrics. Section 4 describes the three correlation measures and their computation using a running example graph. Section 5 introduces the 50 real-world networks used in the correlation study. Section 6 provides a brief outline for the rest of the chapters in this book. Throughout this book, the terms 'node' and 'vertex', 'link' and 'edge', 'network' and 'graph', 'centrality metric' and 'centrality measure' are used interchangeably. They mean the same.

2. NODE CENTRALITY METRICS

In this section, we describe the notion behind the five node centrality metrics (degree centrality: DEG, eigenvector centrality: EVC, betweenness centrality: BWC, closeness centrality: CLC and local clustering coefficient complement-based degree centrality: LCC'DC), their computation procedures and their theoretical computational time complexities as well as illustrate their computation with a running example graph. While the EVC and LCC'DC values range from 0 to 1, there are no upper or lower bounds for the values of the DEG, BWC and CLC metrics. Table 1 presents an outline of the classification of the centrality metrics to the three categories (neighborhood-based, shortest path-based and hybrid: that encompasses the features of both neighborhood-based and shortest path-based metrics).

2.1 Degree Centrality

The degree centrality (DEG) of a vertex is the number of neighbors incident on the vertex. Figure 1 presents the degree centrality of the vertices in the running example graph. One could compute the degree centrality of a vertex by counting the number of edges incident on that vertex. For a graph of V vertices and E edges, the theoretical time complexity to compute DEG is $\Theta(V+E)$.

Degree centrality is the most computationally-light metric among the centrality metrics that are covered in this book. However, a key weakness associated with the degree centrality metric is that the values are integer-based

Table 1. Classification of the centrality metrics

Node Centrality Metric	Neighborhood-Based	Shortest Path-Based	Hybrid
Degree Centrality (DEG)	X		
Eigenvector Centrality (EVC)	X		
Betweenness Centrality (BWC)		X	
Closeness Centrality (CLC)		X	
Local Clustering Coefficient Complement-based Degree Centrality (LCC'DC)			X

Figure 1. Degree centrality of the vertices in an example graph

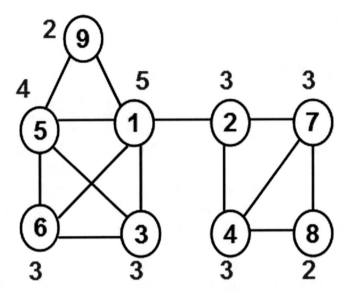

and two or more vertices could have identical values for degree centrality (for example, in Figure 1, five of the nine vertices have a degree centrality of 3). Because of this inherent weakness, degree centrality is not a viable alternative to rank the vertices in the network in lieu of the computationally-heavy centrality metrics.

2.2 Eigenvector Centrality

The eigenvector centrality (EVC) of a vertex is a measure of the degree of the vertex as well as the degree of its neighbors (Bonacich, 1987). We could use the power-iteration algorithm (Lay, 2011) to determine the EVC of the vertices in a network. The algorithm starts with an estimated EVC column vector of all 1s and goes through a sequence of iterations by multiplying the adjacency matrix (an entry $A[v_i, v_j] = 1$ if there is an between the two vertices v_i and v_j; otherwise, $A[v_i, v_j] = 0$) of the graph with an updated EVC column vector in each iteration. In each iteration, we update the EVC column vector as follows: We multiply the adjacency matrix of the graph with the EVC column vector at the end of the previous iteration and obtain a temporary product column vector. The EVC column vector for the next iteration is the normalized version of the product column vector. We continue the iterations until the entries in the EVC column vector between successive iterations converge to a certain level of decimal precision. The EVC column vector at the time of convergence is referred to as the principal eigenvector and the entries in this vector correspond to the eigenvector centrality of the vertices. The normalized value for the principal eigenvector is referred to as the spectral radius for the network graph, and it is bounded between the maximum and minimum degrees of the vertices in the graph.

The time complexity of the power-iteration algorithm is $\Theta(V^3)$ as we do $\Theta(V^2)$ multiplications in each iteration and one would need to proceed for at most V iterations for convergence. Figure 2 presents the computation of the EVC of the vertices in the running example graph. Consider the two vertices 8 and 9 that have the same degree, but have different EVC values. This could be attributed to vertex 9 having two neighbors (vertices 1 and 5) that have a larger DEG and EVC values, whereas the two neighbors of vertex 8 (vertices 4 and 7) have relatively lower DEG and EVC values.

2.3 Betweenness Centrality

The betweenness centrality (BWC) of a vertex is a measure of the number of shortest paths between any two vertices that go through the vertex (Freeman, 1977). We calculate the BWC of a vertex v_i as follows:

Figure 2. Eigenvector centrality of the vertices in an example graph

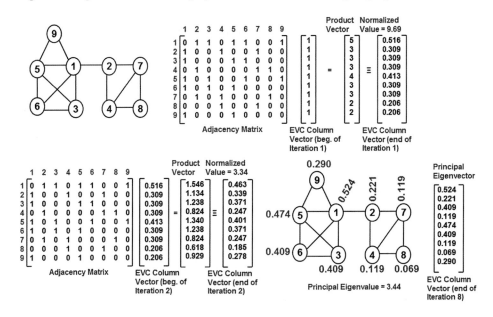

5

$$BWC(v_i) = \sum_{\substack{v_j \neq v_i \\ v_k \neq v_i}} \frac{\# sp_{v_i}(v_j, v_k)}{\# sp(v_j, v_k)},$$

where $\# sp(v_j, v_k)$ is the total number of shortest paths between vertices v_j and v_k, and $\# sp_{v_i}(v_j, v_k)$ is the number of such shortest paths from v_j to v_k that go through v_i. We sum the $\# sp_{v_i}(v_j, v_k) / \# sp(v_j, v_k)$ across all pairs of vertices v_j and v_k (where $v_j \neq v_i$ and $v_k \neq v_i$).

BWC is a computationally-heavy metric and the most fundamental as well as the most efficient algorithm known so far to compute the metric is the Brandes' algorithm (2011). We now briefly describe a Breadth First Search (BFS)-based implementation (Cormen et al., 2009) of the Brandes' algorithm. We determine the BFS trees for each vertex v_i (v_i is also the root of such a BFS tree). The level number of a vertex v_j in the BFS tree rooted at v_i is the number of edges on the (shortest) path from v_i to v_j in the tree. A vertex v_y is a immediate predecessor of a vertex v_x in a BFS tree rooted at v_i if there is an edge (v_x, v_y) in the original graph and the level number of v_x is one more than the level number of v_y in the tree. The number of shortest paths from the root v_i to itself is considered to be 1. The number of shortest paths from the root v_i to some other node v_j is the sum of the number of shortest paths from v_i to the immediate predecessors of v_j in the BFS tree rooted at v_i. We use the above procedure to calculate the number of shortest paths between any two vertices. Due to the graph being undirected, the number of shortest paths from v_i to v_j is the same as the number of shortest paths from v_j to v_i. The number of shortest paths from v_j to v_k that go through v_i (i.e., $\# sp_{v_i}(v_j, v_k)$) is then computed as the product of the number of shortest paths from v_j to v_i and the number of shortest paths from v_k to v_i. Figure 3 illustrates the computation of the BWC of the vertices in the running example graph. To avoid cluttering, we show only the non-zero shortest path fractions incurred for the vertices.

The time complexity of the BFS-based implementation to compute the BWC of the vertices would be $\Theta(V^2 + VE)$ as we would need to run BFS of time complexity $\Theta(V+E)$ starting from each vertex, requiring a total of V BFS runs. Note that to compute the BWC of a particular vertex, we need to know the fractions $\# sp_{v_i}(v_j, v_k) / \# sp(v_j, v_k)$ for all pairs of vertices v_j and v_k (where $v_j \neq v_i$ and $v_k \neq v_i$). This would require us to compute the BFS trees rooted at every vertex in the graph even if we want to compute the BWC of

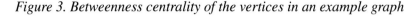

Figure 3. Betweenness centrality of the vertices in an example graph

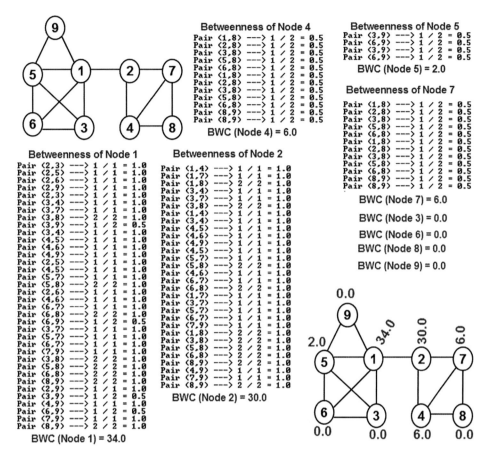

only one or few vertices (and not for all the vertices) in the graph. All of these motivate us to explore computationally-light alternatives for BWC as part of future research.

2.4 Closeness Centrality

The closeness centrality (CLC) of a vertex is a measure of the distance (number of hops on the shortest path) of the vertex to the rest of the vertices in the network and could be computed by running the BFS algorithm starting from the vertex. The CLC of a vertex is the inverse of the sum of the level numbers (which also corresponds to the distance: the number of hops on the shortest paths) of the rest of the vertices in its BFS tree. We take the inverse of the sum to maintain the convention that larger the centrality value for a vertex, more important is the vertex. Figure 4 illustrates the distance matrix of the vertices in the running example graph. Vertex 1 is the closest to the rest of the vertices in the network (the sum of the distances is the lowest value, 12, and its inverse is the largest) and hence has the largest CLC value of 0.083.

The computation time complexity for one run of BFS is $\Theta(V+E)$ and to run it on V vertices, it would take $\Theta(V^2+VE)$ time. Nevertheless, the CLC metric is relatively less time consuming than the BWC metric as there is not much post-processing work (like finding the shortest path fractions for any two pairs of vertices in the case of BWC) to do after we run the BFS algorithm. Also, unlike BWC, the CLC of a vertex could be computed independent of the other vertices in the network by just running BFS only from that vertex.

Figure 4. Closeness centrality of the vertices in an example graph

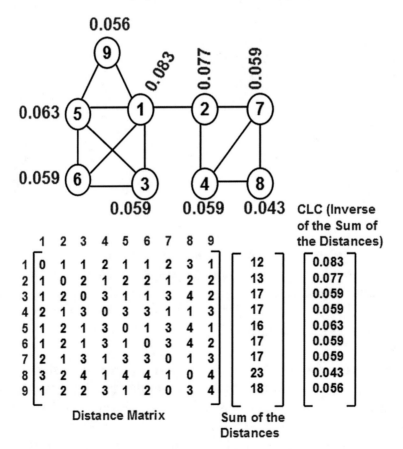

2.5 Localized Clustering Coefficient Complement-Based Degree Centrality

The localized clustering coefficient (LCC) of a vertex is the probability that any two neighbors of the vertex are connected (Newman, 2010). The LCC of a vertex (ranges from 0 to 1) is thus the ratio of the actual number of links between any two neighbors of the vertex and the maximum possible number of links between the neighbors of the vertex. If none of the neighbors of a vertex are not directly connected (i.e., not directly reachable from each other), then the LCC of a vertex is 0.0. If such vertices also have a high degree centrality, then several vertex pairs in the neighborhood of the vertex need to go through the vertex for shortest path communication. We anticipate the BWC of such vertices to be high and has been verified in a prior work (Meghanathan, 2017). The centrality metric related to this idea is called the Localized Clustering Coefficient Complement-based Degree Centrality (LCC'DC) and is computed for a vertex v_i as $(1-LCC(v_i))*DEG(v_i)$. The larger the degree centrality of a vertex and lower its LCC, the larger the LCC'DC of the vertex. Unlike BWC, the LCC'DC of a vertex could be computed locally (just based on the knowledge of the two-hop neighborhood) and only for the vertex of interest. Hence, we claim LCC'DC to be a computationally-light alternative to rank the vertices in lieu of BWC. Figure 4 presents the computation of the LCC'DC values of the vertices in the running example graph.

3. EDGE CENTRALITY METRICS

In this section, we describe the edge centrality metrics that capture the importance of an edge on the basis of their location on the shortest paths

Figure 5. LCC'DC of the vertices in an example graph

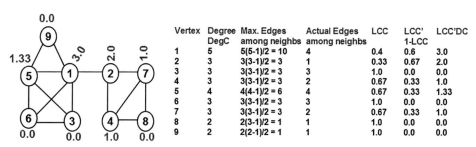

Vertex	Degree DegC	Max. Edges among neighbs	Actual Edges among neighbs	LCC	LCC' 1-LCC	LCC'DC
1	5	5(5-1)/2 = 10	4	0.4	0.6	3.0
2	3	3(3-1)/2 = 3	1	0.33	0.67	2.0
3	3	3(3-1)/2 = 3	3	1.0	0.0	0.0
4	3	3(3-1)/2 = 3	2	0.67	0.33	1.0
5	4	4(4-1)/2 = 6	4	0.67	0.33	1.33
6	3	3(3-1)/2 = 3	3	1.0	0.0	0.0
7	3	3(3-1)/2 = 3	2	0.67	0.33	1.0
8	2	2(3-1)/2 = 1	1	1.0	0.0	0.0
9	2	2(2-1)/2 = 1	1	1.0	0.0	0.0

between any two vertices in the graph. We describe two categories of centrality metrics: the global knowledge-based and the local knowledge-based. The global knowledge-based edge centrality metric is the widely known edge betweenness centrality (EBWC) metric that is a direct measure of the fraction of the number of shortest paths (between any two vertices) on which an edge is located. However, the computation of EBWC is highly time consuming, and we propose to capture the betweenness of an edge in the form of a localized metric called the neighborhood overlap (NOVER), which is the ratio of the fraction of the neighbors that are common to the end vertices of an edge.

3.1 Edge Betweenness Centrality (EBWC)

The betweenness centrality of an edge is a measure of the fraction of the shortest paths (between any two nodes in the network) going through that edge. The EBWC values of the edges are computed en masse by running the Breadth First Search (BFS) algorithm on each of the vertices. Note that the EBWC of any edge could not be computed unless the BFS algorithm is run on all the vertices. The procedure to compute the EBWC of the edges is as follows: (i) We run the BFS algorithm starting from each vertex in the graph and determine the BFS-trees rooted at each vertex; (ii) For each vertex, we determine the number of shortest paths from the root of the different BFS trees to that vertex. For a BFS-tree rooted at a vertex r, the number of shortest paths from r to a vertex i at a level $l > 0$ (number of hops from r to i is l) is the sum of the number of shortest paths from r to the vertices at level l-1 and also directly connected to vertex i through an edge (such nodes are called predecessor nodes). The number of shortest paths from the root of a BFS-tree to itself is 1. (iii) We determine the amount of flow that could originate from the root node of each BFS-tree and propagate to the rest of the nodes through the edges of the tree. To do this, we start with an initial flow of 1 unit to be available at each node and let the flow to aggregate at the root node starting from the nodes at the bottommost level. A node at level l ($l \geq 0$) gathers the flow coming through the edges from nodes at level l+1 (if l is not the bottommost/largest level) and adds to it the one unit of flow originating at itself and divides (if the node is not a root node) the aggregated flow proportionally among all its predecessor nodes (depending on the number of shortest paths from the root node to the predecessor nodes) and forwards their share along the edges to these nodes. Nodes at each level repeat this process and the root node gets the final aggregated flow. The total flow for an edge (EBWC) is the sum (for directed graphs) or half the sum (for undirected graphs) of the flows on the edge determined for all the BFS-trees.

Figure 6 illustrates an example to determine the EBWC of the edges according to the above-described procedure. The graph has six vertices A - F. We first determine the BFS-trees rooted at each vertex and determine the levels of the vertices in each of these BFS-trees. We then determine the amount of flow through the edges on each of the BFS-trees. We use the BFS-tree rooted at vertex A to demonstrate the procedure. Each vertex is assigned an initial flow of one unit. The BFS-tree rooted at A has three levels. Vertex D is the only vertex in the bottommost level (level 3) and has two predecessors G and F (at level 2) that have respectively one and two shortest paths to the root node A. Vertex D divides the 1 unit of flow proportionally (into three sub-flows, each of value 0.33) and sends two sub-flows to F (totaling to 0.67 units of flow) and one sub-flow to G (0.33 units of flow). Vertex F aggregates the 0.67 units of flow with its own one unit of flow and divides the aggregated flow (1.67) proportionally to its two predecessor nodes B and E (at level 1), each of which have one shortest path to the root A. Vertex F sends $1.67/2 = 0.835$ units of sub-flow to each of B and E. On the other hand, vertex G has only one predecessor (vertex B at level 1) and hence simply forwards the aggregated flow of 1.33 units (one unit of flow originating at vertex G plus the 0.33 units of sub-flow that came from vertex D) to vertex B. Vertex B aggregates the 1.33 units of sub flow received from G and the 0.835 units of sub flow received from F along with its own one unit of flow and sends the final aggregated flow of 3.165 units $(1.33 + 0.835 + 1)$ to its only predecessor vertex, the root vertex A. Vertex E has only one descendant node (vertex F) at the immediate next level. Hence, vertex E aggregates the 0.835 units of sub flow received from its descendant vertex F with its own one unit of flow and forwards the final aggregated flow of 1.835 units to its predecessor vertex, the root vertex A. With this, the amount of flow on each of the edges in the graph is calculated. We repeat the calculations for each of the BFS-trees. The EBWC for an edge is the half of the sum of the flows calculated on each of the BFS-trees (as the graph is an undirected graph).

3.2 Neighborhood Overlap

The NOVER score for an edge u-v is quantified as the ratio of the number of nodes who are neighbors of both u and v to that of the number of nodes who are neighbors of at least one of u or v. Note that in the denominator of the

Figure 6. Example to illustrate the calculation of Edge Betweenness Centrality (EBWC)

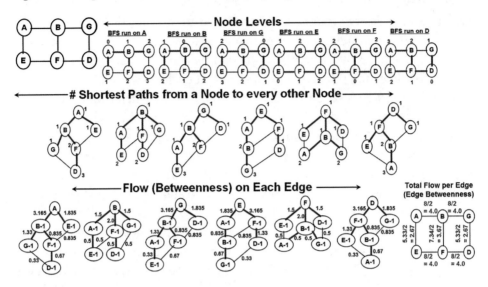

above formulation, the neighbor vertices are to be considered only once and the vertices *u* and *v* have to be excluded from being considered neighbors of each other while computing the denominator.

Figure 7 presents an example to compute the NOVER scores of the edges of the example graph of Figures 1-5. Vertices 1 and 2 of edge 1-2 do not have any common neighbor and hence the NOVER score for edge 1-2 is 0 (NOVER' of 1-2 is 1.0). On the other hand, for edges 3-6 and 4-7, the NOVER scores are 1.0 (all the neighbors are common to both the end vertices) and the NOVER' scores are 0.0 each.

4. CORRELATION MEASURES

We identify three levels of correlation that could be obtained for any two centrality metrics (say, X and Y). They are: pair-wise relative ordering (Kendall's correlation, τ), network-wide ordering (Spearman's correlation, ρ) and linear regression-based prediction (Pearson's correlation, r). All the three correlation coefficients range from -1 to 1, and larger the value, the stronger the correlation and vice-versa. If the correlation coefficient value is in the vicinity of 0, the two metrics are considered to be independent of each other. Among the two centrality metrics of interest, one metric (say, X) could be a computationally-light metric and the other metric (say, Y) could

Figure 7. Example to illustrate the calculation of Neighborhood Overlap (NOVER)

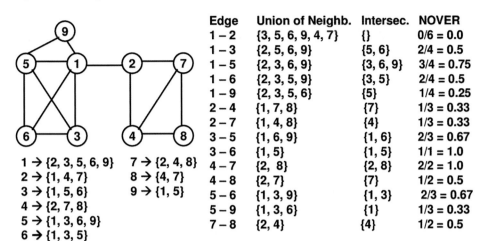

Edge	Union of Neighb.	Intersec.	NOVER
1 – 2	{3, 5, 6, 9, 4, 7}	{}	0/6 = 0.0
1 – 3	{2, 5, 6, 9}	{5, 6}	2/4 = 0.5
1 – 5	{2, 3, 6, 9}	{3, 6, 9}	3/4 = 0.75
1 – 6	{2, 3, 5, 9}	{3, 5}	2/4 = 0.5
1 – 9	{2, 3, 5, 6}	{5}	1/4 = 0.25
2 – 4	{1, 7, 8}	{7}	1/3 = 0.33
2 – 7	{1, 4, 8}	{4}	1/3 = 0.33
3 – 5	{1, 6, 9}	{1, 6}	2/3 = 0.67
3 – 6	{1, 5}	{1, 5}	1/1 = 1.0
4 – 7	{2, 8}	{2, 8}	2/2 = 1.0
4 – 8	{2, 7}	{7}	1/2 = 0.5
5 – 6	{1, 3, 9}	{1, 3}	2/3 = 0.67
5 – 9	{1, 3, 6}	{1}	1/3 = 0.33
7 – 8	{2, 4}	{4}	1/2 = 0.5

1 → {2, 3, 5, 6, 9} 7 → {2, 4, 8}
2 → {1, 4, 7} 8 → {4, 7}
3 → {1, 5, 6} 9 → {1, 5}
4 → {2, 7, 8}
5 → {1, 3, 6, 9}
6 → {1, 3, 5}

be a computationally-heavy metric. The correlation coefficient measures could thus quantify the extent to which a computationally-light centrality metric can be used for pair-wise relative ordering, network-wide ranking or even predicting in lieu of a computationally-heavy centrality metric (e.g., Li et al., 2015; Meghanathan, 2015).

For any two vertices v_i and v_j, the Kendall's correlation coefficient is a quantitative measure of how well we can say that if $X(v_i) < X(v_j)$, then $Y(v_i) < Y(v_j)$. On the other hand, at the global level, if the vertices in the network are ranked based on one centrality metric (say, X), the Spearman's correlation coefficient is a quantitative measure of the similarity of this ranking with respect to the other centrality metric (say, Y). The Pearson's correlation coefficient is a quantitative measure of how well we can predict the values of one centrality metric (say, Y) using the values for another centrality metric (say, X); in this pursuit, we model Y as a linear function of X.

4.1 Kendall's Concordance-Based Correlation

A pair of vertices vi and vj are said to be concordant with respect to two centrality metrics X and Y, if one of the following are true: (i) X(vi) < X(vj) and Y(vi) < Y(vj); (ii) X(vi) > X(vj) and Y(vi) > Y(vj); (iii) X(vi) = X(vj) and Y(vi) = Y(vj). A pair of vertices vi and vj are said to be discordant with respect to two centrality metrics X and Y, if one of the following two conditions are true: (i) X(vi) < X(vj) and Y(vi) ≥ Y(vj); (ii) X(vi) ≥ X(vj) and $Y(vi) < Y(vj)$. To calculate the Kendall's correlation coefficient for any two centrality metrics X and Y, we calculate the number of concordant pairs and the number of discordant pairs of vertices among the vertices in the network and apply the following formulation:

$$\tau(X,Y) = \frac{\#\,conc.pairs(X,Y) - \#\,disc.pairs(X,Y)}{\#\,conc.pairs(X,Y) + \#\,disc.pairs(X,Y)} = f_c(X,Y) - f_d(X,Y)$$

(1)

Figure 8 presents an illustrative example to calculate the Kendall's concordance-based correlation coefficient between the BWC and LCC'DC metrics. There are 9 vertices in the graph; hence, the number of pairs of vertices (also the denominator of formulation 1) considered is 9*(9-1)/2 = 36. Among these 36 pairs of vertices, 34 are concordant and 2 are discordant. Hence, τ (LCC'DC, BWC) = (34 - 2) / 36 = 0.89.

As the denominator of formulation 1 basically adds up to the total number of pairs of vertices in the network, $\tau(X, Y)$ can also be computed as the difference between the fraction of concordant pairs and the fraction of discordant pairs of vertices in the network. Notice that the Kendall's correlation coefficient is very sensitive to the fraction of discordant pairs, $f_d(X, Y)$. Even the presence of a few discordant pairs will lead to a significant reduction in the correlation coefficient. Figure 9 presents the relationship between $\tau(X, Y)$ and $f_d(X, Y)$. For a 1% (0.01) increase in $f_d(X, Y)$, $\tau(X, Y)$ decreases by 0.02.

Figure 8. Example to compute the Kendall's concordance-based correlation coefficient

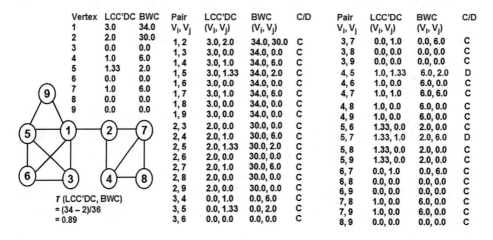

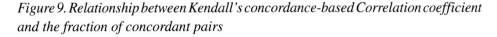

Figure 9. Relationship between Kendall's concordance-based Correlation coefficient and the fraction of concordant pairs

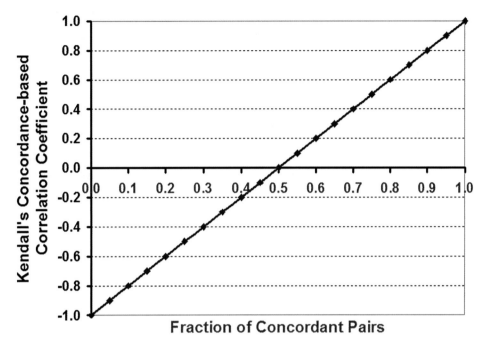

4.2 Spearman's Rank-Based Correlation

The vertices in a network could be ranked with respect to any centrality metric. The Spearman's correlation measure quantifies the extent of similarity between the rankings of the vertices with respect to any two centrality metrics. The procedure to compute the Spearman's rank-based correlation coefficient for any two centrality metrics (say, X and Y) is as follows: For each of the two metrics, we first obtain a tentative ranking of the vertices and use these tentative rank numbers to get the final rank numbers. The tentative rank number assigned is inversely proportional to the centrality value. Vertices with larger values for the centrality metric get a lower tentative rank number. If two or more vertices have the same value for the centrality metric, then the tie (for assigning the tentative rank number) is broken in favor of vertices with lower ID. The final rank number for a vertex with respect to a centrality metric is the same as the tentative rank number if there is no tie. In case of a tie, the final rank number for the vertices that are part of the tie is the average of the tentative rank numbers of the vertices involved in the tie. After obtaining the

15

final rank numbers for the vertices with respect to the two centrality metrics of interest, we determine the difference (d_i) in the two final rank numbers for each vertex v_i and use the formulation below to compute the Spearman's rank-based correlation coefficient (n is the number of vertices in the graph).

$$\rho(X,Y) = 1 - \frac{6\sum_{i=1}^{n} d_i^2}{n(n^2-1)} \qquad (2)$$

Figure 10 presents the computation of the Spearman's rank-based correlation coefficient on the running example graph (Figures 1-5) used to illustrate the computation of the centrality metrics. In the case of BWC, there is a tie between vertices 4 and 7 (each have a BWC of 6). The tentative rank number assigned until then is 2 and we assign tentative rank numbers of 3 and 4 to vertices 4 and 7 respectively (with the tie broken in favor of the vertex with lower ID). However, the final rank number for both 4 and 7 is the average of their tentative rank numbers (i.e., (3+4)/2 = 3.5). Only three of the nine vertices have a non-zero difference in their final rank numbers with respect to BWC and LCC'DC and the differences are not that high either. This justifies the high value for the Spearman's rank-based correlation coefficient (0.95).

4.3 Pearson's Product-Moment Correlation

The Pearson's product-moment correlation (r) is a measure of the linear relationship between two metrics. If the two metrics have a positive linear relationship, then r is closer to 1; if the two metrics have a negative linear

Figure 10. Example to compute the Spearman's rank-based correlation coefficient

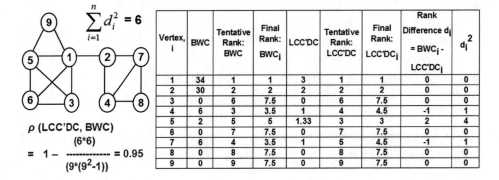

relationship, then r is closer to -1; if the two metrics are independent of each other, then r is closer to 0. If X and Y are the datasets for any two centrality metrics (the centralities of a vertex v_i is denoted X_i and Y_i for $1 \leq i \leq n$, where n is the number of vertices) and the average of the centrality metrics is denoted as $\overline{X}$ and $\overline{Y}$, the Pearson's product-moment correlation coefficient is calculated as shown in formulation (3) below. Note that the term 'product-moment' captures the deviation of the data points from their mean value (in Statistics, mean is also referred to as 'first moment') as seen in the formulation. Figure 11 illustrates the computation of the Pearson's correlation coefficient between BWC and LCC'DC for the running example graph of Figures 1-5. We observe the Pearson's correlation coefficient (0.91) to be between the Spearman's and Kendall's correlation coefficients (of 0.95 and 0.89 respectively) and this is the trend that is also observed for any two centrality metrics across several real-world networks analyzed in this book.

5. REAL-WORLD NETWORKS

This section presents a brief overview of the 50 real-world networks analyzed in the chapters of this book. Table 2 presents the values for some of the fundamental metrics (of graph theory and complex network analysis) for these real-world networks. The metrics listed in the table are as follows: average node degree (k_{avg}), average path length (PL_{avg}), diameter (D), spectral radius ratio for node degree (λ_{sp}; Meghanathan, 2014, 2015a), graph density (G_d), graph modularity (G_m, measured in a scale of 0...1; Newman, 2006b) and the number of components (#comps). The spectral radius ratio ($\lambda_{sp} \geq 1.0$) for node degree is a quantitative measure of the extent of variation in node degree and is measured as the ratio of the principal eigenvalue (Bonacich, 1987) of

Figure 11. Example to compute the Pearson's product-moment correlation coefficient

Vertex, i	BWC	BWC$_i$ - Avg(BWC)	(BWC$_i$ - Avg(BWC))^2	LCC'DC	LCC'DC$_i$ - Avg(LCC'DC)	(LCC'DC$_i$ - Avg(LCC'DC))^2	(BWC$_i$- Avg(BWC))* (LCC'DC$_i$ - Avg(LCC'DC))
1	34	25.33	641.61	3	2.07	4.285	52.433
2	30	21.33	454.97	2	1.07	1.145	22.823
3	0	-8.67	75.17	0	-0.93	0.865	8.063
4	6	-2.67	7.13	1	0.07	0.005	-0.187
5	2	-6.67	44.49	1.33	0.4	0.160	-2.668
6	0	-8.67	75.17	0	-0.93	0.865	8.063
7	6	-2.67	7.13	1	0.07	0.005	-0.187
8	0	-8.67	75.17	0	-0.93	0.865	8.063
9	0	-8.67	75.17	0	-0.93	0.865	8.063
	Avg = 8.67		Sum = 1456	Avg = 0.93		Sum = 9.059	Sum = 104.467

$$r(X,Y) = \frac{104.467}{\sqrt{1456} * \sqrt{9.059}} = 0.91$$

the adjacency matrix of the graph to that of the average node degree. The spectral radius ratio for node degree is independent of the number of nodes or edges in the network. The larger the λ_{sp} value, the larger the variation in node degree and vice-versa. The λ_{sp} values of the 50 real-world networks used in this book range from 1.01 (more common for random networks) to 5.34 (more common for scale-free networks).

The networks considered cover a broad range of categories (as listed below along with the number of networks in each category): Acquaintance network (13), Friendship network (9), Co-appearance network (6), Employment network (4), Citation network (3), Collaboration network (3), Biological network (3), Political network (2), Game network (2), Literature network (2), Transportation network, Geographical network and Trade network (all 1 each). A brief description about each category of networks is as follows: An *acquaintance network* is a kind of social network in which the participant nodes slightly (not closely) know each other, as observed typically during an observation period. A *friendship network* is a kind of social network in which the participant nodes closely know each other, and the relationship is not captured over an observation period. A *co-appearance network* is a network typically extracted from novels/books in such a way that two characters or words (modeled as nodes) are connected if they appear alongside each other. An *employment network* is a network in which the interaction/relationship between people is primarily due to their employment requirements and not due to any personal liking. A *citation network* is a network in which two papers (nodes) are connected if one paper cites the other paper as reference. A *collaboration network* is a network of researchers/authors who are listed as co-authors in at least one publication. A *biological network* is a network that models the interactions between genes, proteins (Dezső et al., 2009), animals of a particular species, etc. A *political network* is a network of entities (typically politicians) involved in politics. A *game network* is a network of teams or players playing for different teams and their associations. A *literature network* is a network of papers/terminologies/authors (other than collaboration, citation or co-authorship) involved in a particular area of literature. A *transportation network* is a network of entities (like airports and their flight connections) involved in public transportation. A *geographical network* is a network of states and their shared borders in a country. A *trade network* is a network of countries/people involved in certain trade. More information about the individual real-world networks is given below:

1.   **Word Adjacency Network (ADJ) (Newman, 2006a):** The network is an undirected graph comprising of 112 words (vertices represent adjectives and nouns) taken from the novel *David Copperfield* by Charles Dickens. Two vertices are linked if the corresponding words appear next to each other at least once in the novel.

2.   **Anna Karnenina Network (AKN) (Knuth, 1993):** The network is an undirected graph comprising of 140 characters (representing the vertices) in the novel *Anna Karnenina*. Two vertices are linked if the corresponding characters appear together for at least one scene in the novel.

3.   **Jazz Band Network (JBN) (Geiser & Danon, 2003):** The network is an undirected graph comprising of 198 Jazz bands (vertices) that did recording sometime between 1912 and 1940. Two vertices are linked if the corresponding bands had at least one common musician in at least one of their recordings.

4.   **C. Elegans Neural Network (CEN) (White et al., 1986):** The network is an undirected graph comprising of 297 neurons (vertices) observed in the neural network of a hermaphrodite by name *Caenorhabditis Elegans*. Two vertices are linked if the corresponding neurons interact with each other (typically in the form of synapses and junctions).

5.   **Centrality Literature Network (CLN) (Hummon et al., 1990):** The network is a directed graph comprising of 118 papers (representing the vertices) that were published on centrality metrics for complex networks from 1948 to 1979. There exists an edge from a vertex v_i to a vertex v_j if vertex v_i represents a paper that has cited the paper represented by vertex v_j as a reference.

6.   **Citation Graph Drawing Network (CGD) (Biedl & Franz, 2001):** The network is a directed graph comprising of 259 papers (representing the vertices) that were published in the proceedings of the GD (Graph Drawing) conferences from 1994 to 2000. There exists an edge from a vertex v_i to a vertex v_j if vertex v_i represents a paper that has cited the paper represented by vertex v_j as a reference.

7.   **Copperfield Network (CFN) (Knuth, 1993):** The network is an undirected graph comprising of 89 characters (vertices) in Charles Dickens' novel *David Copperfield*. Two vertices are linked if the corresponding characters appear together in at least one scene of the novel.

8. **Dolphin Network (DON) (Lusseau et al., 2003):** The network is an undirected graph comprising of 62 dolphins (vertices) that lived in a fiord (Doubtful Sound) in New Zealand. Two vertices are linked if the corresponding dolphins appeared to be moving close to each other during the period of observation.

9. **Drug Network (DRN) (Lee, 2004):** The network is an undirected graph comprising of 212 drug agents (vertices) who are from different ethnic backgrounds. Two vertices are linked if the agents corresponding to these vertices know each other.

10. **Dutch Literature 1976 Network (DLN) (Nooy, 1999):** The network is a directed graph comprising of 37 vertices (representing the Dutch literary authors and critics during the year 1976). There exists an edge from a vertex v_i to a vertex v_j if v_i represents a critic who has either reviewed or interviewed the literature work of the person represented by v_j (who is an author).

11. **Erdos Collaboration Network (ERD) (Batagelj & Mrvar, 2006):** The network is an undirected graph comprising of 433 authors (vertices) who have either directly collaborated with Paul Erdos or linked to Erdos through a chain of collaborators. Two vertices are linked if the corresponding authors have co-authored at least one publication.

12. **Faux Mesa High School Friendship Network (FMH) (Resnick et al., 1997):** The network is an undirected graph comprising of 147 students (vertices) in a high school community in a rural western part of the US. Two vertices are linked if the corresponding students are friends of each other.

13. **Friendship Ties in a Hi-Tech Firm (FHT) (Krackhardt, 1999):** The network is a directed graph comprising of 33 employees (vertices) in a small hi-tech firm that sells, installs and maintains computer systems. There exists an edge from a vertex v_i to a vertex v_j if the former considers the latter as a personal friend.

14. **Flying Teams Cadet Network (FTC) (Moreno, 1960):** The network is a directed graph comprising of 48 vertices (cadet pilots at an US Army school in the year 1943). The cadet pilots are trained in two-seated aircrafts. There exists an edge from a vertex v_i to a vertex v_j if the pilot represented by v_i has indicated preference to train (fly in the same aircraft) with the pilot represented by v_j.

15. **US Football Network (FON) (Girvan & Newman, 2002):** The network is an undirected graph comprising of 115 football teams (vertices) of universities and colleges in the US that played Football during Fall 2000.

Two vertices are linked if the corresponding teams played against each other in the league games.

16. **College Dorm Fraternity Network (CDF) (Bernard et al., 1980):** The network is an undirected graph of 58 residents (vertices) of a college dormitory (at West Virginia College). Two vertices are linked if the corresponding residents were observed to be talking to each other at least one during a 5-day observation period.

17. **GD'96 Network (GD96) (Batagelj & Mrvar, 2006):** The network is a directed graph comprising of 180 vertices representing the AT&T and other WWW websites cited in the 1996 proceedings of the Graph Drawing conference. There exists an edge from a vertex v_i to a vertex v_j if a website represented by vertex v_i has a link to the website represented by vertex v_j.

18. **Marvel Universe Network (MUN) (Gleiser, 2007):** The network is an undirected graph comprising of 167 characters (vertices) that appear in the comic books published by Marvel Universe (a publishing company). Two vertices are linked if the corresponding characters have appeared together in at least one publication.

19. **Graph and Digraph Glossary Network (GLN) (Batagelj & Mrvar, 2006):** The network is a directed graph comprising of 67 vertices representing the terms that appeared in the glossary on Graphs and Digraphs prepared by Bill Cherowitzo. There exists an edge from a vertex v_i to a vertex v_j if the term represented by v_i is cited as the meaning of the term represented by v_j.

20. **Hypertext 2009 Network (HTN) (Isella et al., 2011):** The network is an undirected graph comprising of 115 attendees (vertices) of the 2009 ACM Hypertext conference (held in Turin, Italy from June 29 to July 1). Two vertices are linked if the corresponding attendees had face-to-face contact for at least 20 seconds.

21. **Huckleberry Coappearance Network (HCN) (Knuth, 1993):** The network is an undirected graph comprising of 76 characters (vertices) that appeared in Mark Twain's novel titled *Huckleberry Finn*. Two vertices are linked if the corresponding characters have appeared together in at least one scene.

22. **Infectious Socio-patterns Network (ISP) (Isella et al., 2011):** The network is an undirected graph comprising of 309 visitors (vertices) at the Spring 2009 Science Gallery exhibition held in Dublin, Ireland. Two vertices are linked if the corresponding visitors had face-to-face contact for at least 20 seconds during an event (titled *Infectious Socio-patterns*)

that simulated the spreading of an epidemic through individuals in close proximity.

23. **Karate Club Network (KCN) (Zachary, 1977):** The network is an undirected graph comprising of 34 members (vertices) of a Karate Club at a US university in the 1970s. Two vertices are linked if the corresponding members were observed to interact with each other during an observation period.

24. **Korea Family Planning Network (KFP) (Rogers & Kincaid, 1980):** The network is an undirected graph comprising of 37 women (vertices) at a Mothers' Club in Korea. Two vertices are linked if the corresponding women were observed to talk to each other about family planning methods during an observation period.

25. **Les Miserables Network (LMN) (Knuth, 1993):** The network is an undirected graph comprising of 77 characters (vertices) in the novel *Les Miserables*. Two vertices are linked if the corresponding characters appeared together in at least one chapter in the novel.

26. **Macaque Dominance Network (MDN) (Takahata, 1991):** The network is a directed graph comprising of 62 vertices (representing adult female Japanese macaques in a colony called "Arashiyama B Group" during the non-mating season of April to early October, 1976). There exists an edge from a vertex v_i to a vertex v_j if the macaque represented by v_i exhibited dominance over the macaque represented by v_j.

27. **Madrid Train Bombing Network (MTB) (Hayes, 2006):** The network is an undirected graph comprising of 64 suspected individuals and their relatives (vertices) reconstructed by Rodriguez using press accounts in the two major Spanish daily newspapers (El Pais and El Mundo) regarding the bombing of commuter trains in Madrid on March 11, 2004. There exists an edge between two vertices if the corresponding individuals were observed to have a link in the form of friendship, ties to any terrorist organization, co-participation in training camps and/or wars, or co-participation in any previous terrorist attacks.

28. **Manufacturing Company Employee Network (MCE) (Cross et al., 2004):** The network is an undirected graph of 77 employees (vertices) comprising a research team in a manufacturing company. Two vertices are linked if the corresponding employees are aware of each other's skill sets and knowledge.

29. **Social Networks Journal Co-authors (MSJ) (McCarty & Freeman, 2008):** The network is an undirected graph comprising of 475 authors (vertices) who published a total of 295 articles in the *Social Networks*

journal since 2008. Two vertices are linked if the corresponding authors have published at least one paper in the journal as co-authors.

30. **Author Facebook Network (AFB):** The network is an undirected graph of 171 friends (vertices) of the author in Facebook. Two vertices are linked if the corresponding friends of the author are friends themselves in Facebook.

31. **Mexican Political Elite Network (MPN) (Gil-Mendieta & Schmidt, 1996):** The network is an undirected graph of 35 Mexican president and their close collaborators (modeled as vertices). The two vertices are linked if the corresponding two people have some form of tie (could be political, kinship, friendship or business ties) as part of the collaboration.

32. **ModMath Network (MMN) (Batagelj & Mrvar, 2006):** The network is a directed graph of 30 school superintendents (vertices) from Allegheny County, Pennsylvania, USA during the 1950s and early 1960s. A vertex v_i has a directed edge to another vertex v_j if the superintendent represented by vertex v_i has indicated the superintendent represented by vertex v_j as a friend in a research survey conducted to find the influential superintendents who can effectively spread around some of the modern Math methods among the school systems in the county.

33. **Network Science Co-authorship (NSC) (Newman, 2006a):** The network is an undirected graph of 1589 authors (vertices) who work on network theory and the experiments. Two vertices are linked if the corresponding authors have appeared as co-authors in at least one publication in this area.

34. **US Politics Books Network (PBN) (Krebs, 2003):** The network is an undirected graph of 105 books (vertices) on US politics sold at Amazon. com during the 2004 presidential election. Two vertices are linked if the corresponding books have been purchased together at least once.

35. **Primary School Contact Network (PSN) (Gemmetto et al., 2014):** The network is an undirected graph comprising of children and teachers (238 vertices) who are used for a research study published as an article in the *BMC Infectious Diseases* journal in 2014. Two vertices are linked if the corresponding persons were talking to each other for at least 20 seconds during the observation period.

36. **Prison Friendship Network (PFN) (MacRae, 1960):** The network is a directed graph of 67 prison inmates (vertices) surveyed (on sociometric choices) by John Gagnon in the 1950s. There exists a link from a vertex v_i to a vertex v_j if the inmate corresponding to vertex v_i has indicated the inmate corresponding to vertex v_j as his/her closest friends.

Table 2. Fundamental metrics for real-world network graphs used in correlation analysis

#	Net.	Network Type	λ_{sp}	#nodes	#edges	k_{avg}	D	G_d	G_m	#comps	PL_{avg}
1	ADJ	Co-appearance Net.	1.73	112	425	7.589	5	0.068	0.283	1	2.536
2	AKN	Co-appearance Net.	2.48	140	494	7.057	5	0.051	0.389	2	2.448
3	JBN	Employment Net.	1.45	198	2742	27.697	6	0.141	0.44	1	2.235
4	CEN	Biological Net.	1.68	297	2148	14.465	5	0.049	0.387	1	2.455
5	CLN	Citation Net.	2.03	118	613	10.39	4	0.089	0.297	1	2.374
6	CGD	Citation Net.	2.24	259	640	4.942	11	0.019	0.627	6	4.149
7	CFN	Co-appearance Net.	1.83	89	407	9.146	3	0.104	0.375	2	1.945
8	DON	Acquaintance Net.	1.40	62	159	5.129	8	0.084	0.521	1	3.357
9	DRN	Acquaintance Net.	2.76	212	284	2.679	18	0.013	0.734	9	7.03
10	DLN	Literature Net.	1.49	37	81	4.378	7	0.122	0.299	2	2.703
11	ERD	Collaboration Net.	3.00	433	1314	6.069	11	0.014	0.533	3	4.021
12	FMH	Friendship Net.	2.81	147	202	2.748	16	0.019	0.801	11	6.811
13	FHT	Friendship Net.	1.57	33	91	5.515	5	0.172	0.308	1	2.36
14	FTC	Employment Net.	1.21	48	170	7.083	5	0.151	0.462	1	2.402
15	FON	Game Net.	1.01	115	613	10.661	4	0.094	0.604	1	2.508
16	CDF	Acquaintance Net.	1.11	58	967	33.345	3	0.585	0.066	1	1.419
17	GD96	Citation Net.	2.38	180	228	2.533	8	0.014	0.65	1	4.417
18	MUN	Co-appearance Net.	2.54	167	301	3.605	9	0.022	0.807	20	3.879
19	GLN	Literature Net.	2.01	67	118	3.522	7	0.053	0.502	4	3.099
20	HTN	Acquaintance Net.	1.21	115	2164	37.635	3	0.33	0.095	2	1.662
21	HCN	Co-appearance Net.	1.66	76	302	7.947	4	0.106	0.546	4	2.142
22	ISP	Acquaintance Net.	1.69	309	1924	12.453	10	0.04	0.565	1	3.775
23	KCN	Acquaintance Net.	1.47	34	78	4.588	5	0.139	0.416	1	2.408
24	KFP	Acquaintance Net.	1.70	37	85	4.595	10	0.128	0.444	2	3.23
25	LMN	Co-appearance Net.	1.82	77	254	6.597	5	0.087	0.555	1	2.641
26	MDN	Biological Net.	1.04	62	1167	37.645	2	0.617	0.086	1	1.383
27	MTB	Acquaintance Net.	1.95	64	295	9.219	2	0.146	0.375	1	1.854

continued on following page

Table 2. Continued

#	Net.	Network Type	λ_{sp}	#nodes	#edges	k_{avg}	D	G_d	G_m	#comps	PL_{avg}
28	MCE	Employment Net.	1.12	77	1549	40.23	2	0.529	0.217	1	1.471
29	MSJ	Co-author Net.	3.48	475	625	2.632	17	0.006	0.945	104	6.49
30	AFB	Friendship Net.	2.29	171	940	10.994	7	0.065	0.688	4	3.069
31	MPN	Acquaintance Net.	1.23	35	117	6.686	4	0.197	0.357	1	2.106
32	MMN	Friendship Net.	1.59	30	61	4.067	5	0.14	0.424	1	2.644
33	NSC	Co-author Net.	5.51	1,589	2,743	3.45	17	0.002	0.959	269	5.823
34	PBN	Political Net.	1.42	105	441	8.4	7	0.081	0.525	1	3.079
35	PSN	Acquaintance Net.	1.22	238	5539	46.546	3	0.196	0.39	1	1.941
36	PFN	Friendship Net.	1.32	67	142	4.239	7	0.064	0.581	1	3.355
37	SJN	Acquaintance Net.	1.29	75	155	4.133	7	0.056	0.601	1	3.485
38	SDI	Employment Net.	1.94	230	359	3.122	14	0.014	0.696	5	5.607
39	SPR	Political Net.	1.57	92	477	10.37	5	0.114	0.25	1	2.32
40	SWC	Game Net.	1.45	35	118	6.743	5	0.198	0.231	1	2.123
41	SSM	Acquaintance Net.	1.22	24	38	3.167	6	0.138	0.562	1	2.993
42	TEN	Acquaintance Net.	1.06	22	39	3.545	5	0.169	0.444	1	2.494
43	TWF	Friendship Net.	1.49	47	77	3.277	8	0.071	0.741	4	2.652
44	UKF	Friendship Net.	1.35	83	578	13.928	4	0.17	0.45	2	2.097
45	APN	Transportation Net.	3.22	332	2126	12.807	6	0.039	0.358	1	2.738
46	USS	Geographical Net.	1.25	49	107	4.367	10	0.091	0.571	1	3.935
47	RHF	Friendship Net.	1.27	217	1839	16.949	4	0.078	0.426	1	2.395
48	WSB	Friendship Net.	1.22	43	336	15.628	3	0.372	0.255	1	1.671
49	WTN	Trade Net.	1.38	80	875	21.875	3	0.277	0.220	1	1.724
50	YPI	Biological Net.	3.20	1,870	2,203	2.387	19	0.001	0.841	149	6.810

37. **San Juan Sur Family Network (SJN) (Loomis et al., 1953):** The network is a directed graph of 75 families (vertices) in San Juan Sur, Costa Rica, 1948. There exists an edge from vertex v_i to vertex v_j if the family represented by vertex v_i has visited the house of the family represented by vertex v_j at least once.

38. **Scotland Corporate Interlocks Network (SDI) (Scott, 1980):** The network is an undirected graph comprising of directors and companies (a total of 230 vertices) during 1904-05 in Scotland. Two vertices v_i and v_j are linked if either of the following are true: (i) v_i represents a

director who works in the company represented by vertex v_j; (ii) v_i and v_j represent directors who work together in the board for at least one company.

39. **Senator Press Release Network (SPR) (Grimmer, 2010):** The network is an undirected graph of 92 US senators (vertices) from 2007-2010. Two vertices are linked if the corresponding two senators have issued at least one joint press release.

40. **4Soccer World Cup 1998 Network (SWC) (Batagelj & Mrvar, 2006):** The network is a directed graph of 35 teams (vertices) that played in the 1998 Soccer World Cup. There exists an edge from vertex v_i to vertex v_j if v_j has at least one player (who originated from the country represented by team v_i) who is on contract to play for the team represented by v_i.

41. **Sawmill Strike Communication Network (SSM) (Michael, 1997):** The network is an undirected graph of 24 employees (vertices) working in a sawmill and planning for a strike against the management regarding a new compensation package. Two vertices are linked if the corresponding employees agreed to have met at least three times to discuss about the strike plans during an observation period.

42. **Taro Exchange Network (TEN) (Schwimmer, 1973):** The network is an undirected graph of 22 families (vertices) in a Papuan village. Two vertices are linked if the corresponding families appear to exchange gifts during an observation period.

43. **Teenage Female Friendship Network (TWF) (Pearson & Michell, 2000):** The network is an undirected graph of 47 female teenage students (vertices) who were part of the 1995-97 cohort in a school in Western Scotland. Two vertices are linked if the corresponding students indicated that they are best friends of each other in a survey.

44. **UK Faculty Friendship Network (UKF) (Nepusz et al., 2008):** The network is an undirected graph of 83 faculty members (vertices) at a university in the UK. Two vertices are linked if the corresponding faculty members are friends of each other.

45. **US Airports 1997 Network (APN) (Batagelj & Mrvar, 2006):** The network is an undirected graph f 332 airports (vertices) in the US in 1997. Two vertices are linked if the corresponding airports have at least one direct flight connection.

46. **US States Network (USS) (Meghanathan & Lawrence, 2016):** The network is an undirected graph of the 48 contiguous states in the US and the District of Columbia (DC), totaling to 49 vertices. Two vertices are linked if the corresponding states (or DC) share border.

47. **Residence Hall Friendship Network (RHF) (Freeman et al., 1998):** The network is an undirected graph of 217 students (vertices) living at a residence hall in the campus of the Australian National University. Two vertices are linked if the corresponding student residents are friends of each other.

48. **Windsurfers Beach Network (WSB) (Freeman et al., 1989):** The network is an undirected graph of 43 windsurfers (vertices) on a beach in southern California during Fall 1986. Two vertices are linked if the corresponding windsurfers are perceived to be close to each other (as per surveys).

49. **World Trade Metal Network (WTN) (Smith & White, 1992):** The network is a directed graph of 80 countries (vertices) that were involved in trading miscellaneous metals from 1965 to 1980. There is an edge from a vertex v_i to a vertex v_j if the country represented by v_j was importing metals from the country represented by v_i.

50. **Yeast Protein-Protein Interaction Network (YPI) (Jeong et al., 2001):** The network is an undirected graph of 1870 proteins (vertices) in Yeast used to study the correlation between lethality and centrality in protein-protein interaction networks. Two vertices are linked if the corresponding proteins exhibit mutual interaction.

6. OUTLINE FOR THE BOOK

Chapter 2 provides a comprehensive correlation study of the two computationally-light node centrality metrics (DEG and LCC'DC) vs. the three computationally-heavy node centrality metrics (EVC, BWC and CLC) as well as the computationally-light NOVER vs. the computationally-heavy EBWC metric with respect to all the three levels of correlation. Chapter 3 presents an assortativity analysis of the real-world networks with respect to the four centrality metrics R-DEG (remaining degree), EVC, BWC and CLC. The assortativity index with respect to each centrality metric is computed as the Pearson's correlation coefficient of the centrality values of the end vertices of the edges. We empirically estimate the probabilities with which a real-world network could be assortative, neutral or dissortative with respect to each centrality metric. Chapter 4 analyzes the temporal variation of the DEG, EVC, BWC and CLC centrality metrics during the evolution of a scale-free network under the well-known Barabasi-Albert (BA) model. Chapter 5 proposes edge centrality metrics (based on the notions of bipartivity index and algebraic connectivity) that could be computed locally to quantify the stability of links in a mobile sensor network without requiring the location and mobility information of the nodes; we also illustrate the use of these metrics along with neighborhood overlap to determine stable data gathering trees for mobile sensor networks. Chapter 6 presents an approach to use EVC to track a mobile radioactive dispersal device (RDD) with the aid of static sensor nodes deployed in a region being monitored. This chapter illustrates the use of EVC for intrusion detection. Chapter 7 illustrates an application of the centrality metrics, especially the BWC metric, for a curriculum network graph (CNG), a directed acyclic graph. The chapter proposes a methodology to quantify the relative contribution of the courses in a curriculum and obtain a numerical weight for each course that could be used to compute a weighted average score for the curriculum with respect to assessment, student grade point average, etc.

REFERENCES

Batagelj, V., & Mrvar, A. (2006). *Pajek Datasets*. Retrieved from http://vlado.fmf.uni-lj.si/pub/networks/data/

Bernard, H. R., Killworth, P. D., & Sailer, L. (1980). Informant Accuracy in Social Network Data IV: A Comparison of Clique-level Structure in Behavioral and Cognitive Network Data. *Social Networks*, *2*(3), 191–218. doi:10.1016/0378-8733(79)90014-5

Biedl, T., & Franz, B. J. (2001). *Graph-Drawing Contest Report*. Paper presented at the 9th International Symposium on Graph Drawing, Vienna, Austria.

Bonacich, P. (1987). Power and Centrality: A Family of Measures. *American Journal of Sociology*, *92*(5), 1170–1182. doi:10.1086/228631

Brandes, U. (2001). A Faster Algorithm for Betweenness Centrality. *The Journal of Mathematical Sociology*, *25*(2), 163–177. doi:10.1080/0022250X.2001.9990249

Cormen, T. H., Leiserson, C. E., Rivest, R. L., & Stein, C. (2009). *Introduction to Algorithms* (3rd ed.). MIT Press.

Cross, R. L., Parker, A., & Cross, R. (2004). *The Hidden Power of Social Networks: Understanding How Work Really Gets Done in Organizations* (1st ed.). Harvard Business Review Press.

Dezső, Z., Nikolsky, Y., Nikolskaya, T., Miller, J., Cherba, D., Webb, C., & Bugrim, A. (2009). Identifying disease-specific genes based on their topological significance in protein networks. *BioMed Central Systems Biology*, *3*(1), 1–36. PMID:19309513

Easley, D., & Kleinberg, J. (2010). *Networks, Crowds, and Markets: Reasoning about a Highly Connected World* (1st ed.). Cambridge University Press. doi:10.1017/CBO9780511761942

Fletcher, J. M., & Wennekers, T. (2018). From Structure to Activity: Using Centrality Measures to Predict Neuronal Activity. *International Journal of Neural Systems*, *28*(2), 1750013. doi:10.1142/S0129065717500137 PMID:28076982

Freeman, L. (1977). A Set of Measures of Centrality based on Betweenness. *Sociometry*, *40*(1), 35–41. doi:10.2307/3033543

Freeman, L. (1979). Centrality in Social Networks Conceptual Clarification. *Social Networks*, *1*(3), 215–239. doi:10.1016/0378-8733(78)90021-7

Freeman, L., Freeman, S. C., & Michaelson, A. G. (1989). How Humans See Social Groups: A Test of the Sailer-Gaulin Models. *Journal of Quantitative Anthropology*, *1*, 229–238.

Freeman, L., Webster, C. M., & Kirke, D. M. (1998). Exploring Social Structure using Dynamic Three-Dimensional Color Images. *Social Networks*, *20*(2), 109–118. doi:10.1016/S0378-8733(97)00016-6

Geiser, P., & Danon, L. (2003). Community Structure in Jazz. *Advances in Complex Systems*, *6*(4), 563–573.

Gemmetto, V., Barrat, A., & Cattuto, C. (2014). Mitigation of Infectious Disease at School: Targeted Class Closure vs. School Closure. *BMC Infectious Diseases*, *14*(695), 1–10. PMID:25595123

Gil-Mendieta, J., & Schmidt, S. (1996). The Political Network in Mexico. *Social Networks*, *18*(4), 355–381. doi:10.1016/0378-8733(95)00281-2

Girvan, M., & Newman, M. (2002). Community Structure in Social and Biological Networks. *Proceedings of the National Academy of Sciences of the United States of America, 99*(12), 7821–7826. doi:10.1073/pnas.122653799 PMID:12060727

Gleiser, P. M. (2007). How to become a Superhero. *Journal of Statistical Mechanics: Theory and Experiments, P09020.* doi:10.1088/1742-5468/2007/09/P09020

Grimmer, J. (2010). A Bayesian Hierarchical Topic Model for Political Texts: Measuring Expressed Agendas in Senate Press Releases. *Political Analysis, 18*(1), 1–35. doi:10.1093/pan/mpp034

Hayes, B. (2006). Connecting the Dots. *American Scientist, 94*(5), 400–404. doi:10.1511/2006.61.3495

Hummon, N. P., Doreian, P., & Freeman, L. C. (1990). Analyzing the Structure of the Centrality-Productivity Literature created between 1948 and 1979. *Science Communication, 11*(4), 459–480.

Isella, L., Stehle, J., Barrat, A., Cattuto, C., Pinton, J. F., & Van den Broeck, W. (2011). What's in a Crowd? Analysis of Face-to-Face Behavioral Networks. *Journal of Theoretical Biology, 271*(1), 161–180. doi:10.1016/j.jtbi.2010.11.033 PMID:21130777

Jeong, H., Mason, S. P., Barabasi, A. L., & Oltvai, Z. N. (2001). Lethality and Centrality in Protein Networks. *Nature, 411*(6833), 41–42. doi:10.1038/35075138 PMID:11333967

Knuth, D. E. (1993). *The Stanford GraphBase: A Platform for Combinatorial Computing* (1st ed.). Addison-Wesley.

Krackhardt, D. (1999). The ties that torture: Simmelian tie analysis in organizations. *Research in the Sociology of Organizations, 16*(1), 183–210.

Krebs, V. (2003). Proxy Networks: Analyzing One Network to Reveal Another. *Bulletin de Methodologie Sociologique, 79*(1), 61–70. doi:10.1177/075910630307900105

Lay, D. C. (2011). *Linear Algebra and its Applications* (4th ed.). Pearson.

Lee, J. S. (2004). Generating Networks of Illegal Drug Users using Large Samples of Partial Ego-Network Data. *Intelligence and Security Informatics. Lecture Notes in Computer Science, 3073,* 390–402. doi:10.1007/978-3-540-25952-7_29

Li, C., Li, Q., Van Mieghem, P., Stamey, H. E., & Wang, H. (2015). Correlation between Centrality Metrics and their Application to the Opinion Model. *The European Physical Journal B, 88*(65), 1–13.

Loomis, C. P., Morales, J. O., Clifford, R. A., & Leonard, O. E. (1953). *Turrialba Social Systems and the Introduction of Change* (1st ed.). The Free Press.

Lusseau, D., Schneider, K., Boisseau, O. J., Hasse, P., Slooten, E., & Dawson, S. M. (2003). The Bottlenose Dolphin Community of Doubtful Sound Features a Large Proportion of Long-lasting Associations. *Behavioral Ecology and Sociobiology, 54*(3), 396–405. doi:10.100700265-003-0651-y

MacRae, D. (1960). Direct Factor Analysis of Sociometric Data. *Sociometry, 23*(4), 360–371. doi:10.2307/2785690

McCarty, C., & Freeman, L. (2008). *Network Datasets.* Retrieved from http://moreno.ss.uci.edu/data.html

Meghanathan, N. (2014). *Spectral Radius as a Measure of Variation in Node Degree for Complex Network Graphs.* Paper presented at the 3rd International Conference on Digital Contents and Applications, Hainan, China. 10.1109/UNESST.2014.8

Meghanathan, N. (2015). Correlation Coefficient Analysis of Centrality Metrics for Complex Network Graphs. Paper presented at the 4th Computer Science Online Conference. 10.1007/978-3-319-18503-3_2

Meghanathan, N. (2017). A Computationally-Lightweight and Localized Centrality Metric in lieu of Betweenness Centrality for Complex Network Analysis. *Springer Vietnam Journal of Computer Science, 4*(1), 23–38. doi:10.100740595-016-0073-1

Meghanathan, N., & Lawrence, R. (2016). *Centrality Analysis of the United States Network Graph*. Paper presented at the 3rd International Conference on Electrical, Electronics, Engineering Trends, Communication, Optimization and Sciences, Tadepalligudem, India.

Michael, J. H. (1997). Labor Dispute Reconciliation in a Forest Products Manufacturing Facility. *Forest Products Journal, 47*(11-12), 41–45.

Moreno, J. L. (1960). *The Sociometry Reader* (1st ed.). The Free Press.

Nepusz, T., Petroczi, A., Negyessy, L., & Bazso, F. (2008). Fuzzy Communities and the Concept of Bridgeness in Complex Networks. *Physical Review. E, 77*(1), 016107. doi:10.1103/PhysRevE.77.016107 PMID:18351915

Newman, M. (2006a). Finding Community Structure in Networks using the Eigenvectors of Matrices. *Physical Review. E, 74*(3), 036104. doi:10.1103/PhysRevE.74.036104 PMID:17025705

Newman, M. (2006b). Modularity and Community Structure in Networks. *Proceedings of the National Academy of Sciences of the United States of America, 103*(23), 8557–8582. doi:10.1073/pnas.0601602103 PMID:16723398

Newman, M. (2010). *Networks: An Introduction* (1st ed.). Oxford University Press. doi:10.1093/acprof:oso/9780199206650.001.0001

Nooy, W. (1999). A Literary Playground: Literary Criticism and Balance Theory. *Poetics, 26*(5-6), 385–404. doi:10.1016/S0304-422X(99)00009-1

Pearson, M., & Michell, L. (2000). Smoke Rings: Social Network Analysis of Friendship Groups, Smoking and Drug-taking. *Drugs Education Prevention & Policy, 7*(1), 21–37. doi:10.1080/713660095

Resnick, M. D., Bearman, P. S., Blum, R. W., Bauman, K. E., Harris, K. M., Jones, J., ... Udry, J. R. (1997). Protecting Adolescents from Harm. Findings from the National Longitudinal Study on Adolescent Health. *Journal of the American Medical Association, 278*(10), 823–832. doi:10.1001/jama.1997.03550100049038 PMID:9293990

Rogers, E. M., & Kincaid, D. L. (1980). *Communication Networks: Toward a New Paradigm for Research* (1st ed.). The Free Press.

Schwimmer, E. (1973). *Exchange in the Social Structure of the Orokaiva: Traditional and Emergent Ideologies in the Northern District of Papua* (1st ed.). C Hurst and Co-Publishers Ltd.

Scott, J. P. (1980). *The Anatomy of Scottish Capital: Scottish Companies and Scottish Capital* (1st ed.). Croom Helm. doi:10.2307/j.ctt1w6tfbt

Shavitt, Y., & Singer, Y. (2007). Beyond Centrality - Classifying Topological Significance using Backup Efficiency and Alternative Paths. *New Journal of Physics*, *9*(266), 1–17.

Smith, D. A., & White, D. R. (1992). Structure and Dynamics of the Global Economy: Network Analysis of International Trade 1965-1980. *Social Forces*, *70*(4), 857–893. doi:10.1093f/70.4.857

Takahata, Y. (1991). *Diachronic Changes in the Dominance Relations of Adult Female Japanese Monkeys of the Arashiyama B Group* (1st ed.). Albany, NY: State University of New York Press.

Triola, M. F. (2012). *Elementary Statistics* (12th ed.). Pearson.

White, J. G., Southgate, E., Thomson, J. N., & Brenner, S. (1986). The Structure of the Nervous System of the Nematode *Caenorhabditis Elegans*. *Philosophical Transactions B, 314*(1165), 1-340.

Zachary, W. W. (1977). An Information Flow Model for Conflict and Fission in Small Groups. *Journal of Anthropological Research*, *33*(4), 452–473. doi:10.1086/jar.33.4.3629752

Chapter 2

Computationally Light vs. Computationally Heavy Centrality Metrics:
Correlation Analysis Between Computationally Light and Computationally Heavy Centrality Metrics

ABSTRACT

In this chapter, the authors analyze the correlation between the computationally light degree centrality (DEG) and local clustering coefficient complement-based degree centrality (LCC'DC) metrics vs. the computationally heavy betweenness centrality (BWC), eigenvector centrality (EVC), and closeness centrality (CLC) metrics. Likewise, they also analyze the correlation between the computationally light complement of neighborhood overlap (NOVER') and the computationally heavy edge betweenness centrality (EBWC) metric. The authors analyze the correlations at three different levels: pair-wise (Kendall's correlation measure), network-wide (Spearman's correlation measure), and linear regression-based prediction (Pearson's correlation measure). With regards to the node centrality metrics, they observe LCC'DC-BWC to be the most strongly correlated at all the three levels of correlation. For the edge centrality metrics, the authors observe EBWC-NOVER' to be strongly correlated with respect to the Spearman's correlation measure, but not with respect to the other two measures.

DOI: 10.4018/978-1-5225-3802-8.ch002

1. INTRODUCTION

The computation times for the node centrality metrics such as betweenness centrality (BWC) (Freeman, 1977), eigenvector centrality (EVC) (Bonacich, 1987) and closeness centrality (CLC) (Freeman, 1979) as well as for the edge centrality metric such as the edge betweenness centrality (EBWC; Girvan & Newman, 2002) are of $\Theta(V^3)$ or $\Theta(VE)$ time for network graphs of V vertices and E edges. As a result, the computation times for these node and edge centrality metrics are not scalable with increase in the number of nodes and/ or edges and we refer to these metrics as computationally-heavy metrics. On the other hand, there exist computationally-light centrality metrics such as degree centrality (DEG) (Newman, 2010) and local clustering coefficient complement-based degree centrality (LCC'DC) (Meghanathan, 2017) at the node-level and the complement of the neighborhood overlap (NOVER') (Easley & Kleinberg, 2010) metric at the edge level. The focus of this chapter is to conduct extensive correlation analysis of the computationally-heavy node centrality metrics {BWC, EVC, CLC} vs. the computationally-light node centrality metrics {DEG, LCC'DC} as well as the computationally-heavy EBWC vs. the computationally-light NOVER' at the edge-level.

We conduct the correlation study at three different levels (Triola, 2012): pair-wise ordering (Kendall's correlation coefficient), network-wide ranking (Spearman's correlation coefficient) and linear regression-based modeling (Pearson's correlation coefficient). All the three correlation coefficients are measured in a scale of -1 to 1; (values closer to 1 indicate a stronger positive correlation; values closer to -1 indicate a stronger negative correlation; values closer to 0 indicate no correlation). With Kendall's concordance-based correlation, we seek to quantify the extent to which a pair-wise ordering between any two vertices (or edges) with respect to a computationally-light metric can be used to predict an ordering of the two vertices (or edges) with respect to a computationally-heavy metric. For example, if $LCC'DC(v_i) < LCC'DC(v_j)$, we seek to evaluate the extent, we can claim $BWC(v_i) < BWC(v_j)$? With Spearman's rank-based correlation, we seek to quantify the extent we can use a ranking of the vertices (or edges) with respect to a computationally-light metric (like LCC'DC or NOVER') to rank the vertices (or edges) with respect to a computationally-heavy metric (like BWC or EBWC). With the Pearson's linear regression-based correlation, we seek to quantify the extent to which we can predict the actual values for a computationally-heavy centrality metric at the node or edge level using the actual values for a computationally-light centrality metric at the node or edge level.

Our research objectives in this chapter are as follows: (i) Identify the computationally-light node centrality metric that is strongly correlated with each of the three computationally-heavy node centrality metrics, for the three different levels of correlations; (ii) Identify the correlation level (pairwise, network wide-ranking or linear regression-based modeling) for which we would incur the largest value for the correlation coefficient between a computationally-light and a computationally-heavy centrality metric at the node level. (iii) Evaluate the suitability of using NOVER' as a computationally-light alternative for EBWC for all the three levels of correlation. For correlation analysis involving node centrality metrics, we use a suite of 50 real-world networks (Meghanathan, 2016b) and for correlation analysis involving edge centrality metrics, we use a suite of 47 real-world networks. We omit certain networks for correlation analysis at the edge level due to the computation overhead involved in computing the actual EBWC values.

The rest of the chapter is organized as follows: In Section 2, we tabulate the computation times for the five node centrality and two edge centrality metrics and explain their classification as computationally-heavy or computationally-light. In Section 3, we discuss the results of correlation analysis (at all the three levels) for the computationally-light vs. computationally-heavy node centrality metrics. In Section 4, we discuss the correlation between EBWC vs. NOVER' with respect to the three correlation measures. In Section 5, we discuss related work and highlight the unique contributions of this chapter. Section 6 concludes the chapter and Section 7 discusses future research directions.

2. CLASSIFICATION OF THE CENTRALITY METRICS BASED ON COMPUTATIONAL TIME COMPLEXITY

2.1 Node Centrality Metrics

For each centrality metric and a real-world network, we compute the total time to determine the centrality values for all the nodes and divide by the number of nodes in the network and tabulate as the computation time per node (see Table 1). The computation resources used are as follows: Intel Core i7-2620M CPU @ 2.70 GHz and Main memory (RAM) of 8 GB. To weed out

Table 1. Computation time per node of the centrality metrics for the real-world network graphs

#	Net.	#nodes	#edges	Computation Time per Node (milliseconds)				
				Computationally-Light		Computationally-Heavy		
				DEG	LCC'DC	CLC	EVC	BWC
1	ADJ	112	425	0.00043	0.00723	0.09777	0.30250	2.40223
2	AKN	140	494	0.00068	0.00965	0.05050	0.44021	3.94329
3	JBN	198	2742	0.00017	0.04402	0.12066	0.22212	8.98010
4	CEN	297	2148	0.00018	0.01157	0.07825	0.47899	19.16182
5	CLN	118	613	0.00023	0.00404	0.05186	0.14542	1.45644
6	CGD	259	640	0.00022	0.00083	0.11286	0.48031	19.13170
7	CFN	89	407	0.00017	0.00137	0.06674	0.02854	0.46247
8	DON	62	159	0.00018	0.00071	0.00419	0.02097	0.31935
9	DRN	212	284	0.00025	0.00058	0.10759	0.27104	17.85425
10	DLN	37	81	0.00027	0.00089	0.00216	0.01919	0.12676
11	ERD	433	1314	0.00019	0.00110	0.20591	1.16956	48.16531
12	FMH	147	202	0.00024	0.00050	0.04871	0.12871	5.54497
13	FHT	33	91	0.00024	0.00103	0.00182	0.01485	0.13364
14	FTC	48	170	0.00017	0.00079	0.00292	0.01646	0.18542
15	FON	115	613	0.00019	0.00121	0.01330	0.08209	1.36739
16	CDF	58	967	0.00028	0.00997	0.01810	0.03414	0.67879
17	GD96	180	228	0.00017	0.00052	0.02817	0.09189	4.26378
18	MUN	167	301	0.00018	0.00054	0.02305	0.06587	1.50102
19	GLN	67	118	0.00030	0.00046	0.00910	0.03149	0.32149
20	HTN	115	2164	0.00018	0.00724	0.01165	0.05365	1.79522
21	HCN	76	302	0.00026	0.00074	0.00855	0.02579	0.32276
22	ISP	309	1924	0.00017	0.00130	0.10476	0.55414	21.06320
23	KCN	34	78	0.00018	0.00047	0.00147	0.00529	0.06882
24	KFP	37	85	0.00030	0.00097	0.00324	0.01216	0.16216
25	LMN	77	254	0.00016	0.00083	0.00545	0.01792	0.37195
26	MDN	62	1167	0.00026	0.00560	0.00694	0.03210	0.67774
27	MTB	64	295	0.00017	0.00063	0.00500	0.01609	0.32844
28	MCE	77	1549	0.00017	0.00516	0.00558	0.02377	0.74909
29	MSJ	475	625	0.00020	0.00038	0.18269	0.63120	28.86568
30	AFB	171	940	0.00019	0.00137	0.03135	0.38982	3.36468
31	MPN	35	117	0.00017	0.00086	0.00171	0.00743	0.10314

continued on following page

Table 1. Continued

#	Net.	#nodes	#edges	Computation Time per Node (milliseconds)				
				Computationally-Light		Computationally-Heavy		
				DEG	LCC'DC	CLC	EVC	BWC
32	MMN	30	61	0.00027	0.00047	0.00233	0.00700	0.08767
33	NSC	1,589	2,743	0.00016	0.00072	2.52165	31.21962	457.18801
34	PBN	105	441	0.00020	0.00092	0.01848	0.07352	1.05924
35	PSN	238	5539	0.00016	0.01128	0.04836	0.31601	13.87235
36	PFN	67	142	0.00016	0.00048	0.00567	0.01925	0.33701
37	SJN	75	155	0.00017	0.00055	0.00573	0.02573	0.42813
38	SDI	230	359	0.00018	0.00049	0.05117	0.22422	10.97583
39	SPR	92	477	0.00058	0.00133	0.03793	0.14533	0.79196
40	SWC	35	118	0.00017	0.00054	0.00143	0.00743	0.08714
41	SSM	24	38	0.00021	0.00033	0.00125	0.00417	0.03292
42	TEN	22	39	0.00018	0.00032	0.00091	0.00364	0.03045
43	TWF	47	77	0.00017	0.00032	0.00255	0.00979	0.07106
44	UKF	83	578	0.00016	0.00149	0.00675	0.02675	0.62578
45	APN	332	2126	0.00016	0.00323	0.09518	0.49545	18.50593
46	USS	49	107	0.00041	0.00045	0.00265	0.01224	0.17469
47	RHF	217	1839	0.00016	0.00212	0.04083	0.24429	9.31433
48	WSB	43	336	0.00019	0.00128	0.00209	0.00977	0.17558
49	WTN	80	875	0.00058	0.00283	0.02513	0.10938	0.67938
50	YPI	1,870	2,203	0.00018	0.00086	3.45965	77.53588	834.37062
Fraction of Networks for which Average Computation Time per Node ≥ 0.01 ms				0/50 = 0.0	3/50 = 0.06	26/50 = 0.52	42/50 = 0.84	50/50 = 1.00

any statistical variations due to randomizations that might be involved during the execution of the algorithms, we ran the algorithms for each centrality metric (other than DEG) for 25 iterations and tabulated the average values. There is no prescribed value for a threshold computation time above which a centrality metric can be referred to as computationally-heavy. However, a closer look at Table 1 indicates that 0.01 milliseconds could be used as an appropriate threshold value for the classification purpose with regards to the centrality metrics and real-world networks analyzed in this chapter. Accordingly, we classify a centrality metric as computationally-light if its computation time per node is less than 0.01 milliseconds for at least 50% of the real-world networks analyzed. Per this scale, we observe the DEG metric to be computationally-light for all the 50 real-world networks and the LCC'DC metric to be computationally-light for 94% of the real-world networks analyzed. Hence, we classify DEG and LCC'DC to be computationally-light. On the other hand, we observe the CLC and EVC metrics to be computationally-light for only 48% and 16% of the real-world networks and the BWC metric is not computationally-light for any of the real-world networks. Hence, we classify the CLC, EVC and BWC metrics as computationally-heavy.

2.2 Edge Centrality Metrics

The simulations were run on a computer with Intel Core i7-2620M CPU @ 2.70 GHz and an installed memory (RAM) of 8 GB. Table 2 presents the results of the computation time for the EBWC and NOVER metrics for these real-world networks. The computation times for NOVER are appreciably smaller for all the real-world networks. For about 50% of the networks, the computation times for NOVER are even less than the logarithm of the computation times for EBWC. This vindicates our categorization of EBWC and NOVER as computationally-heavy and computationally-light edge centrality metrics respectively and the interest to investigate the correlation between these two metrics. Figure 1 shows a comparison of the computation times of EBWC and NOVER on a log-log scale (natural logarithm). We observe the data points to fall way below the diagonal line, indicating the logarithm of the EBWC computation times are significantly larger than the logarithm of the NOVER computation times. Figure 2 captures the impact of the number of edges in a real-world network graph on the computation times of NOVER and EBWC (plotted on the logarithmic scale). We observe the computation times to grow exponentially with the number of edges, albeit at different rates. The R^2 of the exponential models are observed to be 0.89 and 0.83 for NOVER and EBWC respectively. The two exponential models are shown in formulations (1) and (2). The growth rate of the computation times is controlled by the two parameters of the exponential models: the exponent and the coefficient. One can notice the values for both the parameters of the model to be lower for NOVER vis-a-vis EBWC, again vindicating our categorization of EBWC to be a computationally-heavy metric and NOVER to be a computationally-light metric.

Table 2. Computation time for EBWC and NOVER for the real-world network graphs

#	Net.	Computation Time for EBWC, ms	Computation Time for NOVER, ms	ln(Computation Time for EBWC)	ln(Computation Time for NOVER)
1	ADJ	148.55	5.67	2.17	0.75
2	AKN	160.54	3.97	2.21	0.60
3	JBN	883.79	45.82	2.95	1.66
4	CEN	1001.60	13.97	3.00	1.15
5	CLN	78.74	2.35	1.90	0.37
6	CGD	322.51	2.61	2.51	0.42
7	CFN	33.62	2.51	1.53	0.40
8	DON	14.03	0.39	1.15	-0.41
9	DRN	149.96	0.45	2.18	-0.35
10	DLN	3.26	0.12	0.51	-0.92
11	ERD	1296.50	3.54	3.11	0.55
12	FMH	39.57	0.47	1.60	-0.33
13	FHT	3.03	0.32	0.48	-0.49
14	FTC	6.06	0.24	0.78	-0.63
15	FON	57.98	0.88	1.76	-0.06
16	CDF	29.53	4.75	1.47	0.68
17	MUN	35.18	0.42	1.55	-0.38
18	GLN	8.37	0.28	0.92	-0.55
19	HTN	147.65	13.99	2.17	1.15
20	HCN	10.67	0.61	1.03	-0.21
21	ISP	779.37	5.11	2.89	0.71
22	KCN	1.69	0.10	0.23	-0.98
23	KFP	2.07	0.11	0.32	-0.98
24	LMN	21.03	0.74	1.32	-0.13
25	MDN	37.46	5.42	1.57	0.73
26	MTB	13.25	0.81	1.12	-0.09
27	MCE	48.76	10.01	1.69	1.00
28	MSJ	110.71	0.65	2.04	-0.19
29	AFB	71.47	1.79	1.85	0.25
30	MPN	2.37	0.20	0.38	-0.70
31	MMN	1.39	0.08	0.14	-1.11
32	NSC	3028.60	3.56	3.48	0.55
33	PBN	39.58	1.23	1.60	0.09
34	PSN	1245.10	45.06	3.10	1.65

continued on following page

Table 2. Continued

#	Net.	Computation Time for EBWC, ms	Computation Time for NOVER, ms	ln(Computation Time for EBWC)	ln(Computation Time for NOVER)
35	PFN	12.96	0.36	1.11	-0.45
36	SJN	15.81	0.31	1.20	-0.51
37	SPR	45.43	1.78	1.66	0.25
38	SWC	4.41	0.35	0.64	-0.45
39	SSM	1.13	0.07	0.05	-1.14
40	TEN	0.97	0.10	-0.01	-0.98
41	TWF	1.59	0.23	0.20	-0.64
42	UKF	49.01	1.36	1.69	0.13
43	APN	806.42	14.26	2.91	1.15
44	USS	6.68	0.20	0.82	-0.69
45	RHF	550.40	4.97	2.74	0.70
46	WSB	10.76	1.32	1.03	0.12
47	WTN	45.69	3.23	1.66	0.51

Figure 1. Comparison of the computation time: ln(EBWC) vs. ln(NOVER)

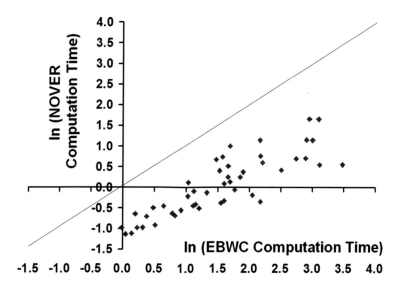

Figure 2. Impact of the number of edges on the NOVER and EBWC computation times

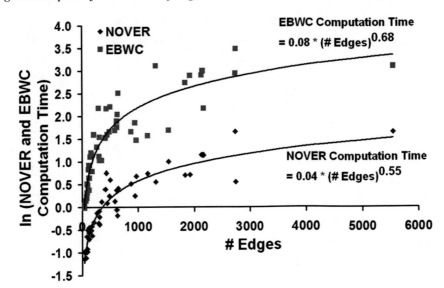

NOVER Computation Time $= 0.04 * (\# \text{Edges})^{0.55}$ (1)

EBWC Computation Time $= 0.08 * (\# \text{Edges})^{0.68}$ (2)

3. CORRELATION ANALYSIS OF NODE CENTRALITY METRICS

Tables 3-5 present respectively the correlation coefficient values obtained for the BWC, EVC and CLC metrics with the DEG and LCC'DC metrics with respect to the three levels of correlation. Figures 3-5 plot the distribution of the correlation coefficient values with respect to the three correlation measures.

In the case of BWC, we observe the LCC'DC metric to be relatively strongly correlated compared to the DEG metric for all the 50 real-world networks and with respect to all the three levels of correlation. This could be attributed to the characteristic of LCC'DC to effectively capture the betweenness of a node among its neighbors and use it as the basis to predict the betweenness of the node for the entire network. The median of the correlation coefficient values observed for BWC-LCC'DC with respect to the Kendall's, Pearson's and Spearman's correlation measures are 0.83, 0.88 and 0.95 respectively. Thus, LCC'DC is an apt metric to be used in lieu of BWC for all the three

Table 3. Correlation analysis of BWC vs. {DEG, LCC'DC}

#	Net.	Kendall's		Pearson's		Spearman's	
		DEG	LCC'DC	DEG	LCC'DC	DEG	LCC'DC
1	ADJ	0.773	0.789	0.915	0.930	0.901	0.916
2	AKN	0.657	0.951	0.892	0.948	0.759	0.994
3	JBN	0.579	0.717	0.610	0.757	0.744	0.860
4	CEN	0.736	0.774	0.780	0.816	0.889	0.923
5	CLN	0.750	0.837	0.825	0.887	0.903	0.954
6	CGD	0.745	0.846	0.797	0.860	0.890	0.956
7	CFN	0.697	0.954	0.808	0.897	0.818	0.993
8	DON	0.667	0.711	0.598	0.709	0.814	0.861
9	DRN	0.758	0.894	0.649	0.696	0.875	0.975
10	DLN	0.672	0.755	0.791	0.846	0.804	0.872
11	ERD	0.708	0.810	0.782	0.831	0.860	0.936
12	FMH	0.711	0.888	0.630	0.718	0.832	0.973
13	FHT	0.755	0.863	0.816	0.900	0.902	0.959
14	FTC	0.582	0.784	0.783	0.913	0.723	0.918
15	FON	0.260	0.447	0.282	0.673	0.336	0.608
16	CDF	0.809	0.869	0.857	0.935	0.940	0.968
17	GD96	0.759	0.769	0.951	0.962	0.859	0.869
18	MUN	0.603	0.955	0.704	0.861	0.699	0.995
19	GLN	0.773	0.856	0.932	0.944	0.888	0.952
20	HTN	0.899	0.939	0.829	0.884	0.983	0.994
21	HCN	0.552	0.948	0.829	0.938	0.656	0.993
22	ISP	0.566	0.611	0.469	0.509	0.737	0.787
23	KCN	0.811	0.886	0.918	0.930	0.905	0.960
24	KFP	0.370	0.663	0.467	0.705	0.500	0.807
25	LMN	0.612	0.923	0.747	0.931	0.745	0.987
26	MDN	0.807	0.950	0.935	0.982	0.936	0.995
27	MTB	0.622	0.896	0.729	0.874	0.746	0.981
28	MCE	0.701	0.955	0.885	0.942	0.834	0.996
29	MSJ	0.453	0.955	0.392	0.610	0.520	0.996
30	AFB	0.424	0.726	0.259	0.543	0.576	0.871
31	MPN	0.780	0.830	0.892	0.941	0.905	0.938
32	MMN	0.781	0.868	0.842	0.888	0.903	0.962
33	NSC	0.416	0.963	0.431	0.703	0.485	0.997
34	PBN	0.515	0.691	0.712	0.779	0.677	0.864

continued on following page

Table 3. Continued

#	Net.	Kendall's		Pearson's		Spearman's	
		DEG	LCC'DC	DEG	LCC'DC	DEG	LCC'DC
35	PSN	0.749	0.824	0.838	0.883	0.913	0.955
36	PFN	0.659	0.811	0.849	0.882	0.804	0.929
37	SJN	0.577	0.708	0.812	0.861	0.722	0.851
38	SDI	0.660	0.665	0.737	0.740	0.792	0.793
39	SPR	0.723	0.763	0.835	0.880	0.872	0.905
40	SWC	0.742	0.771	0.905	0.927	0.863	0.883
41	SSM	0.584	0.795	0.851	0.867	0.708	0.906
42	TEN	0.624	0.850	0.859	0.942	0.750	0.939
43	TWF	0.338	0.795	0.218	0.696	0.433	0.904
44	UKF	0.624	0.818	0.782	0.908	0.794	0.949
45	APN	0.719	0.882	0.705	0.825	0.863	0.973
46	USS	0.730	0.751	0.744	0.770	0.864	0.889
47	RHF	0.669	0.787	0.841	0.903	0.843	0.934
48	WSB	0.866	0.912	0.895	0.948	0.964	0.986
49	WTN	0.845	0.956	0.908	0.944	0.949	0.995
50	YPI	0.834	0.910	0.847	0.849	0.917	0.980

levels of correlation. On a relative scale, we also observe the correlation coefficients to be relatively more different with respect to the Kendall's pair-wise concordance-based correlation compared to the other two correlation measures. The median of the difference in the correlation coefficient values (between BWC-LCC'DC vs. BWC-DEG) with respect to the Kendall's, Spearman's and Pearson's correlation measures are 0.12, 0.08 and 0.05 respectively.

In the case of EVC, barring 4-5 real-world networks, we observe the DEG metric to be relatively strongly correlated compared to the LCC'DC metric for the rest of the real-world networks with respect to all the three levels of correlation. This could be attributed to the consideration of the degree of the neighbor vertices as part of the formulation to compute the EVC of a vertex. The median of the EVC-DEG correlation coefficient values observed with respect to the Kendall's, Pearson's and Spearman's measures are 0.70, 0.89 and 0.84 respectively. Thus, we observe DEG to be relatively more suitable to predict the EVC values of the vertices using linear regression as well as rank the vertices in lieu of EVC. The median of the difference in the correlation

Figure 3. Distribution of the correlation coefficient values: BWC vs. {DEG, LCC'DC}

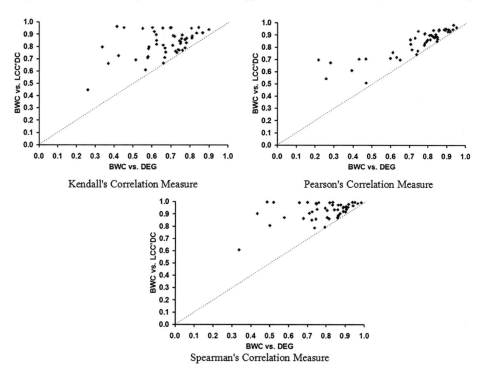

Table 4. Correlation analysis of EVC vs. {DEG, LCC'DC}

#	Net.	Kendall's		Pearson's		Spearman's	
		DEG	LCC'DC	DEG	LCC'DC	DEG	LCC'DC
1	ADJ	0.801	0.676	0.957	0.920	0.929	0.850
2	AKN	0.763	0.540	0.936	0.855	0.897	0.664
3	JBN	0.750	0.608	0.901	0.793	0.890	0.788
4	CEN	0.629	0.535	0.871	0.825	0.811	0.719
5	CLN	0.892	0.759	0.961	0.907	0.976	0.908
6	CGD	0.722	0.633	0.810	0.744	0.876	0.797
7	CFN	0.870	0.622	0.935	0.823	0.965	0.766
8	DON	0.522	0.513	0.720	0.703	0.627	0.663
9	DRN	0.603	0.495	0.650	0.613	0.758	0.610
10	DLN	0.768	0.654	0.947	0.845	0.904	0.817
11	ERD	0.675	0.581	0.916	0.870	0.827	0.741
12	FMH	0.541	0.463	0.558	0.511	0.704	0.586
13	FHT	0.812	0.646	0.937	0.829	0.920	0.827
14	FTC	0.596	0.432	0.822	0.700	0.730	0.579

continued on following page

Table 4. Continued

#	Net.	Kendall's		Pearson's		Spearman's	
		DEG	LCC'DC	DEG	LCC'DC	DEG	LCC'DC
15	FON	0.606	-0.009	0.750	0.011	0.722	-0.007
16	CDF	0.972	0.850	0.997	0.946	0.991	0.967
17	GD96	0.568	0.578	0.844	0.860	0.684	0.694
18	MUN	-0.356	-0.344	-0.712	-0.548	-0.479	-0.440
19	GLN	0.578	0.411	0.853	0.753	0.718	0.530
20	HTN	0.954	0.864	0.994	0.963	0.995	0.972
21	HCN	0.791	0.486	0.936	0.784	0.922	0.603
22	ISP	0.644	0.583	0.893	0.848	0.813	0.771
23	KCN	0.647	0.549	0.917	0.867	0.775	0.680
24	KFP	0.843	0.521	0.931	0.736	0.945	0.674
25	LMN	0.738	0.525	0.847	0.585	0.868	0.683
26	MDN	0.940	0.711	0.994	0.913	0.990	0.871
27	MTB	0.682	0.431	0.924	0.701	0.835	0.548
28	MCE	0.874	0.546	0.977	0.790	0.957	0.638
29	MSJ	0.090	0.061	0.508	0.082	0.120	0.076
30	AFB	-0.267	-0.044	-0.720	-0.224	-0.361	-0.045
31	MPN	0.692	0.597	0.907	0.838	0.838	0.778
32	MMN	0.734	0.573	0.877	0.761	0.851	0.701
33	NSC	-0.092	0.003	-0.511	0.020	-0.107	0.005
34	PBN	0.515	0.381	0.670	0.591	0.663	0.516
35	PSN	0.895	0.786	0.982	0.943	0.983	0.941
36	PFN	0.733	0.485	0.843	0.677	0.863	0.632
37	SJN	0.413	0.333	0.664	0.579	0.536	0.432
38	SDI	0.398	0.391	0.324	0.318	0.512	0.502
39	SPR	0.866	0.713	0.976	0.914	0.968	0.886
40	SWC	0.874	0.597	0.968	0.848	0.964	0.767
41	SSM	0.585	0.390	0.780	0.613	0.714	0.494
42	TEN	0.650	0.401	0.776	0.636	0.774	0.520
43	TWF	0.235	0.177	0.523	0.388	0.294	0.241
44	UKF	0.799	0.554	0.944	0.801	0.928	0.719
45	APN	0.725	0.579	0.956	0.827	0.864	0.735
46	USS	0.667	0.579	0.832	0.766	0.799	0.733
47	RHF	0.715	0.596	0.892	0.808	0.876	0.777
48	WSB	0.909	0.810	0.982	0.940	0.983	0.947
49	WTN	0.851	0.672	0.983	0.948	0.954	0.827
50	YPI	0.330	0.324	0.349	0.333	0.422	0.414

Figure 4. Distribution of the correlation coefficient values: EVC vs. {DEG, LCC'DC}

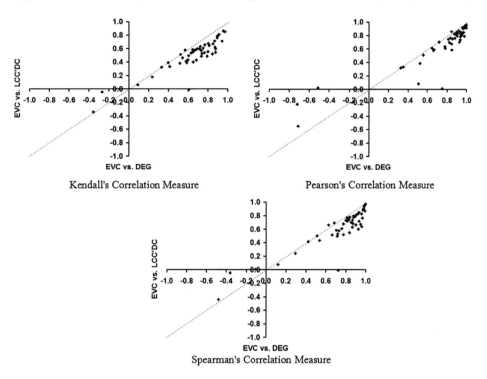

Kendall's Correlation Measure   Pearson's Correlation Measure

Spearman's Correlation Measure

Table 5. Correlation analysis of CLC vs. {DEG, LCC'DC}

#	Net.	Kendall's		Pearson's		Spearman's	
		DEG	LCC'DC	DEG	LCC'DC	DEG	LCC'DC
1	ADJ	0.764	0.655	0.841	0.799	0.901	0.824
2	AKN	0.626	0.507	0.846	0.769	0.767	0.621
3	JBN	0.736	0.726	0.859	0.782	0.890	0.891
4	CEN	0.553	0.499	0.700	0.661	0.738	0.685
5	CLN	0.847	0.720	0.282	0.221	0.956	0.874
6	CGD	0.754	0.697	0.497	0.432	0.893	0.852
7	CFN	0.882	0.649	0.908	0.903	0.945	0.767
8	DON	0.548	0.604	0.713	0.765	0.718	0.780
9	DRN	0.718	0.573	0.608	0.490	0.856	0.700
10	DLN	0.856	0.768	0.908	0.882	0.953	0.903
11	ERD	0.709	0.639	0.261	0.221	0.858	0.798
12	FMH	0.739	0.560	0.624	0.464	0.871	0.684
13	FHT	0.866	0.787	0.409	0.303	0.956	0.923
14	FTC	0.650	0.652	0.837	0.845	0.802	0.821

continued on following page

Table 5. Continued

#	Net.	Kendall's		Pearson's		Spearman's	
		DEG	LCC'DC	DEG	LCC'DC	DEG	LCC'DC
15	FON	0.272	0.366	0.291	0.552	0.344	0.506
16	CDF	0.998	0.895	0.990	0.982	1.000	0.981
17	GD96	0.552	0.572	0.513	0.562	0.659	0.669
18	MUN	0.395	0.379	0.303	0.222	0.486	0.472
19	GLN	0.664	0.498	0.366	0.307	0.806	0.642
20	HTN	0.990	0.914	0.993	0.990	0.999	0.987
21	HCN	0.743	0.539	0.241	0.100	0.874	0.645
22	ISP	0.602	0.559	0.722	0.692	0.786	0.756
23	KCN	0.786	0.759	0.772	0.766	0.895	0.874
24	KFP	0.766	0.600	0.470	0.408	0.877	0.749
25	LMN	0.551	0.516	0.800	0.757	0.675	0.639
26	MDN	0.997	0.792	0.992	0.950	1.000	0.925
27	MTB	0.737	0.528	0.341	0.186	0.872	0.662
28	MCE	0.990	0.679	0.982	0.946	1.000	0.802
29	MSJ	0.488	0.331	0.217	0.277	0.580	0.401
30	AFB	0.272	0.429	0.083	0.123	0.303	0.549
31	MPN	0.643	0.618	0.881	0.862	0.782	0.780
32	MMN	0.865	0.732	0.733	0.705	0.943	0.856
33	NSC	0.595	0.312	0.240	0.281	0.711	0.383
34	PBN	0.418	0.479	0.582	0.627	0.585	0.674
35	PSN	0.869	0.881	0.952	0.954	0.974	0.981
36	PFN	0.761	0.628	0.875	0.777	0.884	0.788
37	SJN	0.486	0.462	0.672	0.670	0.618	0.615
38	SDI	0.416	0.407	0.379	0.363	0.520	0.514
39	SPR	0.870	0.747	0.930	0.882	0.968	0.904
40	SWC	0.864	0.621	0.941	0.841	0.954	0.768
41	SSM	0.610	0.570	0.782	0.804	0.696	0.686
42	TEN	0.524	0.562	0.612	0.717	0.629	0.703
43	TWF	0.279	0.382	0.326	0.344	0.344	0.478
44	UKF	0.759	0.637	0.918	0.848	0.904	0.806
45	APN	0.670	0.583	0.803	0.687	0.823	0.733
46	USS	0.582	0.528	0.755	0.693	0.746	0.701
47	RHF	0.724	0.748	0.891	0.902	0.881	0.907
48	WSB	0.904	0.850	0.975	0.967	0.971	0.962
49	WTN	0.993	0.820	0.987	0.992	0.999	0.929
50	YPI	0.398	0.390	0.191	0.199	0.506	0.496

coefficient values (between EVC-DEG vs. EVC-LCC'DC) with respect to the Kendall's, Spearman's and Pearson's correlation measures are 0.12, 0.10 and 0.08 respectively.

In the case of CLC, for at least 35 real-world networks, we observe the DEG metric to be relatively strongly correlated compared to the LCC'DC metric with respect to all the three levels of correlation. For at least 10 of the real-world networks, we observe LCC'DC to be relatively more strongly correlated with CLC. The median of the CLC-DEG (CLC-LCC'DC) correlation coefficient values observed with respect to the Kendall's, Pearson's and Spearman's measures are 0.72 (0.60), 0.72 (0.70) and 0.86 (0.76) respectively. Thus, we observe DEG to be relatively more suitable to rank the vertices in lieu of CLC. The median of the difference in the correlation coefficient values (between CLC-DEG vs. CLC-LCC'DC) with respect to the Kendall's, Spearman's and Pearson's correlation measures are 0.08, 0.04 and 0.07 respectively, and not as high as those observed for BWC and EVC.

The total number of combinations for the two computationally-light {DEG, LCC'DC} vs. the three computationally-heavy {CLC, EVC, BWC} centrality

Figure 5. Distribution of the correlation coefficient values: CLC vs. {DEG, LCC'DC}

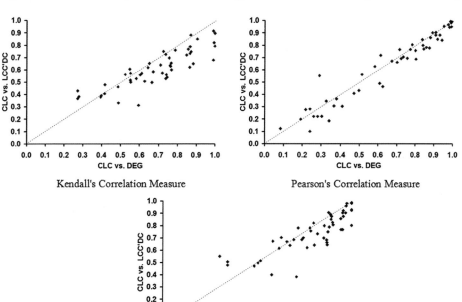

Kendall's Correlation Measure

Pearson's Correlation Measure

Spearman's Correlation Measure

Figure 6. Kendall's vs. Spearman's and Pearson's Correlation Coefficients: {DEG, LCC'DC} vs. CLC

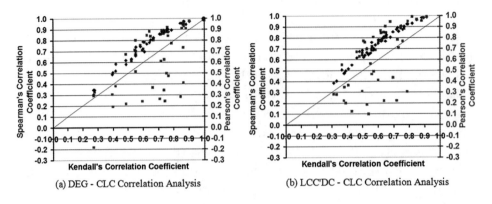

(a) DEG - CLC Correlation Analysis   (b) LCC'DC - CLC Correlation Analysis

Figure 7. Kendall's vs. Spearman's and Pearson's Correlation Coefficients: {DEG, LCC'DC} vs. EVC

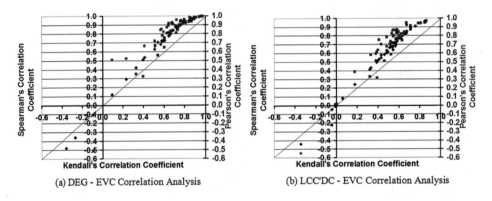

(a) DEG - EVC Correlation Analysis   (b) LCC'DC - EVC Correlation Analysis

metrics evaluated on the 50 real-world network graphs is 2 computationally-light * 3 computationally-heavy * 50 real-world network graphs = 300 combinations. Out of these 300 combinations, for 225 combinations, the Kendall's correlation measure has been observed to incur the lowest values for the correlation coefficient and the Pearson's correlation measure incur the lowest correlation coefficient values for the remaining 75 of the 300 combinations. The Spearman's correlation measure did not incur the lowest correlation coefficient value for any of the 300 combinations. Also, from Tables 1-2, we observe the Kendall's correlation measure to incur the largest values for the correlation coefficient for only 8 of the 300 combinations. Hence, we conclude that the Kendall's correlation measure is likely to serve as a lower bound for the correlation coefficient between any computationally-light vs. computationally-heavy centrality metric with a probability of 0.75 and not an upper bound for the correlation coefficient with a probability of 1 - 8/300 = 0.97. We can also conclude that the Spearman's correlation measure is not likely to incur the lowest values for the correlation coefficient. The Kendall's correlation measure could be hence the first correlation measure that could be computed between a computationally-light vs. computationally-heavy centrality metric; higher values for the Kendall's correlation coefficient between two centrality metrics is more likely an indication that the two centrality metrics would be strongly correlated with respect to the Spearman's and Pearson's correlation measures too.

Figures 6-8 present a visual comparison of the correlation coefficient values incurred for the three correlation measures with respect to the computationally-light vs. computationally-heavy centrality metrics and further corroborate our above assertions. In each of the sub plots of Figures 6-8, the Kendall's correlation measure is compared with the other two correlation measures. If a data point lies above (below) the diagonal line, it implies the other correlation measure (Spearman's for blue colored data points or Pearson's for red colored data points) incurred correlation coefficient value larger (lower) than that of Kendall's. As mentioned above, the blue colored data points pertaining to Spearman's correlation measure are consistently distributed above the diagonal line in all the sub plots of Figures 6-8. Among the three computationally-heavy centrality metrics, the Kendall's correlation coefficient is the lowest (compared to the other two correlation measures) for more than 90% of the data points with respect to EVC (see Figure 7).

4. CORRELATION ANALYSIS OF EDGE CENTRALITY METRICS

This section presents in detail the results of the correlation analysis conducted for the computationally-light NOVER' vs. computationally-heavy EBWC metric for 47 real-world network graphs. Table 6 lists the values for the correlation coefficient incurred with the three correlation measures for EBWC vs. NOVER'. We observe 33 of the 47 real-world networks (about 70%) to exhibit correlation coefficient values of 0.60 or above with respect to the Spearman's measure for network-wide ranking. On the other hand, only 16-17 real-world networks (about 35%) exhibit correlation coefficient

Figure 8. Kendall's vs. Spearman's and Pearson's correlation coefficients: {DEG, LCC'DC} vs. BWC

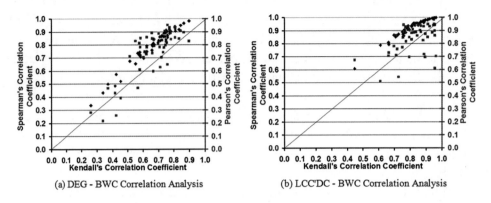

(a) DEG - BWC Correlation Analysis   (b) LCC'DC - BWC Correlation Analysis

Table 6. EBWC vs. NOVER': Correlation coefficient values for real-world networks

#	Net.	Spearman's	Kendall's	Pearson's
1	ADJ	0.320	0.227	0.280
2	AKN	0.819	0.665	0.471
3	JBN	0.755	0.566	0.459
4	CEN	0.616	0.442	0.405
5	CLN	0.655	0.475	0.488
6	CGD	0.571	0.427	0.436
7	CFN	0.897	0.747	0.596
8	DON	0.641	0.476	0.465
9	DRN	0.340	0.270	0.210
10	DLN	0.615	0.458	0.472
11	ERD	0.557	0.408	0.312
12	FMH	0.278	0.217	0.256
13	FHT	0.594	0.432	0.546
14	FTC	0.759	0.566	0.660
15	FON	0.774	0.593	0.753
16	CDF	0.912	0.742	0.741
17	MUN	0.745	0.640	0.339
18	GLN	0.432	0.338	0.376
19	HTN	0.715	0.532	0.431
20	HCN	0.888	0.742	0.684
21	ISP	0.539	0.382	0.189
22	KCN	0.603	0.434	0.528

continued on following page

Table 6. Continued

#	Net.	Spearman's	Kendall's	Pearson's
23	KFP	0.783	0.611	0.600
24	LMN	0.873	0.710	0.535
25	MDN	0.947	0.806	0.896
26	MTB	0.814	0.641	0.577
27	MCE	0.924	0.761	0.804
28	MSJ	0.645	0.567	0.238
29	AFB	0.804	0.641	0.303
30	MPN	0.649	0.484	0.632
31	MMN	0.467	0.340	0.465
32	NSC	0.806	0.706	0.226
33	PBN	0.560	0.401	0.411
34	PSN	0.825	0.643	0.648
35	PFN	0.626	0.489	0.612
36	SJN	0.652	0.492	0.571
37	SPR	0.560	0.398	0.475
38	SWC	0.510	0.384	0.446
39	SSM	0.566	0.451	0.448
40	TEN	0.793	0.653	0.778
41	TWF	0.812	0.661	0.662
42	UKF	0.780	0.586	0.639
43	APN	0.738	0.565	0.353
44	USS	0.547	0.403	0.393
45	RHF	0.759	0.564	0.612
46	WSB	0.809	0.628	0.739
47	WTN	0.873	0.692	0.723
Median		0.715	0.564	0.475

values of 0.60 or above with respect to pair-wise relative ordering and linear regression-based prediction.

We observe the EBWC-NOVER' correlation is best expressed when the edges are to be ranked network-wide and the Spearman's correlation coefficient between EBWC and NOVER' could be considered the upper bound for the correlation coefficient (Figure 9 presents the distribution of the correlation coefficient values in a sorted order for each of the three correlation measures) that could be expected of the two edge centrality metrics for any real-world network graph. Thus, the higher levels of EBWC-NOVER' correlation with respect to the Spearman's correlation measure could be exploited to use the NOVER' scores to rank the edges in a network graph in lieu of EBWC. Figures 10-12 present plots of the Pearson's vs. Spearman's, Pearson's vs. Kendall's and Spearman's vs. Kendall's measures respectively. For all the 47 real-world networks, the correlation coefficient values incurred for the Spearman's correlation measure have been observed to be larger compared to the values incurred for the Kendall's and Pearson's correlation measures. The median of the Spearman's, Kendall's and Pearson's correlation coefficient values are respectively 0.715, 0.564 and 0.475.

One can observe from Figure 11 that real-world networks either have larger correlation coefficient values for both the Spearman's and Kendall's measures or lower values for both the correlation measures. There is no real-world network whose Spearman's correlation coefficient value is above the median (0.715) and Kendall's correlation coefficient value is below the median (0.564) or vice-versa. This vindicates that a real-world network with lower (higher) correlation among edges with respect to pair-wise relative ordering are more likely to also incur lower (higher) correlation among edges with respect to network-wide ranking. On the other hand, from Figures 10 and 12, one can observe that there are some appreciable number of real-world networks that

Figure 9. Distributed of the sorted order of the correlation coefficient values

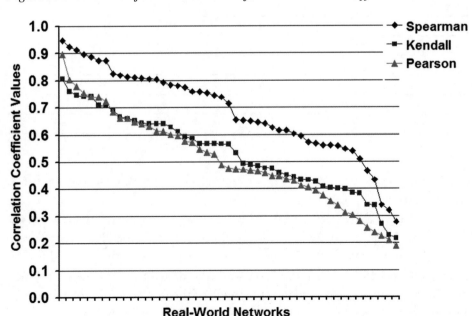

Figure 10. EBWC vs. NOVER': Spearman's vs. Pearson's correlation coefficient values

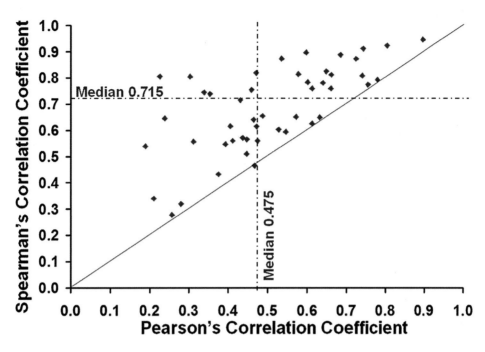

Figure 11. EBWC vs. NOVER': Spearman's vs. Kendall's correlation coefficient values

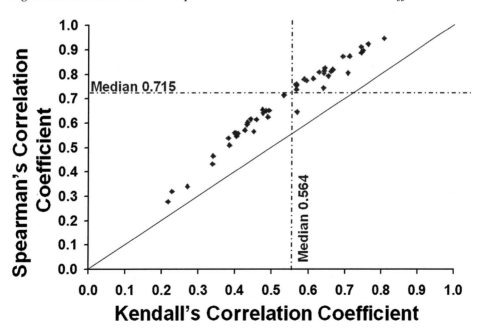

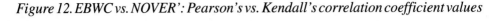

Figure 12. EBWC vs. NOVER': Pearson's vs. Kendall's correlation coefficient values

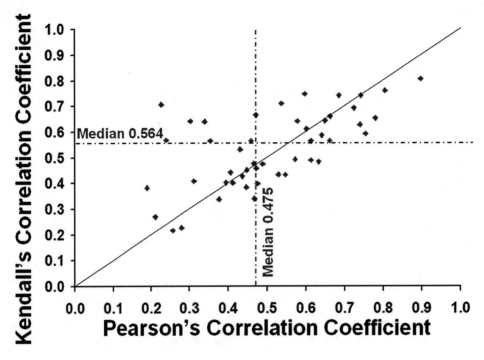

had larger correlation coefficient values with respect to one measure and lower correlation coefficient values with respect to another measure.

Figures 13-15 present the difference in the correlation coefficient values between any two correlation measures to facilitate visual analytics of the results. For all the real-world networks, we observe the Spearman's correlation coefficient values to be appreciably larger (or at the worst equal) than that of the Pearson's correlation coefficient values. We observe 21 of the 47 real-world networks to exhibit larger values for the Pearson's correlation coefficient compared to Kendall's correlation coefficient. To further corroborate this, we also observe that for about 28 of the 47 real-world networks, the difference between the Spearman's correlation coefficient and the Kendall's correlation coefficient (no more than 0.20) is typically lower than the difference between the Spearman's correlation coefficient and the Pearson's correlation coefficient (as large as 0.58). It is interesting to observe from Figure 14 that the Pearson's correlation coefficient is larger than the Kendall's correlation coefficient for real-world networks for which the Pearson's correlation coefficient is significantly lower than the Spearman's correlation coefficient.

Figure 13. Difference in correlation coefficient values: Spearman's vs. Kendall's & Pearson's measures

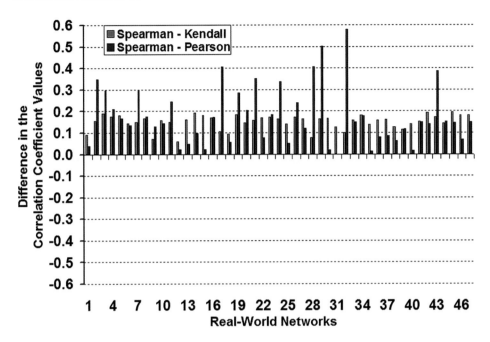

Figure 14. Difference in correlation coefficient values: Pearson's vs. Kendall's & Spearman's measures

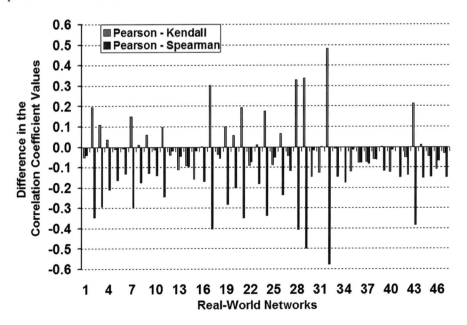

Figure 15. Difference in correlation coefficient values: Kendall's vs. Pearson's & Spearman's measures

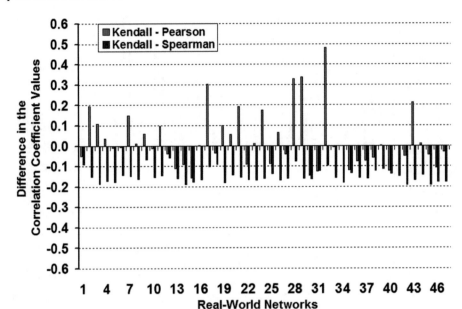

Figure 16 presents the distribution of the spectral radius ratio for node degree vs. the correlation coefficients based on the three correlation measures. The general trend of the distribution is that real-world networks with a lower variation in node degree are likely to exhibit a larger value for the EBWC-NOVER' correlation coefficient compared to networks with larger variation in node degree. Such a trend is more evident in the case of the Pearson's correlation measure. Also, among the 24 real-world networks that had spectral radius ratio for node degree values less than 1.5, the Spearman's correlation coefficient values for 19 of these networks are observed to be 0.60 or above.

5. RELATED WORK

To the best of our knowledge, ours is the first attempt to comprehensively present correlation analysis of the computationally-light vs. computationally-heavy node as well as edge centrality metrics with respect to all the three levels of correlation. Below, we describe the related work in the literature for correlation studies involving the node centrality metrics and edge centrality metrics.

Figure 16. Spectral radius ratio for node degree vs. the correlation coefficient values

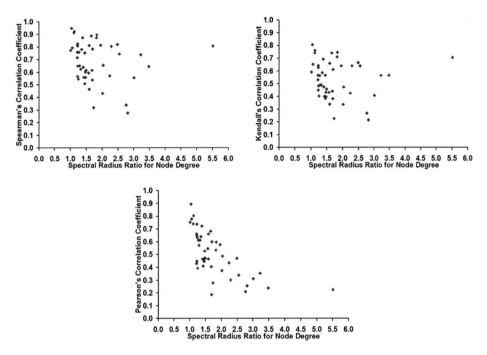

5.1 Node Centrality Metrics

Li et al. (2015) recently started analyzing the correlations between centrality metrics from the point of view of computationally-light DEG vs. the computationally-heavy CLC, EVC and BWC metrics. Meghanathan (2015) also conducted a correlation study of the computationally-heavy maximal clique size for a node (the largest sized clique a node is part of) vs. the computationally-light DEG and the computationally-heavy CLC, EVC and BWC metrics. In both these works, the LCC'DC metric was not considered as well as the Spearman's and Kendall's correlation measures were not used (only the DEG metric is used for the computationally-light metric and the Pearson's correlation measure was the only correlation measure used). The use of Spearman's and Kendall's correlation measures for centrality metrics was recently advocated by Aprahamian et al. (2016) who observed the Kendall's measure to be more suitable for analyzing the correlations involving the top-k ranked vertices, whereas the Spearman's measure was suitable for all rank-based correlation involving all the vertices (especially if there are ties). The three correlation measures were also used by Sajitz-Hermstein and Nikoloski (2016) to analyze the extent to which the flux changes could predict the *functional centrality* metric that could quantify the functional relevance of individual biochemical reactions in metabolic networks.

Wang et al. (2014) developed a new centrality metric (called CIRank) to track the changes propagating among the classes in a software dependency network. They observed larger Spearman's correlation coefficient values for CIRank vs. degree and PageRank centrality metrics. Koschutzki and Schreiber (2008) analyzed the pair-wise correlation (using Kendall's measure) between any two of a suite of eight centrality metrics appropriate for gene regulatory networks. The Kendall's correlation coefficient values were observed to be much lower for any two centrality metrics, especially when genes with non-zero out degree were only considered. In a related study, Dawyer et al. (2006) studied the pair-wise correlation of protein-protein interaction networks in *M. musculus* with respect to DEG, CLC, EVC and BWC metrics. Nomikos et al. (2014) observed that removing the top-k vertices with respect to the locally computable degree centrality metric and the globally computable centrality metrics had a similar impact on the traffic-carrying capacity of the remaining nodes in the network.

Though some of the related work have considered the use of the three correlation measures for correlation studies involving centrality metrics, ours is the first effort to study the correlation from the point of view of computationally-light vs. computationally-heavy centrality metrics involving all the three correlation measures (Kendall's, Spearman's and Pearson's) as well as the LCC'DC metric included along with DEG as a computationally-light centrality metric. One of the key observations from the correlation studies is that the Kendall's correlation measure is more likely to serve as a lower bound (with a probability of 0.75) and not an upper bound (with a probability of 0.97) for the correlation coefficient between a computationally-light vs. computationally-heavy centrality metric.

5.2 Edge Centrality Metrics

To the best of our knowledge, all the correlation studies in the literature on centrality metrics are exclusively focused on node-level metrics. Even for correlation studies that analyze the similarity among the end nodes of the links from the assortativity perspective (Meghanathan, 2016b), it is only the node centrality metrics that are used and the edge centrality metrics are not used.

Ours is the first study to exclusively focus on directly analyzing the correlation between two edge centrality metrics, especially from a computationally-heavy vs. computationally-light metric perspective as well as with respect to the three different levels of correlation.

The two edge centrality metrics that are analyzed in this chapter have been considered for several networking applications. Recently, Meghanathan (2016a) used the neighborhood overlap (NOVER) metric to identify stable links in a mobile sensor network without the need of the location and mobility information of the nodes. It has been observed that links with larger NOVER scores (the end nodes of such links are more likely to be closer to each other) are relatively more stable than links with lower NOVER scores. In the context of social networks (Easley & Kleinberg, 2010), edges with larger NOVER scores are considered to be strong ties (friendships) and edges with lower NOVER scores are considered to be weak ties (acquaintances). The weak ties are sometimes categorized as "local bridges" (Easley & Kleinberg, 2010) as they have been observed to be influential to spread the information from one community of nodes to other communities of nodes in a social network. Fu et al. (2016) observed that the top 10% of the nodes with the largest degree are "leader nodes" of a community and link the community with the other communities in a network.

The edge betweenness centrality (EBWC) metric is an integral part of the well-known Girvan Newman (GN) algorithm for community detection (Girvan & Newman, 2002). EBWC-based community detection has been observed to determine highly modular communities compared to community detection algorithms based on other edge-level metrics (Girvan & Newman, 2002). The tradeoff is that the GN algorithm requires the EBWC of the edges to be repeatedly computed after the removal of each edge. In addition to community detection, some of the other applications of EBWC are as follows: EBWC-based clustering has been used to identify functionally unannotated proteins on the basis of their close association with functionally annotated proteins in protein-protein interaction networks (Dunn et al., 2005). Cuzzocrea et al. (2012) used the EBWC metric to identify the potential utility of edges (for information flow, message delivery, power dissipation, etc.) in wireless sensor networks and implement topology control (adjusting the transmission range of nodes to conserve energy; Pan et al., 2003). EBWC has been observed to be superior to the graph planarization techniques that have been traditionally used for topology control. In a recent work, Vukicevic et al. (2017) propose the notion of "relative edge betweenness" as the ratio of the EBWC of the edge to that of the square root of the product of the adjusted BWCs of the end vertices of the edge. The adjusted BWC for a vertex is the sum of the EBWCs of the edges to the neighbors of the vertex. While the traditional EBWC captures the global importance of an edge, relative edge betweenness has the potential to effectively capture the importance of an edge in a local neighborhood. Though some alternative measures (like running the BFS algorithm on randomly selected nodes instead of all the nodes)(Bader et al., 2007) to approximate EBWC have been proposed in the literature, all these measures are still computationally-heavy. Alternative proposals to capture edge betweenness (like the number of minimum spanning trees that an edge is part of; Mavroforakis et al., 2015) instead of shortest paths are also computationally-heavy.

Owing to the observation of weak ties as local bridges, the neighborhood overlap metric has been recently (Meghanathan, 2016c) used as part of a greedy strategy (just remove the edges in the increasing order of the NOVER scores until the network disintegrates into two or more components) for community detection and the overall modularity score of the NOVER-based communities has been observed to be comparable to that of the EBWC-based communities (Girvan & Newman, 2002) for several real-world networks. The results of the above work indeed motivated us to directly explore the correlation between EBWC and NOVER' (1-NOVER). The results of the correlation study in this chapter prove our claim that the NOVER' scores could indeed be used to rank the edges (network-wide) in lieu of EBWC.

6. CONCLUSION

The key conclusions one could draw from the correlation studies are as follows: With respect to the node centrality metrics, for all the three correlation measures, the LCC'DC metric exhibits relatively stronger levels of correlation (compared to DEG) with the computationally-heavy BWC metric; the DEG metric exhibit relatively stronger levels of correlation with the EVC and CLC metrics. The Kendall's correlation measure is more likely to serve as the lower bound (with a probability of 0.75) and not the upper bound (with a probability of 0.97) for the correlation coefficient values between the computationally-light vs. computationally-heavy centrality metrics. The Spearman's correlation measure is more likely to be not the lower bound for the correlation coefficient values. With respect to the edge centrality metrics, we observe NOVER' to be an appropriate computationally-light edge centrality metric for the computationally-heavy EBWC metric only for network-wide ranking of the edges and not with respect to pair-wise comparison or linear regression-based prediction.

7. FUTURE RESEARCH DIRECTIONS

The strongly positive EBWC-NOVER' correlation with respect to network-wide ranking could be exploited by the computationally-heavy community detection algorithms (like the Girvan-Newman algorithm), as these algorithms could be henceforth adapted to use NOVER' to rank the edges of a network in lieu of EBWC; this will be evaluated as part of our future work. In addition, we plan to develop one or more computationally-light centrality metrics that exhibit strong correlation with edge betweenness centrality for pair-wise correlation and regression-based prediction. As of now, NOVER' is only suitable for network-wide ranking of the edges in lieu of EBWC and is not suitable to do pair-wise correlation and regression-based prediction for EBWC. We also plan to use one or more supervised machine learning algorithms to build models that could predict the betweenness centrality of the vertices and edges in networks that have similar characteristics like spectral radius ratio for node degree, average clustering coefficient, etc.

REFERENCES

Aprahamian, M., Higham, D. J., & Higham, N. J. (2016). Matching Exponential-based and Resolvent-based Centrality Measures. *Journal of Complex Networks*, *4*(2), 157–176. doi:10.1093/comnet/cnv016

Bader, D. A., Kintali, S., Madduri, K., & Mihail, M. (2007). Approximating Betweenness Centrality. *Proceedings of the 5th International Conference on Algorithms and Models for the Web-Graph*. 10.1007/978-3-540-77004-6_10

Bonacich, P. (1987). Power and Centrality: A Family of Measures. *American Journal of Sociology*, *92*(5), 1170–1182. doi:10.1086/228631

Cuzzocrea, A., Papadimitriou, A., Katsaros, D., & Manolopoulos, Y. (2012). Edge Betweenness Centrality: A Novel Algorithm for QoS-based Topology Control over Wireless Sensor Networks. *Journal of Network and Computer Applications*, *35*(4), 1210–1217. doi:10.1016/j.jnca.2011.06.001

Dawyer, T., Hong, S.-H., Koschutzki, D., Schreiber, F., & Xu, K. (2006). *Visual Analytics of Network Centralities*. Paper presented at the Asia-Pacific Symposium on Information Visualization, Tokyo, Japan.

Dunn, R., Dudbridge, F., & Sanderson, C. M. (2005). The Use of Edge-Betweenness Clustering to Investigate Biological Function in Protein Interaction Networks. *BMC Bioinformatics, 6*(39), 1–14. PMID:15740614

Easley, D., & Kleinberg, J. (2010). *Networks, Crowds, and Markets: Reasoning about a Highly Connected World* (1st ed.). Cambridge University Press. doi:10.1017/CBO9780511761942

Freeman, L. (1977). A Set of Measures of Centrality based on Betweenness. *Sociometry, 40*(1), 35–41. doi:10.2307/3033543

Freeman, L. (1979). Centrality in Social Networks Conceptual Clarification. *Social Networks, 1*(3), 215–239. doi:10.1016/0378-8733(78)90021-7

Fu, J., Wu, J., Liu, C., & Xu, J. (2016). Leaders in Communities of Real-World Networks. *Physica A, 444*, 428–441. doi:10.1016/j.physa.2015.09.091

Girvan, M., & Newman, M. (2002). Community Structure in Social and Biological Networks. *Proceedings of the National Academy of Sciences of the United States of America, 99*(12), 7821–7826. doi:10.1073/pnas.122653799 PMID:12060727

Koschutzki, D., & Schreiber, F. (2008). Centrality Analysis Methods for Biological Networks and their Application to Gene Regulatory Networks. *Gene Regulation and Systems Biology*, (2): 193–201. PMID:19787083

Li, C., Li, Q., Van Mieghem, P., Stamey, H. E., & Wang, H. (2015). Correlation between Centrality Metrics and their Application to the Opinion Model. *The European Physical Journal B, 88*(65), 1–13.

Mavroforakis, C., Garcia-Lebron, R., Koutis, I., & Terzi, E. (2015). *Spanning Edge Centrality: Large-Scale Computation and Applications*. Paper presented at the 24th International Conference on World Wide Web, Florence, Italy. 10.1145/2736277.2741125

Meghanathan, N. (2015). *Maximal Clique Size vs. Centrality: A Correlation Analysis for Complex Real-World Network Graphs*. Paper presented at the 3rd International Conference on Advanced Computing, Networking, and Informatics, Orissa, India.

Meghanathan, N. (2016a). Neighborhood Overlap-based Stable Data Gathering Trees for Mobile Sensor Networks. *International Journal of Wireless Networks and Broadband Technologies*, *5*(1), 1–23. doi:10.4018/IJWNBT.2016010101

Meghanathan, N. (2016b). Assortativity Analysis of Real-World Network Graphs based on Centrality Metrics. *Computer and Information Science*, *9*(3), 7–25. doi:10.5539/cis.v9n3p7

Meghanathan, N. (2016c). A Greedy Algorithm for Neighborhood Overlap-based Community Detection. *Algorithms, 9*(8), 1-26.

Meghanathan, N. (2017). A Computationally-Lightweight and Localized Centrality Metric in lieu of Betweenness Centrality for Complex Network Analysis. *Springer Vietnam Journal of Computer Science*, *4*(1), 23–38. doi:10.100740595-016-0073-1

Newman, M. (2010). *Networks: An Introduction* (1st ed.). Oxford University Press. doi:10.1093/acprof:oso/9780199206650.001.0001

Nomikos, G., Pantazopoulos, P., Karaliopoulos, M., & Stavrakakis, I. (2014). *Comparative Assessment of Centrality Indices and Implications on the Vulnerability of ISP Networks*. Paper presented at the 26th International Teletraffic Congress, Karlskrona, Sweden. 10.1109/ITC.2014.6932932

Pan, J., Hou, Y. T., Cai, L., Shi, Y., & Shen, S. X. (2003). *Topology Control for Wireless Sensor Networks*. Paper presented at the 9th Annual International Conference on Mobile Computing and Networking, San Diego, CA.

Sajitz-Hermstein, M., & Nikoloski, Z. (2016). Functional Centrality as a Predictor of Shifts in Metabolic Flux States. *BMC Research Notes*, *9*(317), 1–4. PMID:27328671

Triola, M. F. (2012). *Elementary Statistics* (12th ed.). Pearson.

Vukicevic, D., Skrekovski, R., & Tepeh, A. (2017). Relative Edge Betweenness Centrality. *Ars Mathematica Contemporanea*, *12*(2), 261–270.

Wang, R., Huang, R., & Qu, B. (2014). Network-Based Analysis of Software Change Propagation. *The Scientific World Journal*, (237243), 1–10. PMID:24790557

Chapter 3
Centrality–Based Assortativity Analysis of Complex Network Graphs

ABSTRACT

In this chapter, the author analyzes the assortativity of real-world networks based on centrality metrics (such as eigenvector centrality, betweenness centrality, and closeness centrality) other than degree centrality. They seek to evaluate the levels of assortativity (assortative, dissortative, neutral) observed for real-world networks with respect to the different centrality metrics and assess the similarity in these levels. The author observes real-world networks are more likely to be neutral (neither assortative nor dissortative) with respect to both R-DEG and BWC, and more likely to be assortative with respect to EVC and CLC. They observe the chances of a real-world network to be dissortative with respect to these centrality metrics to be very minimal. The author also assesses the extent to which they can use the assortativity index (A.Index) values obtained with a computationally light centrality metric to rank the networks in lieu of the A.Index values obtained with a computationally heavy centrality metric.

DOI: 10.4018/978-1-5225-3802-8.ch003

1. INTRODUCTION

Assortativity analysis of a complex network is about evaluating the extent of similarity between the end vertices of the edges in the network with respect to a particular node-level metric (Newman, 2002). The assortativity index (*A. Index*) of a network has been traditionally computed as the Pearson's correlation coefficient (Strang, 2005) of the remaining degree centrality (R-DEG) of the end vertices of the edges in the network (Piraveenan et al., 2014; Piraveenan et al., 2015). The R-DEG of a vertex is one less than the degree centrality of the vertex. Networks with larger *A. Index* values (closer to 1) are considered to be assortative and networks with lower *A. Index* values (closer to -1) are considered to be dissortative. In this chapter, we focus on analyzing the assortativity of real-world networks with respect to some of the well-known centrality metrics (such as EVC, CLC and BWC) other than R-DEG.

Our hypothesis in this chapter is that the *A. Index* of real-world networks could differ based on the centrality metric used to evaluate the Pearson's correlation coefficient of the centrality values of the end vertices. In this regard, we first compute the *A. Index* values of a suite of 50 real-world networks with respect to EVC, CLC, BWC as well as R-DEG and then qualitatively assess the *A. Index* values with respect to an assortativity scale as well as rank the real-world networks based on the *A. Index* values. We observe real-world networks to be more likely to be neutral with respect R-DEG and BWC, but weakly assortative and strongly assortative with respect to EVC and CLC respectively. We thus observe the ranking of the real-world networks based on the *A. Index* values to be not the same with respect to any two centrality metrics. We evaluate the extent of similarity in the ranking of the real-world networks using the Spearman's rank-based correlation coefficient and observe the correlation coefficient values to range from 0.61 to 0.85. We observe the R-DEG-based *A. Index* values to be a computationally-light alternative to rank the networks based on the *A. Index* values of computationally-heavy metrics such as EVC and BWC, but not with respect to CLC.

The rest of the chapter is organized as follows: Section 2 presents the formulation to calculate assortativity index (*A. Index*) and the range of *A. Index* values and the corresponding qualitative levels of assortativity as well as illustrates an example to determine the *A. Index* of a network graph based on the R-DEG and BWC metrics (to also show that the *A. Index* values could be different). Section 3 presents the results of the assortativity analysis conducted on the 48 real-world networks. Section 4 discusses related work and highlights the unique contributions of this chapter. Section 5 concludes the chapter. We model all the real-world networks as undirected graphs.

2. ASSORTATIVITY INDEX FORMULATION AND EXAMPLE

The assortative index (*A. Index*) of a real-world network with respect to a centrality metric is computed as the Pearson's correlation coefficient of the centrality values of the end vertices of the edges. The Pearson's product-moment correlation coefficient between two sets of vertices X and Y (whose entries represent the centrality values for one or more vertices with respect to a particular metric C) is calculated as follows. The jth element in the sets X and Y is denoted by x_j and y_j respectively. Let $C_{\overline{X}}$ and $C_{\overline{Y}}$ (calculated as in formulation-1 below) be respectively the average values for the centrality metric of interest (C) among the vertices constituting the sets X and Y.

$$C_{\overline{X}} = \frac{1}{|X|}\sum_{x_j \in X} C(x_j) \quad C_{\overline{Y}} = \frac{1}{|Y|}\sum_{y_j \in Y} C(y_j) \qquad (1)$$

$$Pearson_C(X,Y) = \frac{\sum\limits_{x_j \in X, y_j \in Y}\left[C(x_j) - C_{\overline{X}}\right]\left[C(y_j) - C_{\overline{Y}}\right]}{\sqrt{\sum\limits_{x_j \in X, y_j \in Y}\left[C(x_j) - C_{\overline{X}}\right]^2}\sqrt{\sum\limits_{x_j \in X, y_j \in Y}\left[C(y_j) - C_{\overline{Y}}\right]^2}} \qquad (2)$$

Table 1 presents the range of values used to qualitatively assess the assortativity levels of the real-world networks based on the *A. Index* values. We use five different levels (strongly assortative, weakly assortative, neutral, weakly dissortative, strongly dissortative) wherein the range of *A. Index* values are equally distributed for each level. We color code the assortativity levels as shown in Tables 1-2.

Figures 1-2 illustrate the computation of the *A. Index* values of a graph based on the R-DEG and BWC metric values of the end vertices of the edges. The DEG and BWC values for the vertices are shown next to the node IDs in Figures 1 and 2 respectively. We observe the *A. Index* values to be different

Table 1. Range of Assortative Index values and the levels of assortativity

Range of *A. Index* Values	Level of Assortativity
0.60 ... 1.00	Strongly Assortative
0.20 ... 0.59	Weakly Assortative
-0.19 ... 0.19	Neutral
-0.59 ... -0.20	Weakly Dissortative
-1.00 ... -0.60	Strongly Dissortative

Figure 1. Calculation of the Assortativity Index of the graph based on the Remaining Degree Centrality (R-DEG) values of the end vertices of the edges

Edge (x_j, y_j)	Lists x_j	y_j	R-DEG $C(x_j)$	$C(y_j)$	$C(x_j)-\bar{C}_X$	$C(y_j)-\bar{C}_Y$	$[C(x_j)-\bar{C}_X]^2$	$[C(y_j)-\bar{C}_Y]^2$	$[C(x_j)-\bar{C}_X][C(y_j)-\bar{C}_Y]$
[1-2]	1	2	2	1	0.3	-0.5	0.09	0.25	-0.15
[1-3]	1	3	2	2	0.3	0.5	0.09	0.25	0.15
[1-4]	1	4	2	2	0.3	0.5	0.09	0.25	0.15
[2-3]	2	3	1	2	-0.7	0.5	0.49	0.25	-0.35
[3-4]	3	4	2	2	0.3	0.5	0.09	0.25	0.15
[4-5]	4	5	2	1	0.3	-0.5	0.09	0.25	-0.15
[5-6]	5	6	1	2	-0.7	0.5	0.49	0.25	-0.35
[6-7]	6	7	2	1	0.3	-0.5	0.09	0.25	-0.15
[6-8]	6	8	2	1	0.3	-0.5	0.09	0.25	-0.15
[7-8]	7	8	1	1	-0.7	-0.5	0.49	0.25	0.35
Avg			1.7 ($\bar{C}_X$)	1.5 ($\bar{C}_Y$)	Sum		2.10	2.50	-0.50

$$\textbf{\textit{A.Index}(R-DEG)} = \frac{-0.50}{\sqrt{2.1} * \sqrt{2.5}} = -0.22$$

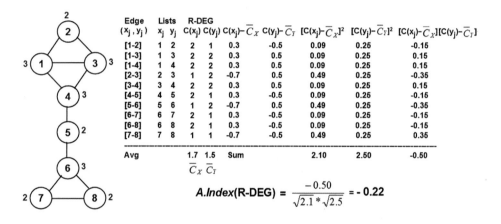

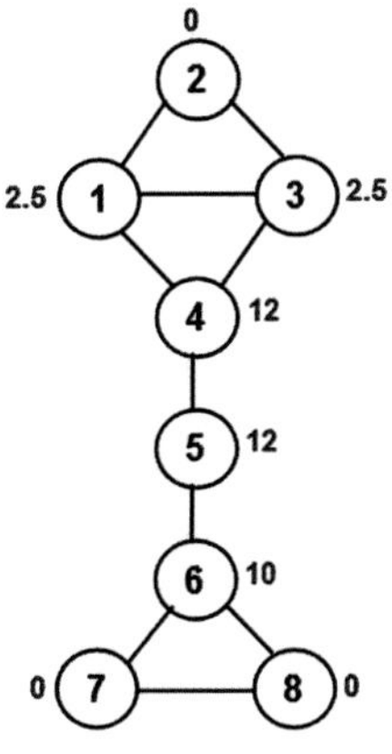

Figure 2. Calculation of the Assortativity Index of the graph based on the Betweenness Centrality (BWC) values of the end vertices of the edges

Edge (x_j, y_j)	BWC Values $C(x_j)$	$C(y_j)$	$C(x_j)-\bar{C}_X$	$C(y_j)-\bar{C}_Y$	$[C(x_j)-\bar{C}_X]^2$	$[C(y_j)-\bar{C}_Y]^2$	$[C(x_j)-\bar{C}_X][C(y_j)-\bar{C}_Y]$
[1-2]	2.5	0	-2.9	-5.1	8.41	26.01	14.79
[1-3]	2.5	2.5	-2.9	-2.6	8.41	6.76	7.54
[1-4]	2.5	12	-2.9	6.9	8.41	47.61	-20.01
[2-3]	0	2.5	-5.4	-2.6	29.16	6.76	14.04
[3-4]	2.5	12	-2.9	6.9	8.41	47.61	-20.01
[4-5]	12	12	6.6	6.9	43.56	47.61	45.54
[5-6]	12	10	6.6	4.9	43.56	24.01	32.34
[6-7]	10	0	4.6	-5.1	21.16	26.01	-23.46
[6-8]	10	0	4.6	-5.1	21.16	26.01	-23.46
[7-8]	0	0	-5.4	-5.1	29.16	26.01	27.54
Avg	5.4 ($\bar{C}_X$)	5.1 ($\bar{C}_Y$)	Sum		221.40	284.40	54.85

$$\textbf{\textit{A.Index}(BWC)} = \frac{54.85}{\sqrt{221.40} * \sqrt{284.40}} = 0.22$$

(-0.22 for R-DEG and 0.22 for BWC) even for this toy example graph. A similar trend is also seen for the real-world networks analyzed in this chapter.

3. RESULTS OF ASSORTATIVITY ANALYSIS

Table 2 lists the centrality-based *A. Index* values obtained for the 50 real-world networks used in this study. The entries in Table 2 are color-coded to be in sync with the ranges and assortativity levels introduced in Table 1. For more than 50% of the real-world networks, we observe two levels of assortativity with respect to any centrality metric (for most cases, the two levels are: neutral and weakly assortative). For about 25% of the real-world networks, we observe three different levels of assortativity. For another 25% of the real-world networks, the assortativity level does not change with the centrality metric. Very few real-world networks (less than 15%) are weakly or strongly dissortative with respect to any centrality metric. If a real-world network exhibits two or three assortativity levels for the centrality metrics, the level of assortativity transitions from neutral to weakly dissortative to strongly dissortative if the centrality metrics are considered in this order: BWC, R-DEG, EVC, CLC.

Figure 3 illustrates the distribution of the centrality-based *A. Index* values. We empirically estimate the probability of observing a real-world network at a particular level of assortativity as the fraction of the real-world networks whose *A. Index* values fall within the range for the level of assortativity. Overall, we observe at least 50% of the real-world networks to be neutral (i.e., neither assortative nor dissortative) with respect to R-DEG and BWC. On the other hand, we observe at least 50% of the real-world networks to be assortative (i.e., weakly or strongly assortative) with respect to EVC and CLC. More specifically, real-world networks are neutral with respect to BWC and R-DEG with estimated empirical probabilities of 0.72 and 0.58 respectively. With respect to EVC, real-world networks are more likely to be weakly assortative (with the largest probability of 0.38 among the different levels). In the case of CLC, real-world networks are more likely to be strongly assortative (with the largest probability of 0.38 among the different levels). Figure 4 presents a comprehensive comparison of the empirically estimated probability values for the different assortativity levels and the four centrality metrics.

We also determine the rankings of the real-world networks with respect to the assortativity index (*A.Index*) values computed with the four centrality metrics and evaluate the Spearman's rank-based correlation coefficients of

Table 2. Centrality-based Assortativity Index values of the real-world networks

#	Net.	BWC	R-DEG	EVC	CLC	#	Net.	BWC	R-DEG	EVC	CLC
1	ADJ	-0.10	-0.10	0.04	0.13	26	LMN	-0.02	-0.08	0.43	0.21
2	AKN	-0.08	-0.08	0.09	0.12	27	MDN	-0.10	-0.05	-0.02	-0.05
3	JBN	-0.04	0.03	0.35	0.18	28	MTB	0.25	0.73	0.79	1.00
4	CEN	-0.06	-0.09	0.22	0.22	29	MCE	0.05	0.72	0.79	0.94
5	CLN	-0.12	-0.11	0.06	0.06	30	MSJ	0.24	0.35	0.94	1.00
6	CGD	0.07	0.14	0.59	1.00	31	AFB	0.09	0.35	0.89	1.00
7	CFN	-0.07	-0.17	-0.09	-0.09	32	MPN	-0.12	-0.16	0.13	0.09
8	DON	0.12	-0.04	0.64	0.53	33	MMN	0.00	0.10	0.50	0.47
9	DRN	0.30	0.35	0.62	1.00	34	PBN	0.04	-0.02	0.54	0.37
10	DLN	-0.08	0.07	0.34	0.33	35	PSN	0.10	0.22	0.29	0.26
11	ERD	0.05	0.18	0.40	1.00	36	PFN	0.23	0.59	0.67	0.96
12	FMH	0.39	0.65	0.84	1.00	37	SJN	0.03	-0.14	0.51	0.41
13	FHT	0.25	0.60	0.69	1.00	38	SDI	0.22	0.08	0.95	1.00
14	FTC	-0.07	-0.03	0.45	0.23	39	SPR	-0.06	0.02	0.14	0.16
15	FON	0.06	0.19	0.69	0.31	40	SMN	-0.20	-0.23	-0.22	-0.23
16	CDF	-0.10	-0.11	-0.10	-0.12	41	SWC	-0.23	-0.17	-0.02	-0.02
17	GD96	-0.24	-0.32	-0.03	0.47	42	SSM	0.04	-0.02	0.50	0.33
18	MUN	0.04	0.14	0.64	1.00	43	TEN	-0.16	-0.36	0.26	0.23
19	GLN	-0.16	-0.13	0.30	1.00	44	TWF	0.55	0.84	0.93	1.00
20	GD01	-0.92	-0.98	-0.75	-0.54	45	UKF	-0.08	0.00	0.22	0.12
21	HTN	-0.10	-0.12	-0.10	-0.12	46	APN	-0.15	-0.21	-0.02	0.06
22	HCN	0.01	0.03	0.18	1.00	47	USS	0.23	0.23	0.62	0.65
23	ISP	0.14	0.29	0.56	0.77	48	RHF	0.00	0.10	0.38	0.25
24	KCN	-0.36	-0.48	-0.24	-0.08	49	WSB	0.02	0.45	0.50	0.89
25	KFP	0.17	0.24	0.53	0.73	50	WTN	-0.26	-0.39	-0.37	-0.35

the network rankings with respect to any two centrality metrics (see Table 3). There are a total of 50 networks; a network is assigned a higher rank number if it has a larger *A.Index* value. Hence, the network with the largest *A.Index* value gets a rank number of 50 and the network with the lowest *A.Index* value gets a rank number of 1. Any ties are broken according to the procedure explained in Chapter 1 for Spearman's rank-based correlation coefficient. From Table 3, we can infer that the *A.Index*(R-DEG) based ranking of the real-world networks has a strong correlation with that of the *A.Index*(BWC) based ranking of the networks. Likewise, we observe the *A.Index*(CLC) based

Figure 3. Distribution of the centrality based Assortativity Index values for the real-world networks

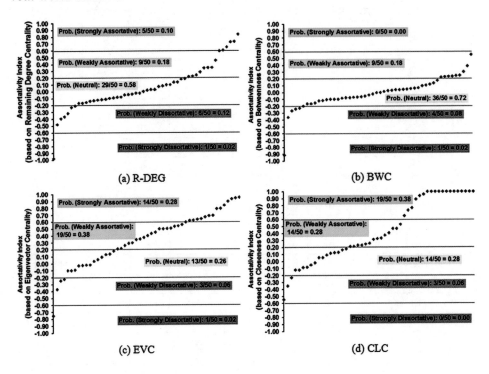

Figure 4. Empirically estimated probability for observing a real-world network at a particular level of assortativity with respect to a centrality metric

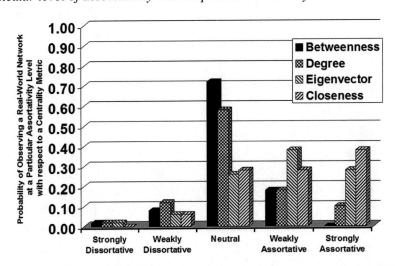

Table 3. Spearman's correlation coefficient for the ranking of real-world networks using the centrality-based Assortativity Index values

	R-DEG	BWC	EVC	CLC
R-DEG		0.90	0.84	0.77
BWC			0.90	0.78
EVC				0.84

ranking of the real-world networks has a strong correlation with that of the *A.Index*(EVC) based ranking of the networks. Among the four centrality metrics, CLC is computationally-heavy than R-DEG, but computationally-light than BWC and EVC (refer to Chapter 1 for the computational time per node for the different centrality metrics). Hence, we can say that R-DEG and CLC could be the computationally-light alternatives to determine an assortativity-based ranking of the real-world networks in lieu of BWC and CLC.

4. RELATED WORK AND OUR CONTRIBUTIONS

The focus of the literature so far (e.g., Newman, 2010; Newman & Girvan, 2003; Noldus & Van Mieghem, 2015) is to study the assortativity of real-world network graphs using the degree centrality metric and its variant, the remaining degree centrality (R-DEG). In this chapter, we study the assortativity of real-world networks with respect to other commonly used centrality metrics such as eigenvector centrality, betweenness centrality and closeness centrality. We estimate the empirical probability of observing a network to be assortative, dissortative or neutral with respect to these centrality metrics (including R-DEG). We observe real-world networks to be more assortative with respect to EVC and CLC and neutral with respect to BWC and R-DEG. We also evaluate the extent to which a computationally-light centrality metric could be alternative to rank the networks based on assortativity and observe strong correlation between R-DEG vs. BWC and CLC vs. EVC. Such results have not been yet reported in the literature. We now discuss the most closely related work on assortativity analysis involving centrality metrics as reported in the literature.

Typically, social networks have been observed to be assortative and the technological as well as biological networks have been observed to be dissortative with respect to the degree centrality metric (Newman, 2003).

But, such studies did not involve a huge collection of real-world networks with diverse degree distribution and spanning over several domains, as is done in this chapter. Among the 50 real-world networks evaluated, more than 50% of the networks are observed to be neutral with respect to R-DEG. The networks generated from theoretical models such as the random network model (Erdos & Renyi, 1959), scale-free network model (Barabasi & Albert, 1999), small-world network model (Watts & Strogatz, 1998) were also observed to be neutral (rather than assortative or dissortative) with respect to the degree centrality metric. In the case of evolutionary networks, for networks that evolve with time without any constraints were observed to be assortative in their maximum entropy state (state of maximum robustness with heterogeneous connectivity distribution)(Demetrius & Manke, 2005; Johnson et al., 2010) and networks that evolve with constraints were observe to transition from being dissortative to assortative over time (Konig et al., 2010). In a related work, synthetic network graphs generated using the Monte Carlo Metropolis-Hastings type algorithms (Chib & Greenberg, 1995) evolved to a giant component quickly with time if the edges (with respect to R-DEG) are assortative (Newman, 2010; Newman, 2003).

Iyer et al. (2013) analyzed the robustness of real-world networks (whose assortativity had been evaluated based on degree) with respect to targeted node removals. Assortative networks were observed to degrade quickly with time if nodes with higher BWC are removed, whereas dissortative and neutral networks were observed to degrade quickly with time if nodes with higher degree are removed. Real-world networks were observed not to degrade much if nodes with larger EVC were removed.

Zhang et al. (2012) proposed the notion of Universal Assortativity Coefficient (UAC) for a community of vertices computed as the sum of the local assortativity index of the edges (as defined by Newman, 2010) emanating from the vertices that are part of the community. Zhang et al. (2012) observed that a globally assortative network could have one or more communities that are locally dissortative with respect to the UAC. In a related work, Piraveenan et al. (2009) studied the distribution of the node assortativity indexes (Piraveenan et al., 2008) vs. the degree of the vertices to identify assortative hubs in social and biological networks and dissortative hubs in scale-free networks (Barabasi & Albert, 1999) such as the Internet. In both the works, the local edge assortativity index and local node assortativity index were computed based on the remaining degree centrality.

The *leverage centrality* metric (values ranging from -1 to 1) was proposed by Joyce et al. (2010) to quantify the assortativeness of the neighborhood of a node. A node is considered to have an assortative neighborhood if it is connected to more nodes than its neighbors (leverage centrality values closer to 1). A node is considered to have a dissortative neighborhood if it is connected to fewer nodes than its neighbors (leverage centrality values closer to -1). Leverage centrality has been so far computed only on the basis of degree centrality and we believe normalized values of the other centrality metrics (like BWC, EVC, CLC, etc) could be used to compute the leverage centrality of the vertices to assess the assortativeness of the neighborhood with respect to these centrality metrics.

Meghanathan (2015) observed a very strong linear correlation between the degree centrality and betweenness centrality metrics for several real-world networks. The results in this chapter also corroborate the above observation, as more than 50% of the real-world networks exhibit the same level of assortativity (neutral) with respect to both R-DEG and BWC. We also attribute the neutral assortativity of the edges as the reason for the low assortativity index for a maximal assortative matching (Meghanathan, 2016) of the nodes based on degree centrality. The results from this chapter indicate real-world networks are relatively more assortative with respect to EVC and CLC, and we opine a maximal assortative matching of the edges based on EVC and CLC would incur a relatively larger assortative index.

5. CONCLUSION

Assortativity analysis of real-world networks has been so far restricted only to the degree centrality of the vertices and its variant (the remaining degree centrality, R-DEG). In this chapter, we have presented the assortativity analysis of real-world networks based on the other commonly used centrality metrics such as eigenvector centrality (EVC), betweenness centrality (BWC) and closeness centrality (CLC). We use a suite of 50 real-world networks for the correlation study and estimate the empirical probabilities that could be used to predict the chances of a real-world network being assortative, dissortative or neutral with respect to a centrality metric. We observe very minimal chances for a real-world network to be dissortative with respect to any of the four common centrality metrics. We observe real-world networks are more likely to be neutral (neither assortative nor dissortative) with respect to BWC (empirical probability of 0.72) and R-DEG (empirical probability of 0.58). On the other hand, we observe real-world networks to be strongly assortative and weakly assortative with respect to CLC and EVC respectively, each with an empirical probability of 0.38. We also observed that real-world networks could be similarly ranked using the assortativity index values obtained for a computationally-light metric (in lieu of a computationally-heavy metric): i.e., R-DEG (in lieu of BWC) and CLC (in lieu of EVC). The results presented in this chapter could be considered to pick the appropriate centrality metric for use with a maximal assortative matching or maximal dissortative matching algorithm as well as to assess the extent of assortativeness of the neighborhood of a node with respect to centrality metrics other than degree centrality.

REFERENCES

Barabasi, A. L., & Albert, R. (1999). Emergence of Scaling in Random Networks. *Science, 286*(5439), 509–512. doi:10.1126cience.286.5439.509 PMID:10521342

Chib, S., & Greenberg, E. (1995). Understanding the Metropolis-Hastings Algorithm. *The American Statistician, 49*(4), 327–335.

Demetrius, L., & Manke, T. (2005). Robustness and Network Evolution - An Entropic Principle. *Physica A, 346*(3-4), 682–696. doi:10.1016/j.physa.2004.07.011

Erdos, P., & Renyi, A. (1959). On Random Graphs I. *Publicationes Mathematicae, 6*, 290–297.

Iyer, S., Killingback, T., Sundaram, B., & Wang, Z. (2013). Attack Robustness and Centrality of Complex Networks. *PLoS One, 8*(4), e59613. doi:10.1371/journal.pone.0059613 PMID:23565156

Johnson, S., Torres, J. J., Marro, J., & Munoz, M. A. (2010). Entropic Origin of Dissortativity in Complex Networks. *Physical Review Letters, 104*(10), 108702. doi:10.1103/PhysRevLett.104.108702 PMID:20366458

Konig, M. D., Tessone, C. J., & Zenou, Y. (2010). From Assortative to Dissortative Networks: The Role of Capacity Constraints. *Advances in Complex Systems, 13*(04), 483–499. doi:10.1142/S0219525910002700

Meghanathan, N. (2015). Correlation Coefficient Analysis of Centrality Metrics for Complex Network Graphs. *Proceedings of the 4th Computer Science Online Conference, 348*, 11-20. 10.1007/978-3-319-18503-3_2

Meghanathan, N. (2016). Maximal Assortative Matching and Maximal Dissortative Matching for Complex Network Graphs. *The Computer Journal*, *59*(5), 667–684. doi:10.1093/comjnl/bxv102

Newman, M. E. J. (2002). Assortative Mixing in Networks. *Physical Review Letters*, *89*(20), 208701. doi:10.1103/PhysRevLett.89.208701 PMID:12443515

Newman, M. E. J. (2003). Mixing Patterns in Networks. *Physical Review. E*, *67*(2), 026126. doi:10.1103/PhysRevE.67.026126 PMID:12636767

Newman, M. E. J. (2010). *Networks: An Introduction*. Oxford, UK: Oxford University Press. doi:10.1093/acprof:oso/9780199206650.001.0001

Newman, M. E. J., & Girvan, M. (2003). Lecture Notes in Physics: Vol. 625. *Mixing Patterns and Community Structure in Networks. Statistical Mechanics of Complex Networks.*

Noldus, R., & Van Mieghem, P. (2015). Assortativity in Complex Networks. *Journal of Complex Networks*, *3*(4), 507–542. doi:10.1093/comnet/cnv005

Piraveenan, M., Prokopenko, M., & Zomaya, A. (2008). Local Assortativeness in Scale-Free Networks. *Europhysics Letters*, *84*(2), 28002. doi:10.1209/0295-5075/84/28002

Piraveenan, M., Prokopenko, M., & Zomaya, A. Y. (2009). Local Assortativity and Growth of Internet. *Interdisciplinary Physics: The European Physical Journal B*, *70*(2), 275–285.

Strang, G. (2005). *Linear Algebra and its Applications*. Pacific Grove, CA: Brooks Cole.

Watts, D. J., & Strogatz, S. H. (1998). Collective Dynamics of Small-World Networks. *Nature*, *393*(6684), 440–442. doi:10.1038/30918 PMID:9623998

Zhang, G.-Q., Cheng, S.-Q., & Zhang, G.-Q. (2012). *A Universal Assortativity Measure for Network Analysis.* arXiv:1212.6456 [physics.soc-ph]

Chapter 4
Temporal Variation of the Node Centrality Metrics for Scale–Free Networks

ABSTRACT

Scale-free networks are a type of complex networks in which the degree distribution of the nodes is according to the power law. In this chapter, the author uses the widely studied Barabasi-Albert (BA) model to simulate the evolution of scale-free networks and study the temporal variation of degree centrality, eigenvector centrality, closeness centrality, and betweenness centrality of the nodes during the evolution of a scale-free network according to the BA model. The model works by adding new nodes to the network, one at a time, with the new node connected to m of the currently existing nodes. Accordingly, nodes that have been in the network for a longer time have greater chances of acquiring more links and hence a larger degree centrality. While the degree centrality of the nodes has been observed to show a concave down pattern of increase with time, the temporal (time) variation of the other centrality measures has not been analyzed until now.

DOI: 10.4018/978-1-5225-3802-8.ch004

1. INTRODUCTION

Real-world networks, ranging from biological networks to the Internet, exhibit complex relationships among the nodes. The complexity is significantly reduced when we model the real-world network as a graph of vertices (representing the nodes) and edges (representing the vertices). There exists well-known theoretical models to generate synthetic graphs whose degree distribution matches with that of the real-world network graphs. Some of the well-known graph theoretical models are the random graph model (Erdos & Renyi, 1959), scale-free model (Barabasi & Albert, 1999) and small-world network model (Watts & Strogatz, 1998). The degree distribution of the random network graphs follows the Poisson model (Erdos & Renyi, 1959) and real-world networks such as the US road network, citation networks, scientific collaboration networks and etc also exhibit a Poisson model (Bornholdt & Schuster, 2003; bell-shaped pattern whose width is a function of the standard deviation of the distribution) for the degree distribution of the vertices. The degree distribution of the scale-free network graphs (Barabasi & Albert, 1999) follows the Power law model and real-world networks such as the World Wide Web, Airline networks, Social networks, Protein-protein interaction networks and etc. exhibit a Power law model for the degree distribution of the vertices (Caldarelli, 2007; a distribution in which the probability for finding nodes with larger degree decreases at a faster rate but the distribution has a long tail).

Our focus of study in this chapter will be on the Barabsi-Albert (BA) model (Barabasi & Albert, 1999) for generating scale-free networks. We seek to analyze the evolution of a scale-free network (under the BA model) over time with respect to the distribution of the centrality metrics (referred to as temporal variation of the centrality metrics). Most of the results currently available (Barabasi & Albert, 1999) in this regard pertains to the degree centrality metric and we briefly review these below: Scale-free networks are characteristic of having a few nodes (but appreciable number of nodes) that have a significantly larger degree than the rest of the nodes in the network. Such nodes are called the hub nodes. Under the BA model for generating scale-free networks, the probability for an existing node to get a new link is proportional to its degree; i.e., new nodes (at the time of joining the network) are more likely to prefer being linked to nodes that have a larger degree (rather nodes with smaller degree). As a result of this "preferential attachment" phenomenon, nodes that joined the network during the earlier stages of evolution exhibited a relatively faster increase in their degree compared to nodes that joined the network during the later stages. Thus, the hub nodes of a scale-free network that evolved under the BA model are those nodes that joined the network much earlier and the nodes that joined at a later time are less likely to become hub nodes.

Our objective in this chapter is to analyze the temporal variation (time-dependent) of the three commonly studied centrality metrics (in addition to degree centrality), viz., eigenvector centrality (EVC), closeness centrality (CLC) and betweenness centrality (BWC) during the evolution of a scale-free network under the BA model. The simulation procedure we use to generate a scale-free network under the BA model is as follows: We start with n_0 number of nodes that are linked in such a way that each node has at least one edge incident on it. After such an initial setup of the nodes, the new nodes join the network one node at a time (starting from time instants n_0+1 to 1000 time units). Each new node acquires 'm' links at the time of its joining the network; these links are chosen probabilistically based on the degrees of the existing nodes in the network (more details are provided in Section 2.2). The ID of a newly joining node is the time at which the node joins the network. We run the simulation for a duration of $1000-n_0$ time units (i.e., at the end of the simulation, there are a total of 1000 nodes in the network). We compute the centrality values of a few selected nodes (that are chosen in such away that their joining times are spread over the 1000 time units) at every time unit since they join the network. For each of the four centrality metrics, we plot the centrality values of the selected vertices vs. time. We observe different patterns of increase or decrease for each centrality metric. The degree centrality (DEG) metric is observed to exhibit a concave down pattern of increase (i.e., the degree centrality of each vertex increases with time, but the rate of increase decreases with time), with the nodes that joined the network earlier exhibiting a relatively faster rate of increase compared to the nodes that joined the network later. The eigenvector centrality metric exhibits a steep concave up pattern of decrease for nodes that joined earlier and a moderate-slow concave up pattern of decrease for nodes that joined later. With concave up pattern of decrease, the rate of decrease increases with time. For the closeness centrality metric, we observe a linear increase with time: the slope of the line (rate of increase) for the nodes that joined the network earlier is relatively lower than the slope of the line for the nodes that joined later. The betweenness centrality is the only centrality metric that exhibit a concave up pattern of increase (i.e., the rate of increase in the centrality value increases with time) such that the BWC of the nodes that joined earlier increases at a much faster rate than the BWC of the nodes that joined later. To the best of our knowledge, this is the first work to study the temporal variation of the major centrality metrics (other than degree centrality) with respect to the evolution of a scale-free network under the BA model.

The rest of this chapter is organized as follows: Section 2 first presents the characteristics of scale-free networks and then explains in detail the evolution of scale-free network under the Barabasi-Albert model. Section 3 presents the simulation environment/parameters and discusses in detail the temporal variation of each of the four centrality metrics during the evolution of a scale-free network under the BA model. Section 4 highlights the unique contributions of the chapter by discussing the related work on evolutionary models for scale-free networks and the robustness of centrality measures to both random as well as systematic variations in network structure. Section 5 concludes the chapter by reinforcing the importance of the observed results in the overall context of analysis of scale-free networks. Section 6 presents future research directions.

2. SCALE-FREE NETWORKS AND BARABASI-ALBERT (BA) MODEL

2.1 Scale-Free Networks and Their Characteristics

A scale-free network exhibits a power-law pattern for the degree distribution of the vertices. Accordingly, the probability of finding a node with degree k is proportional to k^{γ}, where γ is the power-law exponent whose range is typically (2, ..., 3) (Easley & Kleinberg, 2010). The power-law model for degree distribution justifies the presence of few but appreciable number of nodes with degree values that are significantly larger than the average node degree. As a result, unlike the Poisson model, it is not possible to say that the degree values of the vertices are more likely to be within a certain scale related to the average degree (hence, the name "scale-free" for these networks). As shown in Figure 1, the degree distribution of the vertices for a scale-free network is characteristic of a long tail, corresponding to the hub nodes.

Scale-free networks exhibit certain level of hierarchy: The major hubs are mostly connected to some minor hub nodes of relatively smaller degree and these nodes are further connected to the nodes with even smaller degree and so on. Such a hierarchy could be attributed to the ultra small-world

Figure 1. Sample graph for a scale-free network and power-law distribution for node degree

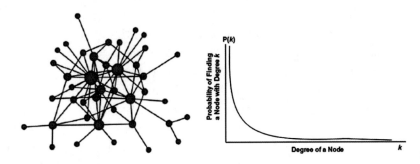

property of the scale-free networks (Watts & Strogatz, 1998) wherein any node is reachable to any other node through a path comprising of the minor hubs and major hubs (a typical example to illustrate the ultra small-world property is the fewer number of intermediate stops one has to make during air travel even between two remote parts of the world). Also, because of this hierarchy, scale-free networks are robust Cohen et al., 2000) to random node failures (as there are only few hub nodes and the majority of the nodes are low-degree nodes, the chances that a randomly chosen node fails is a hub nodes are very minimal). On the other hand, the failure of one or few hub nodes could lead to disintegration of the scale-free network (Cohen et al., 2001). In addition to airline networks, some of the other well-known real-world examples of scale-free networks are World Wide Web (WWW), social networks (like LinkedIn), biological networks (like protein-protein interaction networks) and etc.

Like the degree centrality metric, scale-free networks exhibit a power-law distribution for the clustering coefficient of the nodes. The clustering coefficient of a node is the probability that any two neighbors of the node are connected to each other and is calculated as the ratio of the number of links actually connecting the neighbors of a node to the maximum number of links between any two neighbors of the node. The clustering coefficient of a node ranges from 0 to 1. Due to the hierarchical layout of the nodes in a scale-free network, it is difficult to expect to the neighbors of a hub node (especially those of the minor hub nodes) to be connected to each other. Hence, the hub nodes of a scale-free network typically have a low clustering coefficient. On the other hand, the low-degree nodes (which are in majority) have the hub nodes as their neighbors and these hub nodes are typically connected to each other (e.g., the hub nodes of an airline network are connected to each other, whereas the low-degree nodes are not directly connected to each other). Thus, the low-degree nodes are likely to have a larger clustering coefficient. The probability of finding a node with a larger clustering coefficient is therefore much higher than the probability of finding a node with a lower clustering coefficient. The major hubs of the scale-free networks also serve as structural holes, connecting the disjointed communities of minor hubs and their associated low-degree nodes. The sub graphs of a minor hub and their associated low-degree nodes form denser communities.

2.2 Barabasi-Albert (BA) Model

The Barabasi-Albert (BA) model for evolution of a scale-free network works as follows: To begin with, we have n_0 nodes (with node IDs running from 1 to n_0); each node is connected a randomly chosen node among the remaining nodes. This way, each of the n_0 nodes is guaranteed to have at least one link before the new nodes start joining. After the initial setup, the new nodes start joining the network: one node per time instant. A newly joining node is connected to 'm' of the existing nodes in the network (hence, $m \leq n_0$) and there can be at most one link between any two nodes in the network. The ID of a newly joining node is the time instant at which the node joins. Hence, the joining time instants are counted from $n_0 + 1$ and proceed like $n_0 + 2$, $n_0 + 3$, ..., N, where N is the total number of nodes in the network at the end of the evolution. At time instant i, the probability with which a node $u \in [1...i-1]$ of degree k_u gets a new link to the newly joining node i is given by the probability: $\prod(k_u) = \dfrac{k_u}{\sum_{j=1}^{i-1} k_j}$, where i-1 is the number of nodes in the network before the new node i joins the network. As per the above probability formulation, a newly joining node i is more likely to be attached to a node that already has a higher degree compared to a node that has a lower degree: this justifies the "preferential attachment" pattern of node attachment (Dorogovtsev et al., 2000) in scale-free networks.

The simulation procedure implemented to decide the nodes to which a newly joining node i gets connected to is explained as follows: Before we decide on the first node to which the new node i gets attached to, we compute the sum of the degrees of all the i-1 nodes that currently exist in the network and determine the probability $\prod(k_u)$ for a node u with degree k_u to get the new link, as mentioned above. We then divide the range [0, ..., 1) to sub

ranges $[0, ..., \prod(k_1))$, $[\prod(k_1), ..., \sum_{j=1}^{2}\prod(k_j))$, $[\sum_{j=1}^{2}\prod(k_j), ..., \sum_{j=1}^{3}\prod(k_j))$, ..., [

$\sum_{j=1}^{i-2}\prod(k_j), ..., \sum_{j=1}^{i-1}\prod(k_j))$, where the sub ranges respectively capture the

probability with which nodes 1, 2, ..., i-1 get the new link. The node that has
a larger $\prod(k_u)$ value would have a larger sub range compared to the node
with a lower $\prod(k_u)$ value, justifying the preferential attachment to nodes

having a larger degree. Note that: $\sum_{j=1}^{i-1}\prod(k_j) = 1$. We now generate a random

number in the range [0, ..., 1) and find the sub range (among the above) in
which the random number falls into. If the random number generated falls

in the sub range $[\sum_{j=1}^{x-1}\prod(k_j), ..., \sum_{j=1}^{x}\prod(k_j))$ corresponding to a node $x \in [1, ...,$

i-1], then the first link for node i is with node x. To decide the second of the
'm' links, we follow the above procedure with the only change that node x
chosen for the first link is excluded from the candidate nodes for which the
$\prod(k_u)$ probabilities and the sub ranges are found. Similarly, the first two
nodes chosen for the m links are excluded from the set of nodes considered
for the third link and so on.

3. SIMULATIONS

We conduct the simulations for the BA model as follows: The number of
initial nodes (n_0) is 10 and the number of links (m) added to a newly joining
node is 5. The links among the n_0 nodes is setup before the new nodes are
introduced. For each of the n_0 nodes, we randomly pick a node among the
rest of the nodes to which it has not been already linked to and connect the
two nodes. This way, each of the n_0 nodes is guaranteed to have at least one
link incident on it. The node IDs start from 1 and the initial set of nodes
have ids 1, ..., n_0. The introduction of the new nodes is considered to start
from time instant $n_0 + 1$ and proceed until time instant 1000. We introduce
one node for every time instant and the ID for a node is the time instant it
is being introduced. We follow the procedure described in Section 2.2 (that
involves preferential attachment) to setup the 'm' links for a newly joining
node to the existing nodes. Note that at any time, there is no more than a link

between any two nodes. Due to the preferential attachment phenomenon, the nodes that had been in the network for a longer time (especially the nodes with IDs 1, ..., n_0) are more likely to acquire a larger degree compared to the nodes that joined relatively later.

We measure the centrality values for the nodes introduced at time instants 10, 25, 50, 100, 200 and 300, starting from the time instant they join the network and continue the measurements till the end of the simulation (time instant 1000). Note that only one among the initial set of n_0 nodes is considered for the analysis and the rest of the nodes are the nodes that were introduced as one node per time instant. Note that for centrality metrics such as EVC and BWC, we have to run their respective algorithms on the entire scale-free network graph for every time instant (starting from time instant 10) even though we are interested in the centrality values for the above six vertices. This is because for both EVC and BWC, the centrality value of a vertex cannot be determined in isolation; their computation algorithms are designed in such a way that the algorithms have to be run on the entire graph and as a result, the centrality values for all the vertices would need to be determined even if we want the centrality value for a particular vertex. On the other hand, degree centrality of a vertex can be determined by just counting the number of neighbors for that vertex and closeness centrality of a vertex can be determined by just running the Breadth First Search (BFS) algorithm starting from the vertex. We repeat the simulations for 100 runs and average the results (see Figures 4-7).

Before we discuss the time-dependent variation of the centrality measures, we quickly review the concepts of "concave up" and "concave down" functions and how their curves look like. In our case, the independent variable is the time and the dependent variable is the centrality metric of a particular vertex. We illustrate the typical shapes of the concave up and concave down functions in Figures 2 and 3 respectively. A function is concave up if any tangent drawn to the function is below the curve. A function is concave down if any tangent drawn to the function is above the curve. With a concave up function, the rate of increase (positive slope) or the rate of decrease (negative slope) of the dependent variable would increase with increase in the value of the independent variable. With a concave down function, the rate of increase (positive slope) or the rate of decrease (negative slope) of the dependent variable would decrease with increase in the value of the independent variable.

Figure 4-7 illustrate the time-dependent variation of the centrality measures as a scale-free network evolves under the BA model. The pattern of increase or decrease with time varies with the centrality measures and for a particular

Figure 2. Typical shapes of the curves for "concave up" functions

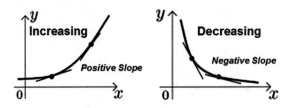

Figure 3. Typical shapes of the curves for "concave down" functions

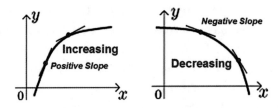

centrality measure, the rate of increase or decrease varies with the vertices considered. We observe vertices that were added to the network in the early stages (typically time instants 10 to 25) had larger values for DEG, EVC and BWC centrality measures and lower CLC values. Note that lower the CLC value for a node, the more closer is the node to the rest of the nodes in the network. Thus, the nodes that were introduced earlier to the network add a lot of significance to the topological structure of the network. We now describe below the nature of the variation with respect to each of the centrality measures.

3.1 Time-Dependent Variation of Degree Centrality

For the degree centrality measure, we observe a "concave down increasing" pattern with time (see Figure 4). This implies, the degree centrality values of a vertex increases with time, but the rate of increase decreases with increase in time. It is also important to node that at any time instant, the rate of increase (i.e., the slope of the curve) is larger for nodes that joined the network earlier. In this context, we observe nodes 10 and 25 to have a faster rate of increase compared to nodes 200 and 300. In addition, we observe nodes 10 and 25 to have an appreciable difference between their degree centrality values throughout the duration of the simulation; on the other hand, the centrality values for nodes 200 and 300 are much lower than those of nodes 10 and 25 as well as converge each other as time progresses. All of these could be attributed to the "preferential attachment" phenomenon due to which nodes that joined the network during the earlier stages of evolution heavily compete with the rest of the nodes in the network and acquire the links with the newly joining nodes as much as possible. The nodes that joined the network during the later stages have to really struggle to acquire new links and their degree centrality continues to remain low. From Figure 4, we observe that the degree centrality values of nodes 200 and 300 remain in the vicinity of 5, where 5 is the value of 'm', the number of new links a node gets at the time of its joining. This implies that the late joining nodes are very less likely to acquire any new links after the initial set of 'm' links.

3.2 Time-Dependent Variation of Eigenvector Centrality

For the eigenvector centrality (EVC) metric, we observe a "concave up decreasing" pattern with time (see Figure 5). The EVC values for the vertices that joined the network during the earlier stages of its evolution are significantly larger than those that joined the network later. The difference in the EVC values decreases with increase in time; nevertheless, the EVC values of the vertices are distinguishable from each other. The decrease in the EVC values for a vertex are more prominent in the time instants immediately following its joining time and after the drastic decrease, the EVC values decrease at

Figure 4. Time-dependent variation of the degree centrality of the nodes [concave down increasing]

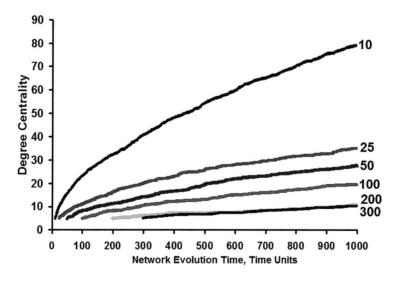

Figure 5. Time-dependent variation of eigenvector centrality of the nodes [concave up decreasing]

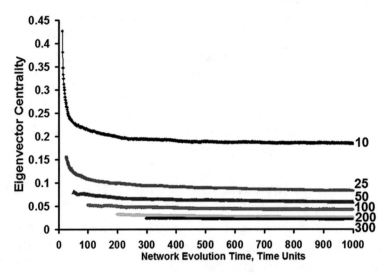

a much slower rate and it looks like they are almost a constant for the rest of the simulation. The steep decline in the EVC values are more prominent for vertices that joined the network in the early stages and for the nodes that joined later, the decline is not at least steep when viewed on a time scale of 1 to 1000 time units. For nodes that joined later, the EVC values only decrease marginally and over the entire time period of the simulation, the EVC values appear to be almost the same.

3.3 Time-Dependent Variation of Betweenness Centrality

For the betweenness centrality measure, we observe a "concave up increasing" pattern with time (see Figure 6). That is, the rate of increase in the BWC values of the vertices increases with increase in time. This could be attributed to the observation that for every new node joining the network, the number of pairs of vertices between which shortest paths are needed increases by the number of nodes in the network. Nodes that joined the network in the earlier stages (most likely to be hub nodes) get preference to be on those shortest paths. We see a huge difference in the BWC values between vertices 10 and 25. As a hierarchy of major hub nodes gets established, even several node pairs establish their shortest paths through the hub nodes and the BWC values of these hub nodes accelerates at an even faster rate. On the other hand, for

Figure 6. Time-dependent variation of betweenness centrality of the nodes [concave up increasing]

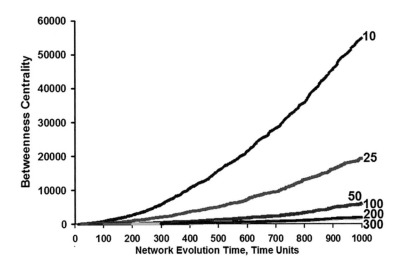

vertices that joined at later stages, it is difficult to be located on the shortest path between any two nodes in the network. On a time scale of 1 to 1000, it looks like the BWC values of vertices 200 and 300 converge. However, we do notice some appreciable difference in the BWC values of the vertices and for all the vertices, we do observe a concave up pattern of increase in the BWC values.

3.4 Time-Dependent Variation of Closeness Centrality

For the closeness centrality (CLC) measure, we observe a "linear increase" with time (see Figure 7). The slopes of the lines for vertices introduced during the earlier time instants were smaller than those introduce during the later time instants. The smaller slope for the CLC line for nodes introduced earlier could be attributed to the preferential attachment phenomenon: as the newly introduced nodes prefer to join the (hub) nodes that were in the network for a longer time, the hub nodes are more likely to incur shortest paths of fewer hops to the majority of the nodes in the network. Nodes that were added later also do not suffer from longer shortest paths; as the new nodes get attached to the hub nodes, they get closer to the rest of the vertices in the network and the length of the shortest paths does not increase significantly. Like EVC and BWC, we could visually observe convergence of the CLC values of the

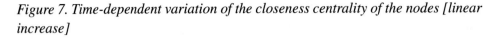

Figure 7. Time-dependent variation of the closeness centrality of the nodes [linear increase]

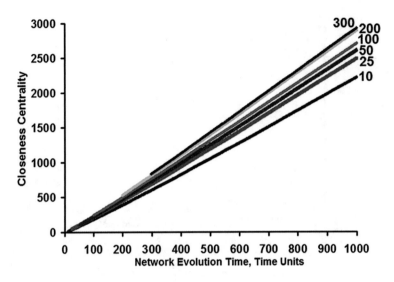

vertices 200 and 300. In other words, there is not much difference between the slopes of the lines for vertices 200 and 300; but, there is appreciable difference between the CLC values of the vertices 10 and 25.

3.5 Contributions of the Simulations to the Literature

The simulation results presented in the earlier sub sections give valuable insights. The most important observation is that the nature and rate of increase or decrease of the centrality values with time varies with the centrality metric considered. This could be a valuable input for the fitness-based generation models for scale-free networks (Dangalchev, 2004). The EVC measure could be considered to be the most stable centrality measure as the scale-free network evolves. There is not much decrease in the EVC values of the vertices over a period of time. On other hand, the CLC values of the vertices continue to linearly increase with increase in time.

The BWC of the nodes added during the earlier stages (compared to the nodes introduced during the middle and later stages) of network evolution increased significantly when new nodes get introduced. Thus, the high-degree nodes are more likely to attain larger BWC values, indicating a strong positive correlation between DEG and BWC for scale-free networks. If the preferential attachment of the nodes in the BA model was according to the

BWC measure, then we opine a power-law pattern of degree distribution that would have a long tail. On the other hand, if we do preferential attachment of the new nodes according to the EVC measure, the EVCs of the vertices would remain highly stable with node introduction. Preferential attachment based on CLC may not introduce the needed diversity in the degree of the nodes to generate a power-law style distribution.

4. RELATED WORK AND OUR CONTRIBUTIONS

Several related works in the literature studied the evolution of scale-free networks as a function of the criteria for the newly added nodes to attach to the existing nodes. In addition to degree, the fitness of a node has been typically considered as the criteria to decide the nodes to which a new node would get attached to. The fitness value for a node could be static or dynamic. Bianconi and Barabasi (2001) introduced a model wherein the fitness of a node is a random number; the probability with which an existing node is likely to get connected to the new node is a function of both the fitness of the node as well as the degree of the node. Nodes that join the network with a larger value of fitness could eventually surpass the degree of the nodes that joined the network earlier, but with a smaller value of fitness. Ranjbar-Sharaei et al. (2014) proposed the Simultaneous Emergence and Evolution (SEE) model according to which the fitness of a node is a dynamic value that is updated every time a new node joins the network. The SEE model enables the study of both structural emergence and behavioral evolution of scale-free networks. Ranjbar-Sharaei et al. (2014) observed that the overall level of cooperation among the nodes in the network (at the end of the evolution) depends primarily on the level of cooperation among the initial set of nodes that existed in the network. With both the above categories of fitness-based generation models, the new nodes are introduced to the network, one at a time. Caldarelli et al. (2002) propose a random network style fitness-based generation model in which each node is assigned a score x_i that is chosen from a certain distribution (exponential distribution is preferred). The probability for a link between two nodes i and j is a function $f(x_i, x_j)$; the preferential attachment phenomenon is captured in the form of the variable x_i statically assigned to the nodes. The temporal variation of the centrality metrics has not been yet studied for these fitness-based generative models for scale-free networks.

Hill and Braha (2010) introduced a dynamic scale-free (DSF) network model to mimic the evolution of dynamic social networks such that the degree centrality of the nodes differed on two scales: a meso-scale (say, daily basis) and a macro-scale (say, weekly basis). To generate a DSF network, the authors proposed to first use an underlay scale-free network generated according to the degree-based preferential attachment phenomenon and study the frequency with which we a neighbor node is visited for every node in the underlay network. The frequency of visiting a neighbor node serves as the probability for the links to exist between any two nodes in the DSF network over a period of time. It has been observed that the degree centrality of the vertices in the underlay scale-free network is different from the degree centrality of the vertices in the DSF network. It would be interesting to study the distribution of the other centrality metrics in both these networks.

Various studies (e.g., Estrada, 2011; Bolland, 1988; Costenbader & Valente, 2003; Borgatti & Everett, 2006; Frantz et al., 2009; Kirsak et al., 2007; Davidsen & Ortiz-Arroyo, 2012) have been conducted to analyze the impact of random and structural variations in the network on the robustness of the centrality measures. The works of Bolland (1988) and Costenbader and Valente (2003) focus only on the impact of addition and/or deletion of links on the centrality measures. The works of Borgatti and Everett (2006), Frantz et al. (2009) and Kitsak et al. (2007) analyze the impact of node addition and deletion on the stability of the centrality measures for different network topologies such as the random networks, small-world networks, core-periphery networks, scale-free networks and cellular networks. Further, Davidsen and Ortiz-Arroyo (2012) examined the impact of different sampling techniques (for deciding on the node or link to be chosen for addition or deletion) on the robustness of the centrality measures. The eigenvector centrality measure has been observed to be the most stable (i.e., robust) measure while considering node and link additions. The degree centrality measure appeared to be more sensible to structural changes in the core-periphery and scale-free networks compared to random networks. Kitsak et al. (2007) observed that even small-degree nodes had a relatively larger betweenness centrality in fractal scale-free networks. However, the BWC of the small-degree nodes decreased significantly with the addition of a few random edges. Overall, the consensus among the works on robustness analysis of centrality measures is along the lines of the conclusions of Estrada (2011) that the betweenness centrality measure is the most sensible of all the centrality measures for node/link addition/deletion.

Liu et al. (2009) studied the generation of scale-free networks using both degree centrality and betweenness centrality of the vertices as the basis of the preferential attachment phenomenon. The scale-free networks generated according to such a model had a relatively larger clustering coefficient and smaller average path length (and still retained the power-law degree distribution of the vertices) compared to the model of just using the degree centrality of the vertices as the basis for preferential attachment. On similar lines, Abbasi et al. (2012) also observed that preferential attachment shifted from degree centrality to betweenness centrality during the evolution of scientific co-authorship networks in the real-world.

Konig and Tessone (2011) proposed the following network evolution model: The network initially comprises of arbitrarily connected nodes. Then, a node i (among the nodes that are not yet chosen for rewiring) is chosen and is rewired (with a probability α) to a node j that has the largest value for a particular centrality measure among the nodes to which node i is not yet connected to as well as is disconnected (with a probability $1-\alpha$) from a node k that has the lowest value for a particular centrality measure among the nodes to which node i is connected to. Koning and Tessone (2011) observed that in the final network (at the end of all the rewiring), the degree distribution of the vertices exhibited an identical power-law pattern irrespective of the centrality measures considered during rewiring. The centrality values of the vertices has been also measured during every step of the evolution from the initial arbitrary network to the final scale-free network.

The focus of our work in this chapter is to analyze the temporal variation in the values of the centrality measures during the evolution of a scale-free network; most of the above works focused on analyzing the robustness of the centrality measures (to node/link additions/deletions) for networks that already exist. If a related work measured the centrality measures during the evolution of a scale-free network, the focus has been mainly on degree centrality and betweenness centrality, and not on all the four centrality measures together. Also, ours is the first work to have analyzed the nature of the temporal variation of each of the four centrality measures as a concave up increasing, concave down increasing, etc. The results presented in this work could be used further for analyzing the temporal changes in the centrality measures during the evolution of the complex networks (such as scale-free networks, dynamic scale-free networks, fractal and non-fractal scale-free networks, small-world networks, cellular networks, core-periphery networks and etc) under the various fitness-based generation models.

5. CONCLUSION

We have analyzed the time-dependent variation of the centrality measures during the evolution of a scale-free network under the Barabasi-Albert (BA) model. Until now, the nature of the temporal variation of the centrality measures (other than degree centrality) is not known in the literature. We observe the temporal variation of the centrality measures to be as follows: The eigenvector centrality (EVC) measure exhibits a concave up decreasing pattern such that the EVC values of the vertices decreases quickly with time, especially for those that joined the network earlier. The betweenness centrality (BWC) measure exhibits a concave up increasing pattern such that the BWC values of the vertices increase quickly with time; nodes that joined the network during the early stages of network evolution are more likely to attain significantly larger BWC values as the network evolves. The closeness centrality (CLC) measure exhibits a linear increase with time; nodes that joined the network during the early stages have a relatively smaller slope, implying that their distances to the newly joining vertices do not increase significantly compared to the CLC of the nodes that joined the network later. As reported in the literature, we also observe a concave down pattern of increase for the degree centrality (DEG) measure with time: i.e., the rate of increase of the DEG values of the vertices decreases with increase in time.

6. FUTURE RESEARCH DIRECTIONS

The results reported in this chapter could be useful to choose an appropriate value for the fitness of the nodes under the fitness-based generation models (e.g., Bianconi & Barabasi, 2001; Dangalchev, 2004). Now that we know the rate of increase of the BWC values of the vertices increases with increase in time (i.e., a concave up increase), we could conclude that the fitness values used to obtain a concave down increase for the DEG metric and make the DEG values of the vertices that joined at the later stages to overtake the DEG values of the vertices that joined at the earlier stages would not be appropriate and sufficient to obtain a concave up increase for the BWC metric. On the other hand, the fitness values to be used to let the BWC values of the vertices that joined at the later stages of a network under evolution to overtake the BWC values of the vertices that joined at the earlier stages of the network need to be substantially larger than those to be used for DEG, and if the BWC-related fitness values are used, then the DEG values of the late joining vertices would soon (after joining the network) overtake the DEG values of the vertices that joined earlier. We conjecture a complex relationship between the joining times of the nodes, their fitness values and the centrality metric under consideration to predict the "overtake time" (the time at which a node that joined the network later overtakes the centrality value of the node that joined the network earlier) under the different fitness-based generation models. It also becomes a complex problem if the fitness values of the nodes changes dynamically with time; the type of function to be used to simulate the change in the fitness values of the nodes need to be differently chosen for each centrality metric.

REFERENCES

Abbasi, A., Hossain, L., & Leydesdorff, L. (2012). Betweenness Centrality as a Driver of Preferential Attachment in the Evolution of Research Collaboration Networks. *Journal of Informetrics, 6*(3), 403–412. doi:10.1016/j.joi.2012.01.002

Barabasi, A. L., & Albert, R. (1999). Emergence of Scaling in Random Networks. *Science, 286*(5439), 509–512. doi:10.1126cience.286.5439.509 PMID:10521342

Bianconi, G., & Barabasi, A. L. (2001). Competition and Multiscaling in Evolving Networks. *Europhysics Letters, 54*(4), 436–442. doi:10.1209/epl/i2001-00260-6

Bolland, J. M. (1988). Sorting out Centrality: An Analysis of the Performance of Four Centrality Models in Real and Simulated Networks. *Social Networks, 10*(3), 233–253. doi:10.1016/0378-8733(88)90014-7

Borgatti, S. P., & Everett, M. G. (2006). A Graph-Theoretic Perspective on Centrality. *Social Networks, 28*(4), 466–484. doi:10.1016/j.socnet.2005.11.005

Bornholdt, S., & Schuster, H. G. (2003). *Handbook of Graphs and Networks: From the Genome to the Internet.* Wiley-VCH Verlag.

Caldarelli, G. (2007). *Scale-Free Networks: Complex Webs in Nature and Technology*. Oxford University Press. doi:10.1093/acprof:o so/9780199211517.001.0001

Caldarelli, G., Capocci, A., Los Rios, P., & Munoz, M. A. (2002). Scale-Free Networks from Varying Vertex Intrinsic Fitness. *Physical Review Letters, 89*(25), 1-4.

Cohen, R., Erez, K., Ben-Avraham, D., & Havlin, S. (2000). Resilience of the Internet to Random Breakdowns. *Physical Review Letters, 85*(21), 4626–4628. doi:10.1103/PhysRevLett.85.4626 PMID:11082612

Cohen, R., Erez, K., Ben-Avraham, D., & Havlin, S. (2001). Breakdown of the Internet under Intentional Attack. *Physical Review Letters, 86*(16), 3682–3685. doi:10.1103/PhysRevLett.86.3682 PMID:11328053

Costenbader, E., & Valente, T. W. (2003). The Stability of Centrality Measures when Networks are Sampled. *Social Networks, 25*(4), 283–307. doi:10.1016/S0378-8733(03)00012-1

Dangalchev, C. (2004). Generation Models for Scale-Free Networks. *Physics A: Statistical Mechanics and its Applications, 338*(3-4), 659-671.

Davidsen, S. A., & Ortiz-Arroyo, D. (2012). Centrality Robustness and Link Prediction in Complex Social Networks. *Computational Social Networks*, 197-224.

Dorogovtsev, S., Mendes, J., & Samukhin, A. (2000). Structure of Growing Networks with Preferential Linking. *Physical Review Letters, 85*(21), 4633–4636. doi:10.1103/PhysRevLett.85.4633 PMID:11082614

Easley, D., & Kleinberg, J. (2010). *Networks, Crowds, and Markets: Reasoning about a Highly Connected World*. Cambridge University Press. doi:10.1017/CBO9780511761942

Erdos, P., & Renyi, A. (1959). On Random Graphs I. *Publicationes Mathematicae, 6*, 290–297.

Estrada, E. (2011). *The Structure of Complex Networks: Theory and Applications*. Oxford Publishing Press. doi:10.1093/acprof:o so/9780199591756.001.0001

Frantz, T. L., Cataldo, M., & Carley, K. M. (2009). Robustness of Centrality Measures under Uncertainty: Examining the Role of Network Topology. *Computational & Mathematical Organization Theory, 15*(4), 303–328. doi:10.100710588-009-9063-5

Hill, S. A., & Braha, D. (2010). Dynamic Model of Time-Dependent Complex Networks. *Physical Review E, 82*(4), 1-7.

Kitsak, M., Havlin, S., Paul, G., Riccaboni, M., Pammolli, F., & Stanley, H. E. (2007). Betweenness Centrality of Fractal and Non-fractal Scale-Free Model Networks and Tests on Real Networks. *Physical Review E, 75*(5), 1-19.

Konig, M. D., & Tessone, C. J. (2011). Network Evolution based on Centrality. *Physical Review E, 84*(5), 1-12.

Liu, Y., Meng, Y., Xu, K., & Li, Y. (2009). *Research on Betweenness: The Model of Scale-Free Networks.* Paper presented at the 4th International Conference on Internet Computing for Science and Engineering, Harbin, China. 10.1109/ICICSE.2009.68

Ranjbar-Sharaei, B., Bloembergen, D., Bou Ammar, H., Tulys, K., & Weiss, G. (2014). *Effects of Evolution on the Emergence of Scale Free Networks.* Paper presented at the 14th International Conference on the Synthesis and Simulation of Living Systems, New York, NY. 10.7551/978-0-262-32621-6-ch060

Watts, D. J., & Strogatz, S. H. (1998). Collective Dynamics of Small-World Networks. *Nature, 393*(6684), 440–442. doi:10.1038/30918 PMID:9623998

Chapter 5

Edge Centrality Metrics to Quantify the Stability of Links for Mobile Sensor Networks

ABSTRACT

In this chapter, we explore the use of neighborhood overlap (NOVER), bipartivity index (BPI) and algebraic connectivity (ALGC) as edge centrality metrics to quantify the stability of links for mobile sensor networks. In this pursuit, we employ the notion of the egocentric network of an edge (comprising of the end vertices of the edge and their neighbors as nodes, and the edges incident on the end vertices as links) on which the above three edge centrality metrics are computed. Unlike the existing approach of using the predicted link expiration time (LET), the computations of the above three edge centrality metrics do not require the location and mobility information of the nodes. For various scenarios of node density and mobility, we observe the stability of the network-wide data gathering trees (lifetime) determined using the proposed three edge centrality metrics to be significantly larger than the stability of the LET-based data gathering trees.

DOI: 10.4018/978-1-5225-3802-8.ch005

1. INTRODUCTION

Mobile sensor networks (MSNs) are a category of wireless sensor networks in which the sensor nodes could move independent of each other. The topology of MSNs changes dynamically with time and hence the communication topologies (like data gathering trees; Meghanathan, 2012) determined for such networks need to be frequently reconfigured. Not much work has been done so far to determine stable communication topologies for MSNs. To determine stable communication topologies in MSNs, it is imperative to quantify the stability of the links. The currently best known approach (Meghanathan, 2014) to quantify link stability has been borrowed from a related field called mobile ad hoc networks (MANETs; Abolhasan et al., 2004) and it is based on the notion of predicted link expiration time (LET, originally proposed by Su & Gerla, 1999 for MANETs). However, to predict the LET of a link, we need to know the location and mobility information of the end vertices of the link and in the case of MSNs, it would be too energy-draining for the sensor nodes to regularly detect their location and mobility information as well as to update their neighbors about the same.

The motivation for the research presented in this chapter is to investigate the use of graph theoretic measures (that would not require the location and mobility information of the nodes) borrowed from complex network analysis to quantify the stability of links in a MSN. In this pursuit, our hypothesis is that links whose end vertices are relatively closer to each other (i.e., have a significant fraction of their neighborhood shared) are more likely to be stable and vice-versa. We could thence use graph theoretic measures that could be used to quantify the extent of shared neighborhood between the end vertices of the edges and use the same as the link stability score (LSS): a measure of the edge weights for the algorithms to determine stable communication topologies. We restrict ourselves to data gathering trees (DG trees) as the communication topology of interest; however, the LSS scores determined based on the graph theoretic measures are independent of the communication topology.

The graph theoretic measures (as measures of edge centrality) used to quantify the extent of shared neighborhood of the end vertices of a link are: Neighborhood Overlap (NOVER)(Easley & Kleinberg, 2010), Bipartivity Index (BPI)(Estrada & Rodriguez-Velazquez, 2005) and Algebraic Connectivity (ALGC)(Fiedler, 1973). All these metrics have been so far used for complex network analysis involving social networks, biological networks, etc and have not been used for mobile sensor networks. Also, BPI and ALGC have been so far used only at the network level and not at the edge level (while NOVER, an edge level metric, has been primarily used for community detection). We capture the neighborhood of the end vertices of an edge *u-v* in the form of an egocentric network comprising of the end vertices and their neighbors (as nodes) and the links incident on the end vertices (as edges). We determine the NOVER, BPI and ALGC scores based on the egocentric edge networks. Simulation studies involving data gathering algorithms indicate edges with larger NOVER and ALGC scores as well as lower BPI scores are observed to be more stable. Hence, we assign the LSS score for an edge *u-v* to be as follows: (i) the NOVER score for the edge *u-v*, (ii) the complement of the BPI, BPI' = 1-BPI, of the egocentric network of the edge *u-v*, and (iii) the ALGC score for the egocentric network of the edge *u-v*.

We use the algorithm (Meghanathan, 2015) for determining maximum bottleneck link weight data gathering trees (MaxBLW-DG trees) to determine DG trees at a node (called the root node, the node that has the largest value for the sum of the LSS scores per link). The bottleneck link weight for a path is the weight that is the lowest among the weights of the constituent links of the path. The maximum bottleneck link weight path between two end vertices *s* and *d* is the path with the largest value for the bottleneck link weight. By running the MaxBLW-DG algorithm starting from a root node, we will be able to determine a data gathering tree that connects the root node to the rest of the nodes in the network such that the paths from the root node to each of the other nodes are the maximum bottleneck link weight paths. We determine the MaxBLW-DG trees using each of the above three edge centrality metrics quantifying the extent of shared neighborhood in MSNs and evaluate the lifetimes of the DG trees. We compare the lifetimes of these DG trees with those incurred by using the predicted LET as a measure of link weight. The predicted link expiration time (LET) of a link $i - j$ between two nodes i and j, currently at (X_i, Y_i) and (X_j, Y_j), and moving with velocities v_i and v_j in directions θ_i and θ_j (with respect to the X-axis) is computed using the formula proposed by Su and Gerla (1999):

$$LET(i - j) = \frac{-(ab + cd) + \sqrt{(a^2 + c^2)R^2 - (ad - bc)^2}}{a^2 + c^2} \qquad (1)$$

$$a = v_i^*\cos\theta_i - v_j^*\cos\theta_j;\ b = X_i - X_j;\ c = v_i^*\sin\theta_i - v_j^*\sin\theta_j;\ d = Y_i - Y_j$$

The rest of the chapter is organized as follows: Section 2 introduces the notion of egocentric network of an edge and illustrates the computation of the graph theoretic metrics (NOVER, BPI and ALGC) on the egocentric network of an edge. Section 3 presents an exhaustive simulation study evaluating the lifetimes of the MaxBLW-DG trees determined using the NOVER, BPI', ALGC and LET metrics. Section 4 concludes the chapter and Section 5 presents future research directions.

2. EGOCENTRIC NETWORK OF AN EDGE AND GRAPH THEORETIC METRICS

2.1 Egocentric Network of an Edge

We propose the egocentric network of an edge *u-v* as the set of vertices comprising of the end vertices *u* and *v* and their neighbors and the set of edges comprising of the links incident on the end vertices. Our notion of egocentric network for an edge is different from the notion of egocentric network for a node (proposed earlier by Marsden, 2002) that comprises of the node as well as its neighbors as vertices and the links incident on both the node and its neighbors as edges. We adopt the unit disk graph model (Clark et al., 1990) to identify the presence of an edge between two vertices. According to this model, there exists an edge between two vertices if the Euclidean distance between the two vertices is within the transmission range per node. We assume all nodes operate at the same transmission range. We illustrate the notion of egocentric network of an edge using an example (see Figure 1). We assume the transmission range of the nodes in this example graph to be 2.25 units. We define the fraction of link distance (*fld*) to be the

Figure 1. Egocentric network of an edge for an example graph

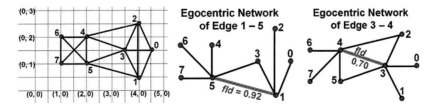

ratio of the Euclidean distance between the end vertices of the edge to that of the transmission range per node.

2.2 Neighborhood Overlap

The neighborhood overlap (NOVER)(Easley & Kleinberg, 2010) score for an edge u-v is the ratio of the number of shared neighbors of the two end vertices u and v to that of the number of unique neighbors of the end vertices u and v (excluding themselves). Figure 2 illustrates the NOVER scores of the edges in the example graph of Figure 1. As expected, the NOVER scores of the edges decrease with increase in the fraction of link distance between the end vertices.

2.3 Bipartivity Index

The bipartivity index (BPI)(Estrada & Rodriguez-Velazquez, 2005) of a graph is a measure of the extent to which the graph is bipartite. A bipartite graph is a graph whose vertices could be partitioned to two disjoint sets such that there are no edges between vertices in the same partition and all the edges in the graph are between vertices in the two partitions. The BPI of a bipartite graph is 1.0. If a graph is not bipartite, it would be attributed to the presence

Figure 2. NOVER-Based LSS scores of edges for the graph of Figure 1

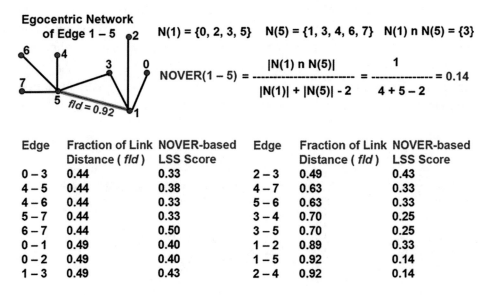

Edge	Fraction of Link Distance (*fld*)	NOVER-based LSS Score	Edge	Fraction of Link Distance (*fld*)	NOVER-based LSS Score
0 – 3	0.44	0.33	2 – 3	0.49	0.43
4 – 5	0.44	0.38	4 – 7	0.63	0.33
4 – 6	0.44	0.33	5 – 6	0.63	0.33
5 – 7	0.44	0.33	3 – 4	0.70	0.25
6 – 7	0.44	0.50	3 – 5	0.70	0.25
0 – 1	0.49	0.40	1 – 2	0.89	0.33
0 – 2	0.49	0.40	1 – 5	0.92	0.14
1 – 3	0.49	0.43	2 – 4	0.92	0.14

of edges (called "frustrated" edges) between vertices in the same partition. The BPI of such graphs is less than 1.0. The presence of frustrated edges between vertices in the smaller partition decreases the BPI relatively faster.

In the case of egocentric network of an edge *u-v*, the vertices *u* and *v* are in one partition and their neighbors are in the other partition. For all egocentric edge networks, the edge connecting the two end vertices is the only frustrated edge. The BPI of egocentric edge networks are hence expected to be larger (closer to 1.0). However, the differences in the fraction of shared neighborhood lead to differences in the BPI values of egocentric edge networks. Egocentric edge networks with a larger fraction of shared neighborhood are observed to have a lower BPI value and vice-versa. Hence, we model the LSS score for an edge *u-v* as BPI' = 1-BPI of the egocentric network of edge *u-v*.

Typically, the BPI value for a network is determined using spectral analysis (Mohar, 1992) of the adjacency matrix of the graph. Spectral analysis of a graph of *n* vertices yields *n* eigenvalues: $\lambda_1, \lambda_2, ..., \lambda_n$. We compute the BPI of the graph using these eigenvalues (as shown in formulation 2). In this chapter, we run spectral analysis on the adjacency matrix representing the egocentric network/graph of an edge to obtain the eigenvalues and then use formulation (2) to compute the BPI score for the egocentric edge network. Figure 3 illustrates the computation of the BPI' score for two egocentric edge networks that differ in the fraction of shared neighbors. The larger the fraction of link distance, the smaller the fraction of shared neighborhood and larger the BPI value (hence, the lower the BPI' value).

$$BPI(G) = \frac{\sum_{j=1}^{n} \cosh(\lambda_j)}{\sum_{j=1}^{n} \cosh(\lambda_j) + \sum_{j=1}^{n} \sinh(\lambda_j)} \qquad (2)$$

Figure 3. BPI-Based LSS scores of edges for the graph of Figure 1

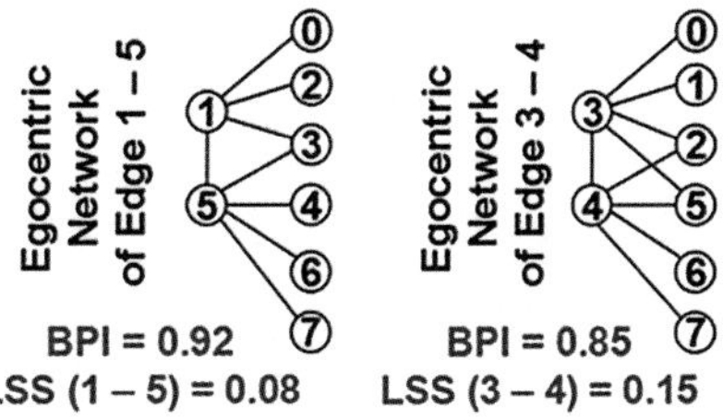

Edge	fld	BPI-based LSS Score	Edge	fld	BPI-based LSS Score
0 – 3	0.44	0.17	2 – 3	0.49	0.21
4 – 5	0.44	0.20	4 – 7	0.63	0.17
4 – 6	0.44	0.17	5 – 6	0.63	0.17
5 – 7	0.44	0.17	3 – 4	0.70	0.15
6 – 7	0.44	0.21	3 – 5	0.70	0.15
0 – 1	0.49	0.18	1 – 2	0.89	0.17
0 – 2	0.49	0.18	1 – 5	0.92	0.08
1 – 3	0.49	0.21	2 – 4	0.92	0.08

Egocentric Network of Edge 1 – 5
BPI = 0.92
LSS (1 – 5) = 0.08

Egocentric Network of Edge 3 – 4
BPI = 0.85
LSS (3 – 4) = 0.15

2.4 Algebraic Connectivity

The algebraic connectivity (ALGC)(Fiedler, 1973) of a graph is a quantitative measure of the robustness of the graph with respect to node or edge removals (Jamakovic & Uhlig, 2007). Graphs with larger ALGC value are expected to stay connected due to the removal of a few nodes and/or edges. In the context of shared neighborhood, we hypothesize that egocentric edge networks with a larger fraction of shared neighborhood would be more robust and have a larger ALGC compared to egocentric edge networks with a relatively lower fraction of shared neighborhood.

We determine the ALGC for an entire graph by computing the eigenvalues of its Laplacian matrix (Mohar, 1992), which is defined as follows: For two different vertices i and j, an entry (i, j) in the Laplacian matrix is 0 if there is no edge between i and j, and is -1 if there is an edge between them. The diagonal entries in the Laplacian matrix correspond to the degree of the vertices. There are n eigenvalues for a Laplacian matrix of n vertices and all these eigenvalues are either 0 or positive. If a graph is connected, then only one eigenvalue of its Laplacian matrix will be 0 and the rest of the eigenvalues will be greater than 0. The ALGC of a connected graph is the smallest non-zero eigenvalue of its Laplacian matrix. We follow the above approach for egocentric edge networks and determine the ALGC value as a measure of the extent of shared neighborhood. If an egocentric edge network has a larger fraction of shared neighbors, then its ALGC value is expected to be high due to the robustness brought in by the edges connecting the end vertices to the shared neighbors. From a distance point of view, the larger the fraction of link distance between the end vertices of an edge, the lower the expected fraction of shared neighbors and lower the ALGC value and vice-versa. Figure 4 illustrates a sample calculation of the ALGC score for an egocentric edge network as well as lists the ALGC scores of all the edges in the example graph of Figure 1.

3. SIMULATIONS

We conducted the simulations in a discrete event simulator implemented in Java for mobile sensor networks. We implemented the MaxBLW-DG algorithm (Meghanathan, 2014) in a distributed fashion and determined the DG trees with the NOVER, BPI', ALGC and LET as the link selection strategies. A

Figure 4. ALGC-based LSS scores of edges for the graph of Figure 1

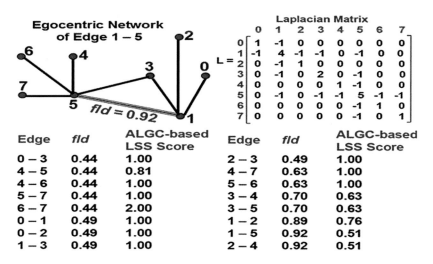

Edge	fld	ALGC-based LSS Score	Edge	fld	ALGC-based LSS Score
0 – 3	0.44	1.00	2 – 3	0.49	1.00
4 – 5	0.44	0.81	4 – 7	0.63	1.00
4 – 6	0.44	1.00	5 – 6	0.63	1.00
5 – 7	0.44	1.00	3 – 4	0.70	0.63
6 – 7	0.44	2.00	3 – 5	0.70	0.63
0 – 1	0.49	1.00	1 – 2	0.89	0.76
0 – 2	0.49	1.00	1 – 5	0.92	0.51
1 – 3	0.49	1.00	2 – 4	0.92	0.51

MaxBLW-DG tree is a rooted maximum spanning tree (Cormen et al., 2009) spanning all the vertices in the graph with the link weights represented by the LSS scores obtained from the link selection strategy used. The medium access control (MAC) channel used for the simulations is assumed to be idle so that there are no collisions of packets. We also assume that sufficient number of TDMA and CDMA slots (Viterbi, 1995) are available so that internal nodes at the same level of DG tree could aggregate data in parallel (an internal node gathers data from its child nodes, one node at a time using different time slots). The sensor nodes are also assumed to operate with infinite energy supply. All of these idealistic assumptions are made to extract the best possible performance (for link stability) from the link selection strategies and the only reason for a tree reconfiguration would be due to the end nodes of a link moving away out of the transmission range of each other. The effectiveness of the link selection strategies lies in quantifying the link stability scores in such a way that stable links (that are expected to last for a longer time) get chosen to be part of the DG trees.

The simulations are conducted in a network of dimensions 100m x 100m; the sink is assumed to be located outside the network, at (50, 300). The number of nodes (N) used is 50 and 100, and the values for the transmission range per node (R) are 25m and 35m. As a result, there are four levels of network densities: low density ($N = 50$ and $R = 25$m), low-moderate density ($N = 50$ and $R = 35$m), moderate-high density ($N = 100$ and $R = 25$m) and high density ($N = 100$ and $R = 35$m). The node mobility model used is the

Random Waypoint model (Bettstetter et al., 2004), with the maximum velocity of the node (v_{max}) varied with values of 1, 3, 5 and 10 m/s. We conduct the simulations for 2000 rounds; the LSS scores of the links are estimated for every round. A round of data aggregation involves data propagating from the leaf nodes towards the root node with aggregation at the internal nodes. The data size is assumed to remain the same throughout the aggregation process at the internal nodes. Whenever a DG tree does not exist, the sink node is assumed to initiate a network-wide broadcast process to construct the MaxBLW-DG tree in a distributed fashion (as per the algorithm explained by Meghanathan, 2014) using the LSS scores estimated for that round.

The lifetime of a DG tree is the number of rounds it could be used for data aggregation without reconfiguration. We measure the average lifetime of the DG tree (in rounds) and present them in Figures 5 (the absolute values) and 6 (the normalized values). The normalized values for the DG tree lifetime could be very useful to evaluate the relative performance of the link selection strategies. We observe all the three graph theory-based link selection strategies to yield DG trees that have appreciably larger lifetime compared to the LET-

Figure 5. Absolute values for the average tree lifetime (in rounds)

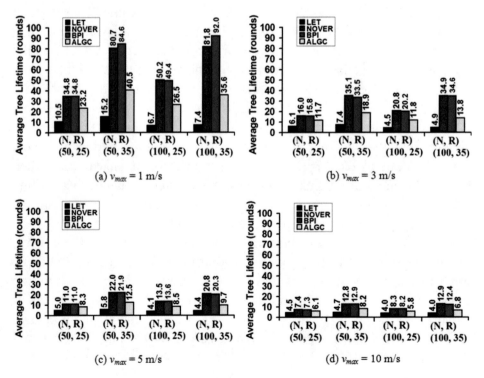

(a) $v_{max} = 1$ m/s

(b) $v_{max} = 3$ m/s

(c) $v_{max} = 5$ m/s

(d) $v_{max} = 10$ m/s

Figure 6. Normalized values for the average tree lifetime

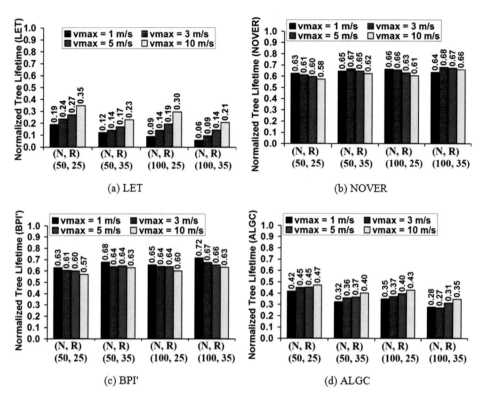

based DG trees. For a given level of node mobility, the NOVER and BPI'-based DG trees incur almost the same average lifetime and are relatively larger compared to the ALGC-based DG trees. The lifetimes of the NOVER and BPI'-based DG trees increase with increase in network density and the lifetimes of the ALGC and LET-based DG trees decrease with increase in network density. The lifetimes of the ALGC-based DG trees decreased at a much reduced rate compared to those of the LET-based DG trees.

The LET and ALGC-based DG trees are relatively more scalable with increase in node mobility for a given network density. For a given network density, the normalized values of the lifetimes of the LET and ALGC-based DG trees increase with increase in node mobility, and the normalized values of the lifetimes of the NOVER and BPI'-based DG trees decrease with increase in node mobility. Nevertheless, the absolute values of the lifetimes of the NOVER and BPI'-based DG trees are much larger than those of the LET and ALGC-based DG trees for all levels of network density and node mobility.

4. CONCLUSION

We have proposed the use of graph theoretic measures (used in Complex Network Analysis) such as neighborhood overlap (NOVER), bipartivity index (BPI) and algebraic connectivity (ALGC) to quantify the extent of shared neighborhood between the end vertices of a link and use it as a measure of the stability of the link. Through extensive simulation study, we observe our hypothesis to be true and the lifetimes of the DG trees determined using all the three graph theoretic measures are larger than the lifetime of the DG trees determined using the currently known approach of predicted link expiration time (LET). We observe the DG trees determined using BPI' and NOVER to be relatively more stable and scalable with increase in network density. The graph theoretic measures could be considered as edge centrality metrics to quantify the extent of shared neighborhood of the end vertices of the edges and could be determined without the location and mobility information of the sensor nodes.

5. FUTURE RESEARCH DIRECTIONS

As part of future research, we plan to develop one or more computationally-light edge centrality metrics that could be used to quantify the stability of links in mobile sensor networks without requiring the location and mobility information of the end nodes. We anticipate tradeoff between the computation time and the link lifetime that could be estimated using the computationally-heavy edge centrality metrics vis-a-vis the computationally-light edge centrality metrics. We plan to develop machine learning models (supervised learning) to predict the BPI and ALGC values for the egocentric edge networks using the NOVER scores of the edges. We also plan to develop machine learning models that could be trained to predict the location and mobility information of the nodes using metrics like predicted link expiration time.

REFERENCES

Abolhasan, M., Wysocki, T., & Dutkiewicz, E. (2004). A Review of Routing Protocols for Mobile Ad hoc Networks. *Ad Hoc Networks*, 2(1), 1–22. doi:10.1016/S1570-8705(03)00043-X

Bettstetter, C., Hartenstein, H., & Perez-Costa, X. (2004). Stochastic Properties of the Random-Way Point Mobility Model. *Wireless Networks*, *10*(5), 555–567. doi:10.1023/B:WINE.0000036458.88990.e5

Clark, B. N., Colbourn, C. J., & Johnson, D. S. (1990). Unit Disk Graphs. *Discrete Mathematics*, *86*(1-3), 165–177. doi:10.1016/0012-365X(90)90358-O

Cormen, T. H., Leiserson, C. E., Rivest, R. L., & Stein, C. (2009). *Introduction to Algorithms* (3rd ed.). MIT Press.

Easley, D., & Kleinberg, J. (2010). *Networks, Crowds, and Markets: Reasoning about a Highly Connected World* (1st ed.). Cambridge, UK: Cambridge University Press. doi:10.1017/CBO9780511761942

Estrada, E., & Rodriguez-Velazquez, J. A. (2005). Spectral Measures of Bipartivity in Complex Networks. *Physical Review. E*, *72*(046105), 1–6. PMID:16383466

Fiedler, M. (1973). Algebraic Connectivity of Graphs. *Czechoslovak Mathematical Journal*, *23*(98), 298–305.

Jamakovic, A., & Uhlig, S. (2007). *On the Relationship between the Algebraic Connectivity and Graph's Robustness to Node and Link Failures.* Paper presented at the 3rd Euro Conference on Next Generation Internet Networks, Trondheim, Norway. 10.1109/NGI.2007.371203

Marsden, P. V. (2002). Egocentric and Sociocentric Measures of Network Centrality. *Social Networks*, *24*(4), 407–422. doi:10.1016/S0378-8733(02)00016-3

Meghanathan, N. (2012). A Comprehensive Review and Performance Analysis of Data Gathering Algorithms for Wireless Sensor Networks. *International Journal of Interdisciplinary Telecommunications and Networking*, *4*(2), 1–29. doi:10.4018/jitn.2012040101

Meghanathan, N. (2014). Stability-based and Energy-Efficient Distributed Data Gathering Algorithms for Mobile Sensor Networks. *Ad Hoc Networks*, *19*, 111–131. doi:10.1016/j.adhoc.2014.02.007

Meghanathan, N. (2015). A Generic Algorithm to Determine Maximum Bottleneck Node Weight-based Data Gathering Trees for Wireless Sensor Networks. *Network Protocols and Algorithms*, *7*(3), 18–51. doi:10.5296/npa.v7i3.7961

Mohar, B. (1992). Laplace Eigenvalues of Graphs - A Survey. *Discrete Mathematics*, *109*(1-3), 171–183. doi:10.1016/0012-365X(92)90288-Q

Su, W., & Gerla, M. (1999). *IPv6 Flow Handoff in Ad hoc Wireless Networks using Mobility Prediction*. Paper presented at the IEEE Global Telecommunications Conference, Rio de Janeiro, Brazil.

Viterbi, A. J. (1995). *CDMA: Principles of Spread Spectrum Communication* (1st ed.). Prentice Hall.

Chapter 6

Use of Eigenvector Centrality for Mobile Target Tracking

ABSTRACT

The author proposes an eigenvector centrality (EVC)-based tracking algorithm to trace the trajectory of a mobile radioactive dispersal device (RDD) in a wireless sensor network. They propose that the sensor nodes simply sum up the strengths of the signals (including those emanating from a RDD) sensed in the neighborhood over a sampling time period and forward the sum of the signals to a control center (called sink). For every sampling time period, the sink constructs an adjacency matrix in which the entry for edge (i, j) is the sum of the signal strengths reported by sensor nodes i and j, and uses this adjacency matrix as the basis to determine the principal eigenvector whose entries represents the EVCs of the vertices with respect to the radioactive signals sensed in the neighborhood. The author proposes that the arithmetic mean (calculated by the sink) of the X and Y coordinates of the suspect sensor nodes (those with higher EVCs) be considered as the predicted location of the RDD at a time instant corresponding to the middle of the sampling time period.

DOI: 10.4018/978-1-5225-3802-8.ch006

1. INTRODUCTION

Wireless sensor networks (WSNs) are useful for several environment monitoring applications, including those require target tracking. In this chapter, we focus on a specific target tracking application wherein the target is a radioactive device (shortly referred to as RDD for the rest of the chapter) that emanates radiations (as signals) in the neighborhood and the sensors deployed in the area of monitoring sense these signals as well as quantify the strength of these signals. The radiation signal strength is expected to be larger in the neighborhood through which the RDD moves and we seek to trace the path of the RDD (the trajectory) through a data gathering mechanism. We construct a data gathering (DG) tree as a rooted spanning tree connecting all the sensor nodes, with the root node randomly chosen by the control center (sink) at the time of constructing the DG tree. Compared to other communication topologies (like mesh, clusters, etc), the use of a DG tree minimizes the energy consumption and the redundancy in the information being propagated. Several efficient data gathering algorithms have been proposed in the literature (see Meghanathan, 2012 for a survey and comparative analysis) of wireless sensor networks.

We assume the sensor nodes to operate within a sensing range that is half their transmission range. Since discerning the radioactive signals from the background signals would be a hard and even erroneous, we let the sensor nodes to transmit the cumulative strength of the signals sensed as the data along the DG tree. The sink node is assumed to know the entire topology (two nodes are connected if they are within the transmission range per node) and hence could fill up an adjacency matrix based on the signal strength data received from the individual sensor nodes along the DG tree. An entry (i, j) in the adjacency matrix contains the sum of the signal strengths reported by nodes i and j that have an edge between them in the network. If the RDD is in the vicinity of a sensor node s, then the entries for node s and its neighbors are expected to be relatively much larger in the adjacency matrix at the sink. We use this idea as the basis and propose to determine the principal eigenvector of the adjacency matrix and the top x number of nodes with the largest values for the eigenvector centrality (EVC), corresponding to the entries in the principal eigenvector, are considered for predicting the location of the RDD. Since the sensor nodes are static, the sink is assumed to have learnt the locations of the sensor nodes a priori (as part of the network initialization) and could predict the location of the RDD as the average of the

X and Y coordinates of the top x nodes that had the largest EVC values for the adjacency matrix at the particular time. We repeat this process throughout the duration of the simulation and build a trajectory for the mobile RDD. We evaluate the effectiveness of the tracking mechanism by computing the difference between the predicted location and the actual location of the RDD across all the sampling time instants and determine the median of the prediction error (Euclidean distance between the actual and predicted locations). We conduct the simulations under both energy-unconstrained and energy-constrained scenarios. Under the energy-constrained scenarios, we observe the prediction error to increase with depletion of sensor nodes and the resulting loss of coverage.

The rest of the chapter is organized as follows: Section 2 presents the system model and an algorithm to determine energy-efficient minimum distance spanning trees-based data gathering trees for wireless sensor networks. Section 3 presents an example to illustrate the computation procedure of the EVCs of the sensor nodes based on the signal strengths reported to the sink node. Section 4 presents the procedures adopted at the individual sensor nodes for target tracking. Section 5 presents the simulation models and the results of the tracking algorithm with respect to various operating parameters. Section 6 reviews related work on mobile target tracking using sensor networks. Section 7 concludes the chapter and Section 8 discusses future research directions.

2. SYSTEM MODEL AND DATA GATHERING ALGORITHM

2.1 System Model

A wireless sensor network of sensor nodes is considered to have been deployed to monitor an area of interest and track the trajectory of any mobile radioactive device (RDD) in the area. A sensor node could sense the signals emanating within its sensing range, but transmit the data (basically, the strength of the sensed signal) to nodes that are within its transmission range. Per Zhang and Hou (2005), for coverage to imply connectivity, the transmission range has to be at least twice the sensing range. For simplicity, we assume the transmission range is twice the sensing range). The sensor nodes are static, battery-operated and are assumed to be aware of their own location. Due to node failures (exhaustion of battery charge), the network topology could change; the sensor nodes maintain a list of the live sensor nodes (sensor nodes that have positive residual energy) within their transmission range.

The sensor nodes sense the signal during every time unit (round) and estimate its strength. A sampling time period is considered to comprise of several such rounds. A sensor node locally updates and maintains the cumulative strength of the signals sensed within its sensing range. At the end of the sampling time period, the sensor nodes report their individual data (the cumulative signal strength for the rounds spread over the sampling time period) to the sink. If the sink does not see data reported from a sensor node at the end of the sampling time period, the sink considers the sensor node to have died due to exhaustion of battery charge.

2.2 Data Gathering Algorithm

We run the algorithm to construct a data gathering tree (DG tree) in a distributed fashion (more details below). The algorithm is run at the time of network startup and is then run periodically (for every $t_{refresh}$ rounds) or whenever a DG tree needs to be reconfigured (due to node failures). The sensor nodes are considered to lose energy for constructing a DG tree (whenever the algorithm is run) as well as to transmit and receive data along the edges of the tree. Based on the identification information of the nodes from which the signal strength message was received during the latest sampling time period, the sink nodes evaluates the availability of the sensor nodes and the connectivity of the DG tree. If the DG tree appears to be no longer connected due to the lack of data from one or more sensor nodes (these nodes are thereby assumed to have failed), the sink decides there is a need to reconstruct the DG tree.

Whenever the sink node decides that a DG tree needs to be constructed, it randomly chooses a live sensor node and sends it a LEADER NODE NOMINATION message. The chosen leader node initiates a network-wide broadcast of the TREE CONSTRUCTION message, records its ID and location information in the *forwarder information* field and broadcasts to its neighbors. Each node waits for a time period after receiving the tree construction message for the first time (i.e., the node has not yet rebroadcast the message in its neighborhood). During this time, the node expects to get some more copies of the tree construction message from its neighbors. A node prefers to join the DG tree through the closest neighbor. Hence, when a node receives several copies of the tree construction message during the waiting time period, it determines the distance between itself and the neighbors who forwarded the tree construction message. The node chooses to join the DG tree through the neighbor node that is closest to it and sets its upstream node id to the id of the chosen neighbor node; the node also overwrites the contents of the *forwarder information* field with its own ID and location information. The tree construction message is then rebroadcast in the neighborhood and the above process is repeated at all the nodes. Each node broadcasts the tree construction message exactly once. By the end of the network-wide broadcast, each node would have joined the DG tree through the neighbor node that is closest to it (and would serve as its upstream node). Such a design for the data gathering algorithm is expected to minimize the energy loss during transmission and save the energy of the nodes.

3. EIGENVECTOR CENTRALITY FOR LOCATION TRACKING

The procedure explained in Chapter 1 to determine eigenvector centrality (EVC) of the vertices used the 0-1 adjacency matrix as the basis. In this chapter, we will use a weighted adjacency matrix as the underlying matrix for calculating the EVC values of the vertices. The weight for a vertex is the cumulative signal strength that it reports to the sink at the end of a sampling time period. The weight for an edge *u-v* entered in the weighted adjacency matrix is the sum of the weights of the vertices *u* and *v*. We then run the power-iteration algorithm on the weighted adjacency matrix to determine the EVC of the vertices. We choose the top 5 vertices that have the largest EVC values and predict the location of the mobile target to be the average of the X and Y coordinates of these nodes.

In Figure 1, we illustrate the working of the above said procedure through an example. In the graph shown in Figure 1, the numbers inside the circles represent the node ID and the numbers outside the circles represent the weights of the vertices (the cumulative signal strengths reported by the nodes). The weighted adjacency matrix is shown next to the graph. We run six iterations of the power-iteration algorithm before the principal eigenvalue converges. Vertex 4 has the largest EVC value (0.521) and its neighbor nodes (vertices 2, 3 and 7) also expectedly have relatively larger EVC values compared to the other vertices that are not directly attached to vertex 4. The target is considered to be in the vicinity of the vertices with the largest EVC values.

Figure 1. Example to illustrate the calculation of eigenvector centrality using power iteration method

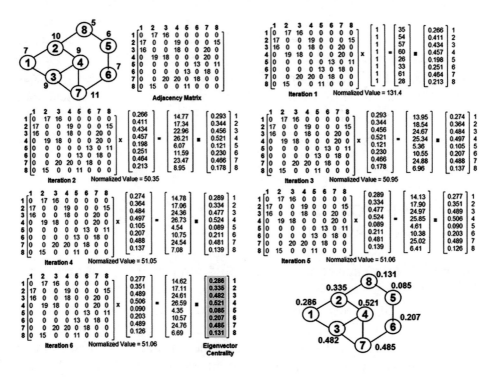

4. PROCEDURE FOR MOBILE TARGET TRACKING

We assume each sensor node to be capable of sensing the radioactive signals emanating in its neighborhood from the mobile target. We assign the strength of the background non-radiation signals to be 1 and the strength of the radiation signals to be also 1. Due to the difficulty in designing sensor nodes that could differentiate between the different signals and accurately estimate the individual signal strengths, we assume a sensor node just estimates the strength of all the signals (put together) sensed in its neighborhood (it could be a 1 or 2 per time unit, as per our model). Each sensor node locally maintains the cumulative signal strength values sensed across a sampling time period.

Whenever it is time to gather the signal strength data, the leader node broadcasts a Query Data message to its neighbors, which further propagate the message down to their neighbors and so on. The Query Data message contains a *Signal Strength Vector* field to which every node will append its cumulative signal strength recorded for the latest sampling time period. An intermediate node waits to receive the updated Query Data message from its downstream child nodes. Hence, the upward propagation of the Query Data message starts from the leaf nodes. A leaf node records the cumulative signal strength in the Signal Strength Vector field and propagates the message to its immediate upstream node. After receiving the Query Data message from all its immediate downstream nodes, an intermediate node records its own cumulative signal strength data in the Signal Strength Vector field and forwards the Query Data message to its own upstream node. The leader node also follows the same procedure for an intermediate node and sends one copy of the Query Data message to the sink node with the signal strength from all the live sensor nodes recorded in it.

The sink node follows the procedure described in Section 3 to determine the top 5 vertices that incur the largest EVC values based on the weighted adjacency matrix of cumulative signal strength values constructed based on the latest Query Data message received from the leader node. The sink node is assumed to know the locations of all the sensor nodes in the network (through an a priori Query message broadcast in the network or through some offline means) and predicts the location of the mobile target during the time instant at the middle of the sampling time period to be the average of the X and Y coordinates of the nodes with the top 5 EVC values. At the end of the simulation, we could get a trajectory (mobility profile) of the mobile RDD and compare it with the actual mobility profile. The *distance error* at a particular sampling time instant is the Euclidean distance between the actual location and the predicted location.

5. SIMULATIONS

5.1 RDD Mobility Profile

At any time, the RDD is assumed to move with a velocity that is uniform-randomly chosen from the range $[0...v_{RDD}]$. The actual mobility profile of the RDD is stored and generated as follows: To begin with, the RDD is set at a randomly chosen location within the monitoring area and it chooses a random velocity from the range $[0...v_{RDD}]$ as well as a random target location (within the boundaries of the area being monitored) to move. The RDD is assumed to move to the target location in a straight line at the chosen velocity. After moving to the targeted location, the RDD repeats the above process (i.e., chooses a new random target location and a random velocity in the range $[0...v_{RDD}]$ to move to the new location) until the end of the simulation. Since the RDD moves in a straight line at a particular velocity before changing directions, it would be sufficient to keep track of the starting and ending locations of the RDD when it moves in a straight line and the corresponding velocity of movement. The location of the RDD at any time instant could be then interpolated using the above mobility profile.

Figure 2 illustrates an example to interpolate the mobility profile of an RDD and determine the exact location of the RDD at a particular time instant (t) wherein $t_i \leq t \leq t_j$; t_i and t_j are respectively the time instants at which the RDD starts from a location (X_i, Y_i) and goes in a straight line with a velocity $v_{ij} \in [0...v_{RDD}]$ to location (X_j, Y_j). We determine the fraction (f) of the straight line (linear distance) that would have been covered from time instant t_i to t and it is calculated as: $f = (t - t_i)/(t_j - t_i)$. The X and Y co-ordinates of the node at time instant t can be then computed as: $X = f * X_j + (1-f) * X_i$; $Y = f * Y_j + (1-f) * Y_i$. Figure 3 presents a visual comparison of the actual mobility profile (determined using the procedure described in this sub section) and the predicted mobility profile (determined using the procedure described in

Figure 2. Procedure to determine the exact location of the RDD at any time instant

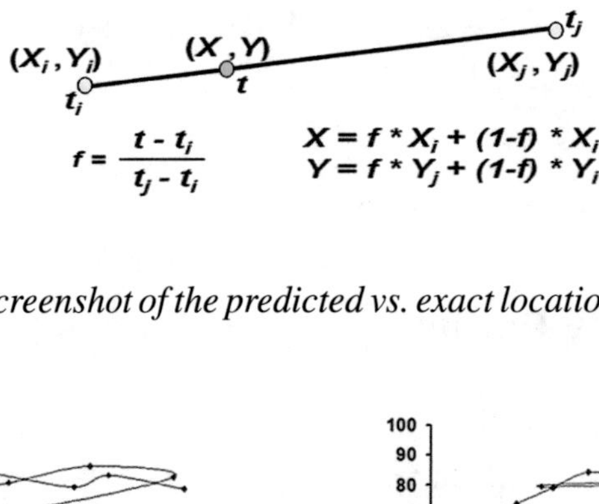

Figure 3. A sample screenshot of the predicted vs. exact locations of the RDD during a simulation run

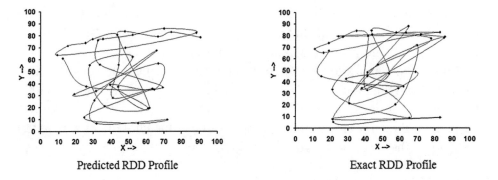

Sections 3 and 4) of an RDD with a maximum velocity v_{RDD} of 5 m/s in a network area of dimensions 100m x 100m.

5.2 Sensor Energy Consumption Model

We use first-order radio model (Rappaport, 2002) for modeling energy consumption that has also been used in several of the previous works (e.g., Heinzelman et al., 2000; Lindsey et al., 2002) in the literature. The energy lost at a sensor node transmit a k-bit message over a distance d is given by: $E_{TX}(k, d) = E_{elec}*k + \in_{amp}*k*d^2$, where $E_{elec} = 50$ nJ/bit is the energy lost in the transmitter or receiver radio circuitry and $\in_{amp} = 100$ pJ/bit/m^2 is the energy lost to run the transmitter amplifier. The energy lost to broadcast over the entire transmission range R of a sensor node is then given by $E_{TX}(k, R)$. To receive a message of size k bits, a sensor node loses energy $E_{RX}(k) = E_{elec}$ $*k$. If there are n neighbors for a sensor node, then the energy lost to receive a broadcast message of size k bits from all its n neighbors will be then $n*$ $E_{RX}(k)$. A sensor node loses energy to transmit and receive the Query Data message along the DG tree as well as loses energy to broadcast and receive the tree construction message every time a DG tree is constructed.

5.3 Network and Data Aggregation Parameters

Simulations are run in a discrete-event simulator implemented in Java by the author. The medium access control (MAC) layer is assumed to be idle: there are no collisions during message broadcasts and transmissions. The sensor nodes are assumed to be able to transmit data as per both TDMA (time division multiple access) as well CDMA (code division multiple access). Intermediate nodes at the same level of the DG tree would use different CDMA codes in parallel (one CDMA code per intermediate node) to communicate with their immediate downstream/child nodes. Nevertheless, an individual intermediate node would need to allocate TDMA timeslots to its immediate child nodes and receive the Query Data messages from one child node per timeslot according to the TDMA schedule.

The number of sensor nodes used in the simulations is 100 and the network area is of dimensions 100m x 100m. The values for the transmission range per node are: 25m (moderate density) and 40m (high density). The network is more likely to be not 100% connected for lower transmission range values and hence we just use the above two values that are also considered as a measure of network density. The maximum velocity of the mobile RDD (v_{RDD}) is varied from 2 m/s (low mobility) to 5 m/s (moderate mobility) and 10 m/s (high mobility). We generate 20 mobility profiles of the RDD for each of these three v_{RDD} values. The values for the sampling time period are: 1, 5, 10, 20, 30, 40, 50, 60, 70, 80, 90, 100, 120, 140, 170 and 200 seconds. The DG tree is refreshed for every 300 seconds (if not refreshed during this period). Simulations are run for both energy-unconstrained and energy constrained scenarios (in the latter case, each sensor node is assumed to have 0.25 Joules of energy). Simulations are run for 6000 seconds (rounds) in the case of energy-unconstrained scenarios or until the network fails for energy-constrained scenarios. A network is considered to have failed if it gets disconnected due to the failure of one or more nodes. For a particular operating condition (transmission range per node, maximum velocity of the RDD and sampling time period), we determine the distance errors at time instants corresponding to the middle of every sampling time period and find the median of the values across all the simulation runs (of the 20 mobility profile files). We expect the simulations under energy-unconstrained scenarios to give us a lower bound for the median distance error under identical conditions (vis-a-vis the energy-constrained scenarios).

5.4 Performance Metrics

We evaluate the following performance metrics in the simulations: (i) *Median Distance Error* - We define the distance error as the distance between the predicted and actual X and Y locations of the mobile target at any particular time instant (middle time instant of every sampling period). We accumulate the distance errors for all the 20 mobility profile files for a particular set of operating conditions and determine the median of these distance error values. (ii) *Node Lifetime* - The node lifetime is the time of first node failure due to exhaustion of battery charge. (iii) *Network Lifetime* - The network lifetime is the time at which the network gets disconnected due to one or more node failures. For node lifetime and network lifetime (measurable only when the simulations are run for energy-constrained scenarios), we average the results for all the 20 mobility profile files for a particular set of operating conditions.

For a fixed value of v_{RDD} and the sampling time period, the median distance error (see Figure 4) for the energy-constrained scenarios decreases with increase in network density and approaches closer to the median distance error obtained under energy-unconstrained scenarios for identical operating conditions. On the other hand, for a fixed sampling time period and network density, the median distance error (for both the energy-constrained and energy-unconstrained scenarios) increases with increase in v_{RDD}. Especially, when operated under energy-constrained scenarios, there is a shortage of live sensor nodes as the simulation progresses and the median distance error of the predictions is bound to increase as the RDD moves faster.

At high RDD mobility, it is thus essential to improve the accuracy of prediction by deploying strategies that would increase the participation of appreciable number of nodes (operate at a larger transmission range per node) and/or decrease the sampling time period (so that the RDD has not moved much farther away from the predicted location). Though both the strategies are likely to consume more energy and lead to premature node failures and sometimes network failure too, they can be very effective in increasing the accuracy of the predictions. Notice that when operating with a sampling time period as low as 1 second, the network lifetime and node lifetime are closer to each other (indicating premature network disconnection and nodes failing in quick succession). One could employ sensor node recharging or replacement (Meghanathan & Judon, 2010) as an alternative to prolong network lifetime in the presence of node failures. At low-moderate RDD mobility, it would be sufficient to operate the network at moderate transmission range per node and/or larger values for the sampling time periods. Since the RDD would be moving slowly with time, it is expected to be in the vicinity of the suspect nodes (that have larger EVC values) for a certain time period facilitating relaxed operating conditions.

From Figure 5, one could notice that the difference between the node lifetime and network lifetime (see Figure 5) is also likely to increase for larger values of the sampling time period. However, too larger values for the sampling time periods could indeed affect the accuracy of the predictions as several nodes could then end up having the similar EVC values. Hence, it is imperative to choose appropriate values for the sampling time period for both energy-constrained and energy-unconstrained scenarios. Based on the simulation results, it appears that 10-40 seconds would be an appropriate range of values for the sampling time period so that we could incur lower values for the median distance error as well as larger values for the network lifetime.

For a fixed RDD velocity and sampling time period, the median distance error decreases with increase in the transmission range/sensing range per node. However, operating at larger values for the transmission range per node leads to substantial increase in the energy consumption at the nodes, leading to premature node failures. Hence, if the RDD mobility is not high,

Figure 4. Median distance error values

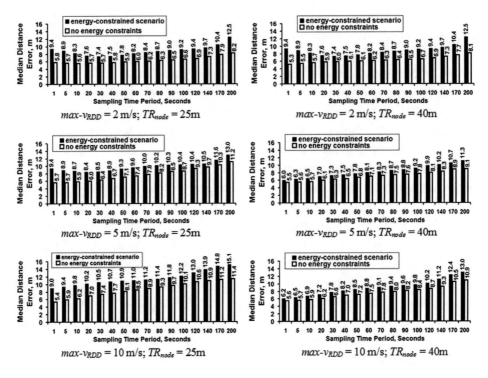

Figure 5. Node lifetime and network lifetime

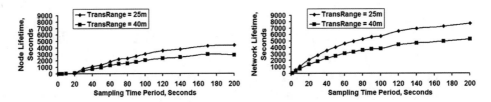

it would be more prudent to operate at moderate values of the transmission range/sensing range per node to prolong network lifetime without incurring too high of a prediction error.

In Figure 4, for scenarios of high RDD mobility, we notice the median distance error metric to exhibit a concave down pattern of increase with increase in the sampling time period. This implies that the rate of increase of the median distance error decreases with increase in the sampling time period. In other words, the median distance error is not just going to blow up (i.e., kind of increase exponentially) with increase in the sampling time period. Hence, it is more prudent to conduct data gathering for moderate sampling time periods (10-40 seconds, as mentioned above) even at high RDD mobility. From Figure 5, we notice the node lifetime and network lifetime to also exhibit a concave down pattern of increase with increase in the sampling time period. In other words, operating at significantly larger values of sampling time period is not going to lead to a significantly longer node lifetime or network lifetime. To keep the median distance error desirably low for an appreciable duration (i.e., for the lifetime of the network), it would be again more prudent to conduct data gathering for moderate sampling time periods.

6. RELATED WORK AND OUR CONTRIBUTIONS

Mobile target tracking is an actively researched topic in the area of wireless sensor networks. Most of the work in the literature (e.g., Chin et al., 2010) require the use of localization techniques such as triangulation and tri-lateration (Savvides et al., 2004) to predict the location of the target. In addition, some algorithms require the nodes to be synchronized with respect to time (Amundson et al., 2007), especially when operated for heterogeneous networks. Some of the works (e.g., Zhang & Cao, 2004) also require considerable coordination among the sensor nodes to track a mobile target. On the other hand, the proposed EVC-based mobile target tracking algorithm does not require the use of localization techniques as well as does not require the sensor nodes to be synchronized with respect to time. The EVC-based tracking algorithm does not require much coordination among the sensor nodes; the nodes just need to broadcast the Query Data message to its neighbors (so that the message reaches the downstream child nodes) and a downstream child node just needs to send updated Query Data message back to its upstream node. The proposed EVC-based tracking algorithm also imposes less overhead on the individual sensor nodes: they have to just measure the cumulative strength of the signals sensed in the neighborhood and simply forward the cumulative signal strength across the duration of the sampling time period to the sink. The sink uses an innovative approach of putting together the cumulative signal strengths received from the individual sensor nodes in a weighted adjacency matrix that is used to compute the EVC of the nodes. The EVC metric accurately captures the neighborhood in which the RDD is moving around.

Some algorithms (e.g., Goshorn et al., 2007) require the use of clusterheads that aggregate the data (like the cumulative signal strengths) from the sensor nodes within the cluster and analyze it further to track the presence of any mobile target. However, to do this, the clusterheads need to be more sophisticated than the non-clusterhead nodes and would still need to forward the processed results to the sink so that the trajectory of the target could be obtained over a larger time period. Chand et al. (2008) employed a mix of smart radioactive sensor nodes (that could act as clusterheads) and regular sensor nodes to detect static targets, but not mobile targets. Wang et al. (2008) proposed an algorithm wherein the sensor nodes are arranged in a hierarchy such that the internal nodes are more sophisticated to obtain some initial results on target tracking before forwarding the data and the initial results to the sink. Instead of requiring certain sensor nodes (like the clusterheads or the intermediate nodes in the hierarchy) to do substantial amount of processing, but still requiring them to forward the results and data to the sink for comprehensive analysis, we believe it would be more prudent to just let the sink handle the bulk of the processing and reduce the overhead at the sensor nodes. The intermediate nodes in our tracking algorithm are just required to be able to assign timeslots to their downstream child nodes under TDMA. Thus, we could employ sensor nodes that are more similar to each other and incur less maintenance overhead. Nevertheless, our proposed EVC-tracking algorithm could be used with nodes of different processing capacities (these will be just complementary to our algorithm and would improve its performance even better); the algorithm could be even adapted to choose the more sophisticated nodes as intermediate nodes and have the less sophisticated nodes as leaf nodes of the DG tree.

Liu et al. (2011) proposed a Bayesian statistics-based method to track a nuclear target; the sensor nodes need to be programmed with the statistical distribution of the different radiations so that the radiation of interest could be sensed and processed for predicting the presence of the target. This method also requires the nodes to be strategically placed and some of the nodes need to be mobile too. Similarly, Rassam et al. (2013) also proposed a tracking mechanism that would require the sensor nodes to be programmed with a priori knowledge of the signals so that the sensor nodes could run some anomaly detection algorithms if they sense signals that differ from what is known. Unlike these related works, our EVC-based tracking algorithm does not require the sensor nodes to know the statistical distribution of the signals a priori and need not be strategically placed or be mobile. The strategies of summing up the signal strengths detected over a sampling time period and then further summing up the signal strengths of the end vertices of the edges to obtain a weighted adjacency matrix and the ensuing the eigenvector centrality values are effective enough to trace the trajectory mobile targets with low distance errors.

7. CONCLUSION

The key contribution of this chapter is the use of eigenvector centrality (EVC) to trace the trajectory of a mobile target in a wireless sensor network. The proposed strategy of EVC-based tracking could be employed with network of homogeneous or heterogeneous sensor nodes and the nodes need not be strategically placed or sophisticated enough for some data processing or be mobile. The sensor nodes need not be able to detect the radioactive signals per se; they simply keep track of the cumulative strengths of the signals sensed in their neighborhood and forward the data to the sink node along the edges of a data gathering tree. The sink node puts together a weighted adjacency matrix based on which the EVC values of the vertices are found. Vertices having larger EVC values are likely suspects (the mobile target is likely to move around the neighborhood of these vertices) and we predict the location of the mobile target as the average of the X and Y coordinates of the top x number of nodes (with respect to their EVC values). We conducted extensive simulation analysis for tracking a mobile target using wireless sensor networks. We observe the median distance error as well as the node lifetime and network lifetime to increase (in a concave down fashion) with increase in the sampling time period and decrease in the transmission range per node. Hence, to incur lower values for the median distance error and be able to run the sensor network for a longer lifetime, it becomes imperative to operate the wireless sensor networks with moderate values for the sampling time period and transmission range/sensing range per node. However, with increase in RDD mobility, the median distance error could be decreased by operating at smaller values of the sampling time period and larger transmission range per node.

8. FUTURE RESEARCH DIRECTIONS

As part of future research, we will investigate the use of localized centrality metrics (those that do not require computation at the global level) that could be computed by the sophisticated sensor nodes randomly deployed along with the regular sensor nodes. The localized centrality metrics could be adapted from the notion of the egocentric edge network and one could compute the principal eigenvalue of the entries in the adjacency matrix representing the egocentric edge network and use this as the basis to predict the neighborhood in which the target would be moving around. Due to the failure of one or more nodes (attributed to the exhaustion of battery charge), it is imperative to operate the live nodes with a larger transmission range as well as sensing range (to provide connectivity among the live sensor nodes across the coverage area). To counter this problem, we plan to consider employing mobile sensor nodes that could move around and compensate for loss of coverage resulting from node failures. However, node mobility comes with the overhead of maintaining stable data gathering trees that could be used for a longer time without the need to frequently reconfigure.

REFERENCES

Amundson, I., Kushwaha, M., Kusy, B., Volgyesi, P., Simon, G., Koutsoukos, X., & Ledeczi, A. (2007). *Time Synchronization for Multi-Modal Target Tracking in Heterogeneous Sensor Networks*. Paper presented at the Workshop on Networked Distributed Systems for Intelligent Sensing and Control, Kalamata, Greece.

Chandy, M., Pilotto, C., & McLean, R. (2008). *Networked Sensing Systems for Detecting People Carrying Radioactive Material*. Paper presented at the 5th International Conference on Networked Sensing Systems, Kanazawa, Japan. 10.1109/INSS.2008.4610916

Chin, J. C., Rao, N. S. V., Yau, D. K. Y., Shankar, M., Yang, Y., Hou, J. C., Srivathsan, S., & Iyengar, S. (2010). Identification of Low-Level Point Radioactive Sources using a Sensor Network. *ACM Transactions on Sensor Networks, 7*(3).

Goshorn, R., Goshorn, J., Goshorn, D., & Aghajan, H. (2007). *Architecture for Cluster-based Automated Surveillance Network for Detecting and Tracking Multiple Persons*. Paper presented at the ACM/IEEE International Conference on Distributed Smart Cameras, Vienna, Austria. 10.1109/ICDSC.2007.4357527

Heinzelman, W., Chandrakasan, A., & Balakarishnan, H. (2000). *Energy-Efficient Communication Protocols for Wireless Microsensor Networks*. Paper presented at the Hawaiian International Conference on Systems Science, Maui, HI. 10.1109/HICSS.2000.926982

Lindsey, S., Raghavendra, C., & Sivalingam, K. M. (2002). Data Gathering Algorithms in Sensor Networks using Energy Metrics. *IEEE Transactions on Parallel and Distributed Systems*, *13*(9), 924–935. doi:10.1109/TPDS.2002.1036066

Liu, A. H., Bunn, J. J., & Chandy, K. M. (2011). *Sensor Networks for the Detection and Tracking of Radiation and Other Threats in Cities*. Paper presented at the 10th International Conference on Information Processing in Sensor Networks, Chicago, IL.

Meghanathan, N. (2012). A Comprehensive Review and Performance Analysis of Data Gathering Algorithms for Wireless Sensor Networks. *International Journal of Interdisciplinary Telecommunications and Networking*, *4*(2), 1–29. doi:10.4018/jitn.2012040101

Meghanathan, N., & Judon, L. P. (2010). Improvement in Network Lifetime for On-Demand Routing in Mobile Ad hoc Networks using either On-Demand Recharging or Transmission Power Control or Both. *Journal of Computer and Information Science*, *3*(1), 3–11.

Rappaport, T. S. (2002). *Wireless Communications: Principles and Practice*. Prentice Hall.

Rassam, M. A., Zainal, A., & Maarof, M. A. (2013). Advancements of Data Anomaly Detection Research in Wireless Sensor Networks: A Survey and Open Issues. *Sensors (Basel)*, *13*(12), 10088–10122. doi:10.3390130810087 PMID:23966182

Savvides, A., Srivastava, M., Girod, L., & Estrin, D. (2004). Localization in Sensor Networks. In C. S. Raghavendra, K. M. Sivalingam, & T. Znati (Eds.), *Wireless Sensor Networks*. Boston, MA: Kluwer Academic Publishers.

Wang, Z., Li, H., Shen, X., Sun, X., & Wang, Z. (2008). *Tracking and Predicting Moving Targets in Hierarchical Sensor Networks*. Paper presented at the IEEE International Conference on Networking, Sensing and Control, Sanya, China. 10.1109/ICNSC.2008.4525393

Zhang, H., & Hou, J. C. (2005). Maintaining Sensing Coverage and Connectivity in Large Sensor Networks. *Wireless Ad hoc and Sensor Networks. International Journal (Toronto, Ont.)*, *1*(1-2), 89–123.

Zhang, W., & Cao, G. (2004). DCTC: Dynamic Convoy Tree-based Collaboration for Target Tracking in Sensor Networks. *IEEE Transactions on Wireless Communications*, *3*(5), 1689–1701. doi:10.1109/TWC.2004.833443

Chapter 7

Use of Centrality Metrics for Ranking of Courses Based on Their Relative Contribution in a Curriculum Network Graph

ABSTRACT

The author proposes a centrality and topological sort-based formulation to quantify the relative contribution of courses in a curriculum network graph (CNG), a directed acyclic graph, comprising of the courses (as vertices), and their pre-requisites (captured as directed edges). The centrality metrics considered are out-degree and in-degree centrality along with betweenness centrality and eigenvector centrality. The author normalizes the values obtained for each centrality metric as well as the level numbers of the vertices in a topological sort of the CNG. The contribution score for a vertex is the weighted sum of the normalized values for the vertex. The author observes the betweenness centrality of the vertices (courses) to have the largest influence in the relative contribution scores of the courses that could be used as a measure of the weights to be given to the courses for curriculum assessment and student ranking as well as to cluster courses with similar contribution.

DOI: 10.4018/978-1-5225-3802-8.ch007

1. INTRODUCTION

The networks that have been commonly analyzed in the literature are social networks, biological networks, co-authorship networks, transportation networks and etc. Very little focus has been on curriculum network graphs that are the focus of this research. We model a curriculum network graph (CNG) as a directed acyclic graph (DAG) of vertices and edges (Cormen et al., 2009): each course in the curriculum is a vertex and there exists a directed edge from vertex u to vertex v (represented as $u \rightarrow v$) if the course corresponding to vertex u (a.k.a. the upstream vertex) is a pre-requisite for the course corresponding to vertex v (a.k.a. the downstream vertex). We define a terminal course as one that has one or more courses as pre-requisites, but is not the pre-requisite for any other course; likewise, we define a seed course as one that serves as a pre-requisite for one or more courses, but does not have any pre-requisite. For the rest of the chapter, the terms 'course' and 'vertex' are used interchangeably.

Most of the analysis on CNGs (e.g., Aldrich, 2014; Lightfood, 2010; Komenda et al., 2015) has been restricted to identifying one or more courses that satisfy a specific requirement, like: courses that could be used for assessment, incorporating changes to the curriculum, introducing core topics, etc. In this chapter, we seek to address the following research question based on the structural analysis of a CNG: *How to comprehensively rank the courses in a curriculum as well as quantify the relative contribution of the courses in the curriculum and cluster them taking into consideration all of these below*:

1.   The order in which the courses are taken,
2.   The number of courses for which a course is a pre-requisite for,
3.   The number of courses that are the pre-requisites for a course,
4.   The courses that have one or more courses as a common pre-requisite
5.   The courses that jointly serve as a pre-requisite for one or more courses
6.   The intermediate courses that have one or more courses as pre-requisites as well as serve as pre-requisites for one or more courses.

We seek to address the above research questions by making use of topological sort (Cormen et al., 2009) and centrality metrics (Newman, 2010):

1.   A topological sort of the vertices (Cormen, et al., 2009) in a DAG like the CNG would comprise of a sequence of courses such that if there is a directed edge from vertex u to vertex v, then vertex u would appear

somewhere before vertex v in the topological sort. We introduce a metric called the *level number* of a vertex in a DAG and we define it as one plus the maximum of the level numbers of the incoming neighbor vertices that appear somewhere before the vertex in the topological sort. In the context of a CNG, the level number for a course (vertex) is a measure of the earliest possible semester a student could take a course as part of a degree plan for the curriculum. A course with a larger value for the level number in the CNG should appear in a later semester in the degree plan compared to a course with a relatively smaller value for the level number. A course with a larger value for the level number would thus reinforce the topics that were studied in the courses taken earlier and hence could be considered a candidate course for evaluating the cumulative knowledgebase attained by the students as a result of taking a sequence of courses leading to the course.

2. The out-degree centrality of a vertex in a directed graph is the number of edges for which the vertex is an upstream vertex. The out-degree centrality of a course is thus a direct measure of the number of courses for which a vertex is a pre-requisite for. Courses that are taken earlier in the curriculum are more likely to get a higher value with respect to the out-degree centrality metric.

3. The in-degree centrality of a vertex in a directed graph is the number of edges for which the vertex is a downstream vertex. The in-degree centrality of a course is thus a direct measure of the number of pre-requisite courses for a course. Courses that are taken later in the curriculum are more likely to get a higher value with respect to the in-degree centrality metric.

4. The cocitation coupling matrix (Gipp & Beel, 2009) of a directed graph is a square matrix (with the number of rows and columns corresponding to the number of vertices) such that the value for an entry (u, v) indicates the number of vertices that are the upstream vertices for both u and v as part of directed edges in the original graph. In the context of a CNG, the value for an entry (u, v) in the cocitation coupling matrix for a CNG indicates the number of courses that are the common pre-requisite courses for courses corresponding to both vertices u and v. We evaluate the contribution of the courses that had one or more common pre-requisites by computing the eigenvector centrality of the vertices in the cocitation coupling matrix of the CNG. Junior and senior-level courses are more likely to get a higher value for the eigenvector centrality of the cocitation coupling matrix of a CNG.

5. The bibliographic coupling matrix (Zhao & Strotmann, 2008) of a directed graph is a square matrix (with the number of rows and columns corresponding to the number of vertices) such that the value for an entry (u, v) is the number of vertices to which both u and v serve as upstream vertices as part of directed edges in the original graph. In the context of a CNG, the value for an entry (u, v) in the bibliographic coupling matrix for a CNG indicates the number of courses for which both u and v serve as pre-requisite courses. We evaluate the contribution of the courses that jointly serve (with another course) as a pre-requisite for one or more courses by computing the eigenvector centrality of the vertices in the bibliographic coupling matrix of the CNG. Courses that are taken in the Freshman and Sophomore years are more likely to get a higher value for the eigenvector centrality of the bibliographic coupling matrix of a CNG.

6. The betweenness centrality (BWC; Brandes, 2001) of a vertex is a measure of the fraction of the shortest paths between any two vertices going through the vertex. We will use the BWC values of the vertices in a CNG to analyze the criticality of an intermediate course in facilitating students to take one or more courses in the curriculum.

Very few works (like Slim et al., 2014a, 2014b) have addressed the problem of identifying courses that satisfy more than one requirement. Slim et al. (2014a) quantify the cruciality of a course as the sum of the out-degree of the course and the length of the longest path to any other course in the curriculum. But the formulation lacks any normalization and it could be misleading to directly add degree with path length. In this chapter, we propose to normalize the scores for courses obtained from the individual graph theoretic metrics and compute the contribution score for a course as a weighted sum of the normalized scores. We define the relative contribution score for a course as the ratio of the contribution score for the course to that of the sum of the contribution scores. We illustrate the use of the relative contribution scores of the courses in a curriculum to determine a cumulative grade score, cumulative assessment score as well as to cluster courses that have comparable contribution to the curriculum.

The rest of the chapter is organized as follows: Section 2 explains the computation of the out-degree and in-degree centrality of the vertices, topological sort and the level numbers of the vertices, BWC values of the vertices, eigenvector centrality of the vertices as well as the cocitation coupling and bibliographic coupling matrices of a directed graph that is also a DAG.

Section 3 presents the formulation to quantify the relative contribution of the vertices (courses) in a curriculum and rank them. Section 4 explains the application of the formulation on two real-world CNGs. Section 5 discusses related work and highlights the contribution of the work presented in this chapter. Section 6 concludes the chapter and Section 7 discusses future research directions.

2. COMPUTATION OF THE GRAPH THEORETIC METRICS

In this section, we explain the computation of the graph theoretic metrics listed from (a)-(f) in Section 1. We use a running example of a DAG (see Figure 1) throughout this section.

2.1 Out-Degree and In-Degree Centrality

The out-degree and in-degree centrality of a vertex are respectively the number of outgoing edges and the number of incoming edges to the vertex. Figure 2 illustrates the out-degree and in-degree centrality of the vertices in the running example of Figure 1. The centrality values are expressed as a 2-element tuple for each vertex, with the first entry indicating out-degree and the second entry indicating in-degree.

Figure 1. Running example of a DAG

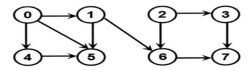

Figure 2. Out-Degree and in-degree centrality of the vertices in the running example of a DAG

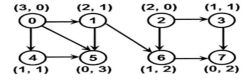

2.2 Topological Sort and Level Number of the Vertices

The topological sort of a DAG is an ordered listing of the vertices (each vertex appears exactly once in the list) such that for any directed edge $u \rightarrow v$ in the DAG, vertex u appears somewhere before vertex v in the list. The topological sort of a DAG is obtained by running the Depth First Search (DFS) algorithm (Cormen et al., 2009) starting from a randomly chosen vertex in the DAG. We use a stack to keep track of the order in which the vertices are visited. When a vertex is visited for the first time, we push the vertex into the stack. We continue the traversals by visiting one of the unvisited out-going neighbors of the vertex and recursively continue the traversals until we can no longer visit any out-going neighbor for a vertex that is currently in the top of the stack. At that time, we pop out the vertex from the stack. We keep track of the order in which the vertices are pushed and popped out of the stack. A topological sort of the DAG is the reverse of the order in which the vertices are popped out of the stack. In Figure 3, we show the order (as a 2-element tuple for each vertex): the first number in the 2-element tuple for a vertex indicates the order in which the vertex was pushed into the stack and the second number in the 2-element tuple for a vertex indicates the order in which the vertex was popped out of the stack.

We define the level number of a vertex in a DAG as one plus the maximum of the level numbers of the upstream vertices (from which there is an incoming edge to the vertex) that are also ahead of the vertex in the topological sort of the DAG. The level number for a seed vertex in a DAG is 1 as there are no incoming edges to this vertex. If more than one seed vertex exists (like vertices 0 and 2 in Figure 3), each of them get a level number of 1. We determine and assign the level numbers for the vertices in the order they are listed in the topological sort of the DAG. For example, consider vertex 5 in the running example of the DAG (shown in Figure 3) that has three incoming neighbors (vertices 0, 1 and 4) that also appear somewhere before vertex 5 in the topological sort of the DAG and their level numbers are already known before determining the level number for vertex 5. The level number for vertex 5 is one plus the maximum of the level numbers (1, 2, 2) of its incoming neighbors: $1 + 2 = 3$.

Figure 3. Computation of the topological sorted list and level numbers of the vertices in a DAG

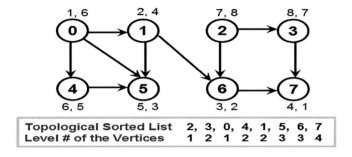

Topological Sorted List	2,	3,	0,	4,	1,	5,	6,	7
Level # of the Vertices	1	2	1	2	2	3	3	4

2.3 Eigenvector Centrality

The eigenvector centrality of a vertex (Bonacich, 1987) is computed only for undirected graphs as a measure of the degree of the vertex and the degrees of its neighbors. As centrality is computable only when we have outgoing edges from each vertex, in the case of directed acyclic graphs (DAGs): the eigenvector centrality of the vertices becomes zero (Zafarani et al., 2014). As undirected graphs have a symmetric adjacency matrix, the above issue is not a concern.

In this chapter, we compute the eigenvector centrality of the vertices using the adjacency matrices generated from the cocitation coupling (see Section 2.4; Gipp & Beel, 2009) and bibliographic coupling (see Section 2.5; Zhao & Strotmann, 2008) of a DAG like the CNG. In this section, we illustrate the computation of the eigenvector centrality metric by treating the DAG of our running example as an undirected graph. We use the Power-iteration algorithm (Lay, 2001) that is also used in Sections 2.4 and 2.5.

The Power-iteration algorithm proceeds as follows: We start with a unit vector of all 1s as the tentative eigenvector (for iteration 0: initialization). In the $(i+1)^{th}$ iteration, we take the product of the adjacency matrix and the tentative eigenvector at the end of the ith iteration. We find the normalized value of the product vector and divide each entry in the product vector by the normalized value. We continue the iterations until the normalized value obtained for a particular iteration converges to the value obtained in the previous iteration (in this chapter: considered for two decimal places). At that point, the entries in the tentative eigenvector are finalized as the eigenvector centrality of the vertices. Figure 4 illustrates the computation of the eigenvector centrality of the example graph of Figure 1 assuming all the edges are undirected.

Figure 4. Example to illustrate computation of Eigenvector centrality using power-iteration algorithm

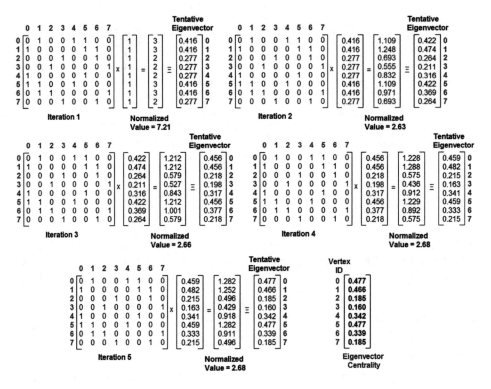

2.4 Cocitation Coupling

The cocitation coupling matrix (CC)(Gipp & Beel, 2009) is a square symmetric matrix (one row/column for each vertex) that captures the common pre-requisite courses for any two courses in the curriculum. To obtain the cocitation and bibliographic coupling matrices, we define the entries in the adjacency matrix A of a directed graph in a slightly different way, explained as follows: $A[i, j] = 1$ if and only if there is a directed edge from vertex j to vertex i. An entry $CC(i, j)$ is greater than 0 if and only if there exists at least one vertex k such that there exist directed edges from vertex k to both vertices i and j. More formally,

$$CC[i, j] = \sum_{k=1}^{n} A[i, k] * A[j, k] = \sum_{k=1}^{n} A[i, k] * A[k, j]^{T} \tag{1}$$

$$CC = A * A^{\mathrm{T}} \tag{2}$$

where A^{T} is the transpose of A.

In Figure 5, we show the computation of the cocitation coupling matrix for the DAG that is being used as the running example in this chapter. We also show the final values for the eigenvector centrality obtained by running the Power-iteration algorithm (illustrated in Figure 4) on the cocitation coupling matrix of this DAG. We notice that vertex 5 had two peers (vertices 1 and 4) - all of which had a common pre-requisite (vertex 0) and another peer (vertex 6) with which it has vertex 1 as a common pre-requisite. Besides, vertex 4 is also a pre-requisite for vertex 5: leading to three incoming neighbors. The vertex with the next largest value for the EVC_CC is vertex 6 and this could be attributed to its sharing a common pre-requisite with two peers (vertex 1 is a common pre-requisite for vertices 5 and 6; vertex 2 is a common pre-requisite for vertices 3 and 6) as well as two incoming neighbors.

2.5 Bibliographic Coupling

The bibliographic coupling matrix (BC)(Zhao & Strotmann, 2008) is a square symmetric matrix (one row/column for each vertex) that quantifies

Figure 5. Eigenvector Centrality of Vertices based on Cocitation Coupling Matrix (EVC_CC)

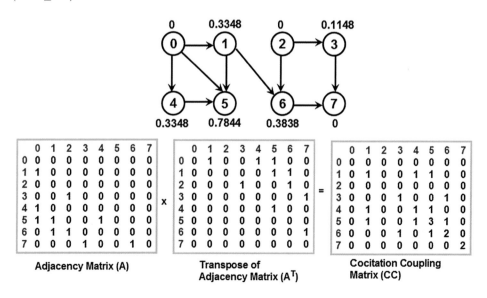

Adjacency Matrix (A)

	0	1	2	3	4	5	6	7
0	0	0	0	0	0	0	0	0
1	1	0	0	0	0	0	0	0
2	0	0	0	0	0	0	0	0
3	0	0	1	0	0	0	0	0
4	1	0	0	0	0	0	0	0
5	1	1	0	0	1	0	0	0
6	0	1	1	0	0	0	0	0
7	0	0	0	1	0	0	1	0

Transpose of Adjacency Matrix (A^{T})

	0	1	2	3	4	5	6	7
0	0	1	0	0	1	1	0	0
1	0	0	0	0	0	1	1	0
2	0	0	0	1	0	0	1	0
3	0	0	0	0	0	0	0	1
4	0	0	0	0	0	1	0	0
5	0	0	0	0	0	0	0	0
6	0	0	0	0	0	0	0	1
7	0	0	0	0	0	0	0	0

Cocitation Coupling Matrix (CC)

	0	1	2	3	4	5	6	7
0	0	0	0	0	0	0	0	0
1	0	1	0	0	1	1	0	0
2	0	0	0	0	0	0	0	0
3	0	0	0	1	0	0	1	0
4	0	1	0	0	1	1	0	0
5	0	1	0	0	1	3	1	0
6	0	0	0	1	0	1	2	0
7	0	0	0	0	0	0	0	2

the extent to which a course serves as a joint pre-requisite with one or more courses. An entry $BC(i, j)$ is greater than 0 if and only if there exists at least one vertex k such that there exist directed edges from both vertices i and j to vertex k. More formally,

$$BC[i, j] = \sum_{k=1}^{n} A[k, i] * A[k, j] = \sum_{k=1}^{n} A[i, k]^{T} * A[k, j] \qquad (3)$$

$$BC = A^{T}*A \qquad (4)$$

where A^{T} is the transpose of A.

In Figure 6, we show the computation of the bibliographic coupling matrix for the DAG that is being used as the running example in this chapter. We also show the final values for the eigenvector centrality obtained by running the Power-iteration algorithm on the bibliographic coupling matrix of this DAG. We notice that vertex 0 (incurring the largest EVC value) has three outgoing edges as well as serves as a joint pre-requisite with vertices 1 and 4 (for vertex 5). Vertex 1 (incurring the second largest EVC value) has two outgoing edges and serves as a joint pre-requisite with vertex 2 for vertex 6 as well as serves as a joint pre-requisite with vertices 0 and 4 (for vertex 5). Notice that though vertex 4 has one outgoing edge and vertex 2 has two outgoing edges, vertex 4 has a relatively larger EVC value: vertex 4 serves as a joint pre-requisite with two vertices (vertices 0 and 1) for vertex 5; but, vertex 2 serves as joint pre-requisite with only vertex 1 (for vertex 6). Thus, the EVC values of the bibliographic coupling matrix appear to be very much dependent on the number of courses with which a vertex serves as a joint pre-requisite.

2.6 Betweenness Centrality

The Betweenness Centrality (BWC) of a vertex (Brandes, 2001) is a measure of the fraction of the shortest paths between any two vertices in the graph. We use the Brandes' algorithm (2001) to determine the BWC of the vertices. The Brandes' algorithm comprises of running the Breadth First Search (BFS) algorithm (Cormen et al., 2009) on every vertex of the graph and determining the level of each vertex on the BFS tree rooted at every vertex. On a particular BFS tree, the root vertex is at level 0 and the number of shortest paths from

Figure 6. Eigenvector Centrality of Vertices based on Bibliographic Coupling Matrix (EVC_BC)

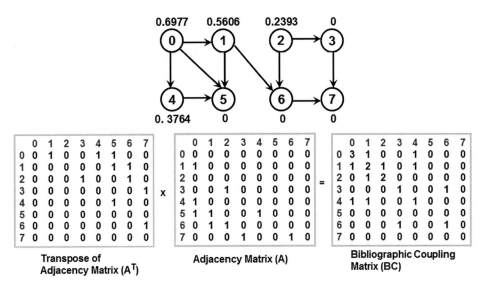

the root vertex to itself is 1. The number of shortest paths from a root vertex r to a vertex k at level l ($l > 0$) is the sum of the number of shortest paths from the root vertex r to each of the pre-requisite vertices (of vertex k) at level l-1. The fraction of shortest paths from vertex i to vertex j in which vertex k is located is the ratio of the maximum of the number of shortest paths from vertex i to vertex k and the number of shortest paths from vertex j to vertex k to that of the number of shortest paths from vertex i to vertex j. The BWC of a vertex k is the sum of the fractions of the shortest paths between any two vertices (as calculated above).

Figure 7 illustrates the calculation of the BWC of the vertices in the running example DAG of this chapter. We show the BFS trees rooted at each of the eight vertices; the tuple on the top of each vertex in a BFS tree indicates the level of the vertex in the BFS tree (if a path exists to the vertex from the root of the BFS tree) and the number of paths to the vertex from the root of the BFS tree (as calculated above). If there is no path to a vertex from the root of the BFS tree, the level for the vertex is indicated as - and the number of shortest paths to the vertex from the root of the BFS tree is 0. We see that only three vertices (vertices 1, 3 and 6) lie on the shortest path between any two vertices. Vertex 1 lies on the shortest paths from vertex 0 to 6 and on the shortest path from vertex 0 to 7; there is only one shortest path between these pairs of vertices; hence the BWC of vertex 1 is 1/1 (accounted for the

139

pair 0→6) + 1/1 (accounted for the pair 0→7) = 2.0. Vertex 3 lies on one of the two shortest paths from vertex 2 to 7 and for no other pair of vertices; hence the BWC of vertex 3 is 1/2 (accounted for the pair 2→7) = 0.5. Vertex 6 lies on the shortest paths from vertex 0 to vertex 7, vertex 1 to vertex 7 and vertex 2 to vertex 7; there is only one shortest path from vertex 0 to vertex 7 and from vertex 1 to vertex 7 and there are two shortest paths from vertex 2 to vertex 7; hence the BWC of vertex 6 is 1/1 (accounted for the pair 0→7) + 1/1 (accounted for the pair 1→7) + 1/2 (accounted for the pair 2→7) = 2.5.

3. FORMULATION TO QUANTIFY THE RELATIVE CONTRIBUTION OF THE COURSES

In this section, we present the formulation (see equations 6...9) to quantify the relative contribution of the courses in a curriculum network graph (CNG) based on each of the six metrics discussed in Section 2. We basically normalize

Figure 7. Computation of the betweenness centrality of vertices for a DAG using Brandes' algorithm

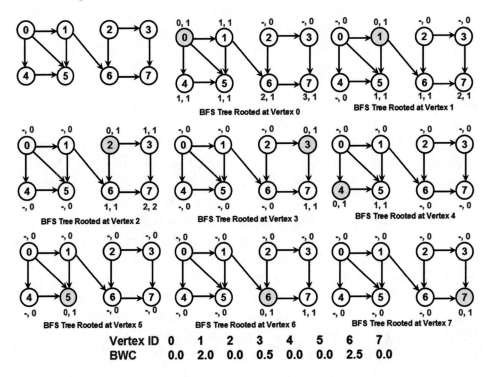

Vertex ID	0	1	2	3	4	5	6	7
BWC	0.0	2.0	0.0	0.5	0.0	0.0	2.5	0.0

the values obtained for each of the graph theoretic metrics and refer to the sum of the normalized values for a course (based on all the metrics) as the Contribution Score of the course to the curriculum. We then determine the relative contribution score of a course in a CNG as the ratio of the Contribution Score for the course to that of the sum of the Contribution Scores of all the courses in the curriculum. In the case of topological sort, we use the level number of the vertices in a DAG itself as the basis to determine the normalized scores. Table 1 displays the actual values for the graph theoretic metrics for the vertices in the running example of a DAG (CNG) used in Figures 1-7. Table 2 illustrates the calculation of the relative contribution scores of the vertices (courses) in this DAG.

The proposed formulation is flexible enough to void the normalized scores obtained for one or more graph theoretic metrics (**GM**) as well as flexible enough to change the weights for the normalized scores obtained for one or more graph theoretic metrics (w_M is the weight assigned to a particular metric $M \in \textbf{GM}$ such that $\sum_{M \in GM} w_M = 1$). In this chapter, we assign equal weight to all the metrics (hence, $w_M = 1/6$ for each $M \in \textbf{GM}$). Note that $M(v)$ is the value for vertex v with respect to a particular metric M. Due to the involvement of six different graph theoretic metrics in the formulation, we opine that each course (vertex) in a CNG is more likely to get a unique relative contribution score.

$$
Graph\ Metrics\left(\textbf{GM}\right) = \begin{cases} Level\ Numbers\ of\ Vertices\ in\ Topological\ Sort, \\ In\text{-}Degree\ Centrality, Out\text{-}Degree\ Centrality, \\ Eigenvector\ Centrality\ based\ on\ Cocitation\ Coupling, \\ Eigenvector\ Centrality\ based\ on\ Bibliographic\ Coupling, \\ Betweenness\ Centrality \end{cases}
$$

(5)

$$
\text{Normalized Score } [v; M \in \textbf{GM}] = \frac{M(v)}{\sqrt{\sum_{v \in V} M(v) * M(v)}}
$$

(6)

$$
\text{Contribution Score}[v] = \sum_{M \in GM} w_M * \text{Normalized Score } [v; M \in \textbf{GM}]
$$

(7)

Table 1. Actual values for the graph theoretic metrics for the vertices in the DAG of Figure 1

ID	Actual Values					
	In-Degree	Out-Degree	Level #	EVC_CC	EVC_BC	BWC
0	0	3	1	0.0000	0.6977	0.0
1	1	2	2	0.3348	0.5606	2.0
2	0	2	1	0.0000	0.2393	0.0
3	1	1	2	0.1148	0.0000	0.5
4	1	1	2	0.3348	0.3764	0.0
5	3	0	3	0.7844	0.0000	0.0
6	2	1	3	0.3838	0.0000	2.5
7	2	0	4	0.0000	0.0000	0.0

Table 2. Calculation of the relative contribution score of the vertices in the DAG of Figure 1

ID	Normalized Values						Contribution Score	Relative Contribution Score
	In-Degree	Out-Degree	Level #	EVC_CC	EVC_BC	BWC		
0	0.0000	0.6708	0.1443	0.0000	0.6977	0.0000	0.2521	0.1216
1	0.2236	0.4472	0.2887	0.3348	0.5606	0.6172	0.4120	0.1987
2	0.0000	0.4472	0.1443	0.0000	0.2393	0.0000	0.1385	0.0668
3	0.2236	0.2236	0.2887	0.1148	0.0000	0.1543	0.1675	0.0808
4	0.2236	0.2236	0.2887	0.3348	0.3764	0.0000	0.2412	0.1163
5	0.6708	0.0000	0.4330	0.7844	0.0000	0.0000	0.3147	0.1518
6	0.4472	0.2236	0.4330	0.3838	0.0000	0.7715	0.3764	0.1816
7	0.4472	0.0000	0.5774	0.0000	0.0000	0.0000	0.1708	0.0824

$$\text{Relative Contribution Score}[v] = \frac{Contribution\ Score[v]}{\sum_{v \in V} Contribution\ Score[v]} \qquad (8)$$

4. APPLICATION OF THE FORMULATION ON REAL-WORLD CURRICULUM NETWORK GRAPHS (CNGs)

We apply the proposed formulation for ranking the vertices in a CNG on two real-world network graphs (CNGs): the Computer Science (CSC) curriculum and Computer Engineering (CPE) curriculum at Jackson State University

(JSU). The pre-requisite chart for the CSC and CPE curricula are respectively shown in Figures 8 and 10. For each curricula, we only list the core courses and elective courses that have one or more pre-requisites and/or serve as pre-requisites for one or more courses. The weight assigned for each of the six graph metrics in the formulation is 1/6.

Tables 3-6 illustrate the application of the proposed formulation to the Computer Science (CSC) curriculum at JSU. Tables 3 and 4 illustrate respectively the actual and normalized values for the graph theoretic metrics obtained for the CSC courses; Tables 7 and 8 do the same for the courses in the CPE curriculum. Tables 4 and 8 also calculate the contribution score for each course as well as the relative contribution score for each course in the CSC curriculum and CPE curriculum respectively. The listing of the courses in Tables 3 and 4 (as well as in Tables 7 and 8) is in the decreasing order of the values for the relative contribution scores and the courses are also ranked based on this order. A course with a larger value for the relative contribution score is ranked high (lower numerical value for the rank). Two or more courses with the same value for the relative contribution score get the same rank. Though we anticipated zero ties among the vertices, we notice ties between vertices that have the same values for all the six graph theoretic metrics; however, the chances of observing a tie are very minimal. We observe

Figure 8. Undergraduate BS Computer Science degree curriculum at JSU

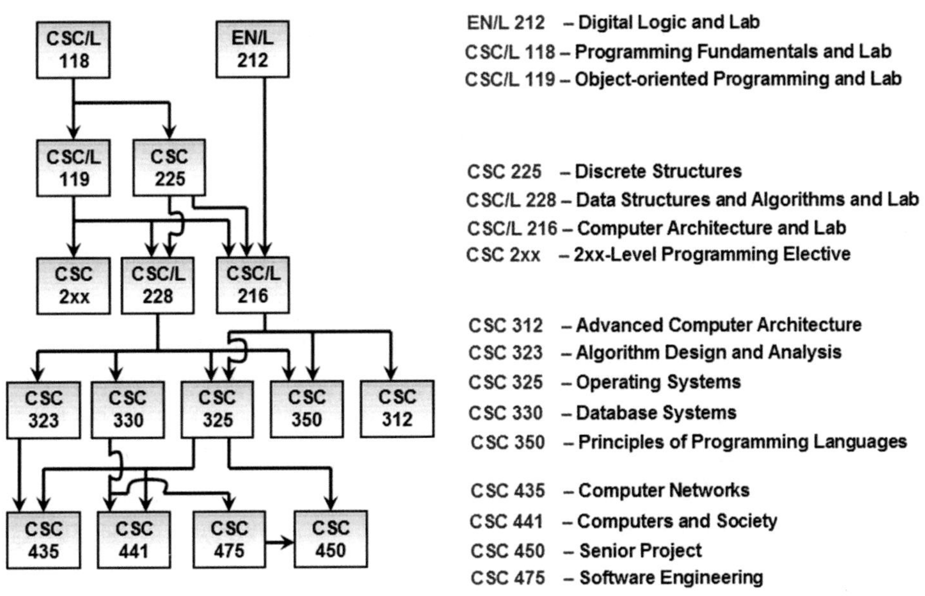
CSC/L 118
EN/L 212
CSC/L 119
CSC 225
CSC 2xx
CSC/L 228
CSC/L 216
CSC 323
CSC 330
CSC 325
CSC 350
CSC 312
CSC 435
CSC 441
CSC 475
CSC 450
EN/L 212 – Digital Logic and Lab
CSC/L 118 – Programming Fundamentals and Lab
CSC/L 119 – Object-oriented Programming and Lab
CSC 225 – Discrete Structures
CSC/L 228 – Data Structures and Algorithms and Lab
CSC/L 216 – Computer Architecture and Lab
CSC 2xx – 2xx-Level Programming Elective
CSC 312 – Advanced Computer Architecture
CSC 323 – Algorithm Design and Analysis
CSC 325 – Operating Systems
CSC 330 – Database Systems
CSC 350 – Principles of Programming Languages
CSC 435 – Computer Networks
CSC 441 – Computers and Society
CSC 450 – Senior Project
CSC 475 – Software Engineering

Table 3. Actual values of the graph theoretic metrics for the courses in the CSC curriculum

Course #	Actual Values					
	In-Degree	Out-Degree	Level #	EVC_CC	EVC_BC	BWC
CSC/L 228	2	4	3	0.0000	0.7882	14.5833
CSC/L 216	3	3	3	0.0000	0.6154	13.9167
CSC 325	2	3	4	0.5952	0.0000	10.9167
CSC 330	1	2	4	0.3342	0.0000	4.8333
CSC 350	2	0	4	0.5952	0.0000	0.0000
CSC/1 119	1	3	2	0.0000	0.0000	6.5000
CSC 323	1	1	4	0.3342	0.0000	1.3333
CSC 225	1	2	2	0.0000	0.0000	5.5000
CSC 450	2	0	6	0.0000	0.0000	0.0000
CSC 312	1	0	4	0.2609	0.0000	0.0000
CSC 475	1	1	5	0.0000	0.0000	1.0000
CSC 441	2	0	5	0.0000	0.0000	0.0000
CSC 435	2	0	5	0.0000	0.0000	0.0000
CSC 2XX	1	0	3	0.0000	0.0000	0.0000
CSC/L 118	0	2	1	0.0000	0.0000	0.0000
EN/L 212	0	1	1	0.0000	0.0000	0.0000

critical courses like Data Structures and Algorithms, Computer Architecture, Operating Systems, Database Systems, Algorithm Design and Analysis and etc are some of the top-ranked courses in the CSC curriculum (see Table 4). Similarly, we also observe critical courses like Computer Architecture, Electronics, Digital Logic, Circuits and etc are some of the top-ranked courses in the CPE curriculum (see Table 8).

Tables 5 and 6 for the CSC curriculum and Tables 9 and 10 for the CPE curriculum illustrate the application of the relative contribution scores to calculate the weighted cumulative grade score for a student and weighted cumulative assessment score of the courses across the curriculum. For the student cumulative grade score application, the cumulative score is the sum of the relative numerical scores (product of the relative contribution score for the course and the numerical equivalent for the grade) of all the courses in the curriculum. For the cumulative curriculum assessment application, the cumulative score is the sum of the relative curriculum average scores (product

Table 4. Normalized values of the graph theoretic metrics for the courses in the CSC curriculum and the relative contribution scores of the courses

Course #	In-Degree	Out-Degree	Level #	EVC_CC	EVC_BC	BWC	Contribution Score	Relative Contribution Score	Rank
CSC/L 228	0.3162	0.5252	0.1987	0.0000	0.7883	0.5837	0.4020	0.1513	1
CSC/L 216	0.4743	0.3939	0.1987	0.0000	0.6155	0.5570	0.3732	0.1405	2
CSC 325	0.3162	0.3939	0.2649	0.5953	0.0000	0.4370	0.3345	0.1259	3
CSC 330	0.1581	0.2626	0.2649	0.3342	0.0000	0.1935	0.2022	0.0761	4
CSC 350	0.3162	0.0000	0.2649	0.5953	0.0000	0.0000	0.1961	0.0738	5
CSC/l 119	0.1581	0.3939	0.1325	0.0000	0.0000	0.2602	0.1574	0.0592	6
CSC 323	0.1581	0.1313	0.2649	0.3342	0.0000	0.0534	0.1570	0.0591	7
CSC 225	0.1581	0.2626	0.1325	0.0000	0.0000	0.2201	0.1289	0.0485	8
CSC 450	0.3162	0.0000	0.3974	0.0000	0.0000	0.0000	0.1189	0.0448	9
CSC 312	0.1581	0.0000	0.2649	0.2609	0.0000	0.0000	0.1140	0.0429	10
CSC 475	0.1581	0.1313	0.3311	0.0000	0.0000	0.0400	0.1101	0.0414	11
CSC 441	0.3162	0.0000	0.3311	0.0000	0.0000	0.0000	0.1079	0.0406	12
CSC 435	0.3162	0.0000	0.3311	0.0000	0.0000	0.0000	0.1079	0.0406	12
CSC 2XX	0.1581	0.0000	0.1987	0.0000	0.0000	0.0000	0.0595	0.0224	14
CSC/L 118	0.0000	0.2626	0.0662	0.0000	0.0000	0.0000	0.0548	0.0206	15
EN/L 212	0.0000	0.1313	0.0662	0.0000	0.0000	0.0000	0.0329	0.0124	16

of the relative contribution score for the course and the average assessment score for the course) of all the courses in the curriculum.

As not all courses in a curriculum are equally important, the cumulative grade score calculated with the proposed relative contribution score approach could be very useful to rank students based on their performance in the courses (with weights corresponding to the relative contribution score). Similarly, the cumulative assessment score calculated with the proposed relative contribution score approach could be very useful to quantitatively capture the overall assessment score as one single value: based on a weighted average of the average assessment scores from the individual courses.

Figures 9 and 11 respectively capture the dependence of the graph theoretic metrics on the relative contribution scores of the courses in the CSC and CPE curriculum network graphs. Overall, for the CSC CNG, we observe the relative contribution scores of the courses tend to increase with increase in the BWC as well as the in-degree and out-degree of the courses (vertices). On the other hand, for the CPE CNG, we observe the relative contribution scores of the courses to be primarily dependent on the BWC and to a certain

Table 5. Sample for computing the cumulative grade score of a student based on the relative contribution scores in the CSC curriculum

Course #	Relative Contribution Score	Student Grade	Numerical Equivalent	Relative Numerical Score
CSC/L 228	0.1513	A	4	0.6051
CSC/L 216	0.1405	B	3	0.4214
CSC 325	0.1259	A	4	0.5036
CSC 330	0.0761	C	2	0.1522
CSC 350	0.0738	A	4	0.2951
CSC/L 119	0.0592	B	3	0.1777
CSC 323	0.0591	A	4	0.2363
CSC 225	0.0485	C	2	0.0970
CSC 450	0.0448	A	4	0.1790
CSC 312	0.0429	C	2	0.0858
CSC 475	0.0414	C	2	0.0829
CSC 441	0.0406	A	4	0.1624
CSC 435	0.0406	C	2	0.0812
CSC 2XX	0.0224	A	4	0.0895
CSC/L 118	0.0206	B	3	0.0619
EN/L 212	0.0124	C	2	0.0248
Cumulative Grade Score				3.2558

extent on the out-degree of the courses. With respect to the level # calculated using topological sort, we observe the relative contribution scores of the courses to be noticeably high for moderate values of the level #s (2-4) of the courses. For courses that have a higher level # (primarily terminal courses that do not serve as pre-requisites for any other course) or have a lower level # (primarily seed courses that do not have any pre-requisites and only serve as pre-requisites for one or more courses), we observe the relative contribution scores of the courses to be relatively low. We observe minimal impact of the EVC values of the cocitation and bibliographic coupling matrices on the relative contribution scores of the courses; for most of the courses, we observe the EVC_CC and EVC_BC values to be zero.

We ran the K-Means algorithm (Marsland, 2009) to identify an appropriate clustering of the courses with similar relative contribution scores for both the CSC and CPE curricula. For each of the two curricula, we ran the K-Means algorithm on the relative contribution scores of the courses with respect to

Table 6. Sample for computing the cumulative assessment score of the courses based on the relative contribution scores in the CSC curriculum

Course #	Relative Contribution Score	Average Assessment Score [1..4]	Relative Assessment Score
CSC/L 228	0.1513	3.5	0.5295
CSC/L 216	0.1405	2.8	0.3933
CSC 325	0.1259	2.6	0.3273
CSC 330	0.0761	3.1	0.2359
CSC 350	0.0738	3.7	0.2730
CSC/L 119	0.0592	2.9	0.1718
CSC 323	0.0591	3.2	0.1890
CSC 225	0.0485	2.4	0.1164
CSC 450	0.0448	3.4	0.1522
CSC 312	0.0429	2.8	0.1201
CSC 475	0.0414	3.1	0.1284
CSC 441	0.0406	3.7	0.1502
CSC 435	0.0406	2.8	0.1137
CSC 2XX	0.0224	2.7	0.0604
CSC/L 118	0.0206	2.5	0.0516
EN/L 212	0.0124	3.5	0.0434
	Cumulative Assessment Score		3.0562

Figure 9. Dependence of the graph theoretic metrics on the relative contribution scores of the courses in the CSC curriculum network graph

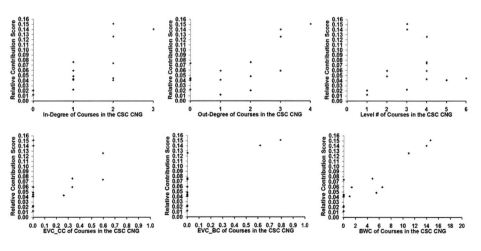

Figure 10. Undergraduate BS Computer Engineering degree curriculum at JSU

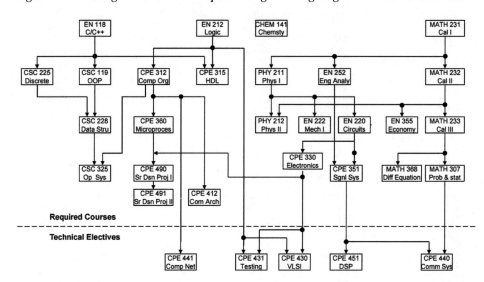

different values of K (ranging from 1 to the number of courses). We determine the Sum of the Squares of Errors (SSE) values for each value of K and use the Elbow-method (Sugar & James, 2003) to identify the appropriate value of K (see Figure 12) that resulted in a drastic decrease of the SSE values to a lower value. Accordingly, we obtained K value of 4 for the CSC curriculum (see Figure 12-a) and 5 for the CPE curriculum (see Figure 12-b). The SSE values were relatively high for the CSC curriculum (that had 4 clusters with a total of 16 courses) compared to the CPE curriculum (that had 5 clusters with a total of 31 courses). Figures 13-(a) and 13-(b) respectively show the clustering of courses along with their relative contribution scores. We observe that courses whose relative contribution scores are proximal enough to each other get clustered together under the K-Means/Elbow-method.

5. RELATED WORK

There has been only very limited work on analyzing curriculum network graphs (CNGs) from a graph theoretic perspective. Slim et al. (2014a) introduce two terms: blocking factor and delay factor to quantify the "cruciality" of courses in a curriculum. The blocking factor for a vertex is simply the out-degree of the vertex and the delay factor for a vertex is the length of the longest path from the vertex to any other vertex in the CNG. The cruciality

Table 7. Actual values of the graph theoretic metrics for the courses in the CPE curriculum

Course #	Actual Values					
	In-Degree	Out-Degree	Level #	EVC_CC	EVC_BC	BWC
CPE 312	2	4	2	0.4919	0.0000	12.0
CPE 330	1	3	4	0.0000	0.4162	14.0
EN 220	2	2	3	0.0000	0.0000	18.0
EN 212	0	4	1	0.0000	0.7239	0.0
CPE 490	2	1	5	0.1898	0.0000	8.5
EN 118	0	4	1	0.0000	0.5452	0.0
CPE 431	2	0	5	0.4419	0.0000	0.0
CPE 430	2	0	5	0.4419	0.0000	0.0
CPE 351	2	2	4	0.0000	0.0000	9.5
MATH 232	1	4	2	0.0000	0.0000	7.5
CPE 315	2	0	2	0.4919	0.0000	0.0
PHY 211	1	3	2	0.0000	0.0000	4.5
CPE 360	1	1	3	0.0000	0.0736	6.0
MATH 233	1	2	3	0.0000	0.0000	4.5
CSC 228	2	1	3	0.0000	0.0000	2.0
CSC 119	1	1	2	0.2113	0.0000	0.5
CSC 225	1	1	2	0.2113	0.0000	0.5
CPE 440	2	0	5	0.0000	0.0000	0.0
MATH 307	1	1	4	0.0000	0.0000	1.5
CSC 325	2	0	4	0.0000	0.0000	0.0
CPE 491	1	0	6	0.0000	0.0000	0.0
EN 252	1	1	2	0.0000	0.0000	3.0
PHY 212	2	0	3	0.0000	0.0000	0.0
CPE 451	1	0	5	0.0000	0.0000	0.0
MATH 368	1	0	4	0.0000	0.0000	0.0
MATH 231	0	3	1	0.0000	0.0000	0.0
EN 222	1	0	3	0.0000	0.0000	0.0
EN 355	1	0	3	0.0000	0.0000	0.0
CPE 441	1	0	3	0.0000	0.0000	0.0
CPE 412	1	0	3	0.0000	0.0000	0.0
CHEM 141	0	0	1	0.0000	0.0000	0.0

Table 8. Normalized values of the graph theoretic metrics for the courses in the CPE curriculum and the relative contribution scores of the courses

Course #	In-Degree	Out-Degree	Level #	EVC_CC	EVC_BC	BWC	Contribution Score	Relative Contribution Score	Rank
CPE 312	0.2582	0.3814	0.1063	0.4919	0.0000	0.3843	0.2704	0.0779	1
CPE 330	0.1291	0.2860	0.2126	0.0000	0.4162	0.4484	0.2487	0.0717	2
EN 220	0.2582	0.1907	0.1594	0.0000	0.0000	0.5765	0.1975	0.0569	3
EN 212	0.0000	0.3814	0.0531	0.0000	0.7240	0.0000	0.1931	0.0557	4
CPE 490	0.2582	0.0953	0.2657	0.1898	0.0000	0.2722	0.1802	0.0519	5
EN 118	0.0000	0.3814	0.0531	0.0000	0.5453	0.0000	0.1633	0.0471	6
CPE 431	0.2582	0.0000	0.2657	0.4419	0.0000	0.0000	0.1610	0.0464	7
CPE 430	0.2582	0.0000	0.2657	0.4419	0.0000	0.0000	0.1610	0.0464	7
CPE 351	0.2582	0.1907	0.2126	0.0000	0.0000	0.3042	0.1610	0.0464	7
MATH 232	0.1291	0.3814	0.1063	0.0000	0.0000	0.2402	0.1428	0.0412	10
CPE 315	0.2582	0.0000	0.1063	0.4919	0.0000	0.0000	0.1427	0.0411	11
PHY 211	0.1291	0.2860	0.1063	0.0000	0.0000	0.1441	0.1109	0.0320	12
CPE 360	0.1291	0.0953	0.1594	0.0000	0.0736	0.1922	0.1083	0.0312	13
MATH 233	0.1291	0.1907	0.1594	0.0000	0.0000	0.1441	0.1039	0.0299	14
CSC 228	0.2582	0.0953	0.1594	0.0000	0.0000	0.0641	0.0962	0.0277	15
CSC 119	0.1291	0.0953	0.1063	0.2113	0.0000	0.0160	0.0930	0.0268	16
CSC 225	0.1291	0.0953	0.1063	0.2113	0.0000	0.0160	0.0930	0.0268	16
CPE 440	0.2582	0.0000	0.2657	0.0000	0.0000	0.0000	0.0873	0.0252	18
MATH 307	0.1291	0.0953	0.2126	0.0000	0.0000	0.0480	0.0808	0.0233	19
CSC 325	0.2582	0.0000	0.2126	0.0000	0.0000	0.0000	0.0785	0.0226	20
CPE 491	0.1291	0.0000	0.3189	0.0000	0.0000	0.0000	0.0747	0.0215	21
EN 252	0.1291	0.0953	0.1063	0.0000	0.0000	0.0961	0.0711	0.0205	22
PHY 212	0.2582	0.0000	0.1594	0.0000	0.0000	0.0000	0.0696	0.0201	23
CPE 451	0.1291	0.0000	0.2657	0.0000	0.0000	0.0000	0.0658	0.0190	24
MATH 368	0.1291	0.0000	0.2126	0.0000	0.0000	0.0000	0.0569	0.0164	25
MATH 231	0.0000	0.2860	0.0531	0.0000	0.0000	0.0000	0.0565	0.0163	26
EN 222	0.1291	0.0000	0.1594	0.0000	0.0000	0.0000	0.0481	0.0139	27
EN 355	0.1291	0.0000	0.1594	0.0000	0.0000	0.0000	0.0481	0.0139	27
CPE 441	0.1291	0.0000	0.1594	0.0000	0.0000	0.0000	0.0481	0.0139	27
CPE 412	0.1291	0.0000	0.1594	0.0000	0.0000	0.0000	0.0481	0.0139	27
CHEM 141	0.0000	0.0000	0.0531	0.0000	0.0000	0.0000	0.0089	0.0026	31

Table 9. Sample for computing the cumulative grade score of a student based on the relative contribution of scores in the CPE curriculum

Course #	Relative Contribution Score	Student Grade	Numerical Equivalent	Relative Numerical Score
CPE 312	0.0779	A	4	0.3117
CPE 330	0.0717	B	3	0.2151
EN 220	0.0569	C	2	0.1138
EN 212	0.0557	C	2	0.1113
CPE 490	0.0519	A	4	0.2078
EN 118	0.0471	A	4	0.1883
CPE 431	0.0464	B	3	0.1392
CPE 430	0.0464	B	3	0.1392
CPE 351	0.0464	C	2	0.0928
MATH 232	0.0412	A	4	0.1647
CPE 315	0.0411	A	4	0.1646
PHY 211	0.0320	A	4	0.1279
CPE 360	0.0312	B	3	0.0936
MATH 233	0.0299	B	3	0.0898
CSC 228	0.0277	A	4	0.1109
CSC 119	0.0268	C	2	0.0536
CSC 225	0.0268	C	2	0.0536
CPE 440	0.0252	A	4	0.1007
MATH 307	0.0233	B	3	0.0699
CSC 325	0.0226	A	4	0.0905
CPE 491	0.0215	C	2	0.0430
EN 252	0.0205	A	4	0.0820
PHY 212	0.0201	B	3	0.0602
CPE 451	0.0190	B	3	0.0569
MATH 368	0.0164	B	3	0.0492
MATH 231	0.0163	A	4	0.0652
EN 222	0.0139	A	4	0.0554
EN 355	0.0139	B	3	0.0416
CPE 441	0.0139	C	2	0.0277
CPE 412	0.0139	A	4	0.0554
CHEM 141	0.0026	B	3	0.0077
Cumulative Grade Score				3.1833

Table 10. Sample for computing the cumulative grade score of a student based on the relative contribution of scores in the CPE curriculum

Course #	Relative Contribution Score	Average Assessment Score [1..4]	Relative Numerical Score
CPE 312	0.0779	3.2	0.2494
CPE 330	0.0717	2.5	0.1792
EN 220	0.0569	2.7	0.1537
EN 212	0.0557	2.9	0.1614
CPE 490	0.0519	3.6	0.1870
EN 118	0.0471	3.2	0.1506
CPE 431	0.0464	2.8	0.1299
CPE 430	0.0464	3.1	0.1438
CPE 351	0.0464	2.4	0.1113
MATH 232	0.0412	2.6	0.1070
CPE 315	0.0411	2.5	0.1029
PHY 211	0.0320	2.7	0.0863
CPE 360	0.0312	2.8	0.0874
MATH 233	0.0299	3.2	0.0958
CSC 228	0.0277	3.1	0.0859
CSC 119	0.0268	3.4	0.0912
CSC 225	0.0268	3.9	0.1046
CPE 440	0.0252	2.7	0.0680
MATH 307	0.0233	2.8	0.0652
CSC 325	0.0226	2.9	0.0656
CPE 491	0.0215	3.0	0.0646
EN 252	0.0205	3.3	0.0677
PHY 212	0.0201	2.5	0.0502
CPE 451	0.0190	2.4	0.0455
MATH 368	0.0164	2.3	0.0378
MATH 231	0.0163	2.7	0.0440
EN 222	0.0139	2.9	0.0402
EN 355	0.0139	3.3	0.0457
CPE 441	0.0139	3.2	0.0444
CPE 412	0.0139	3.4	0.0471
CHEM 141	0.0026	3.2	0.0082
Cumulative Assessment Score			2.9214

Figure 11. Dependence of the graph theoretic metrics on the relative contribution score of the courses in the CPE curriculum network graph

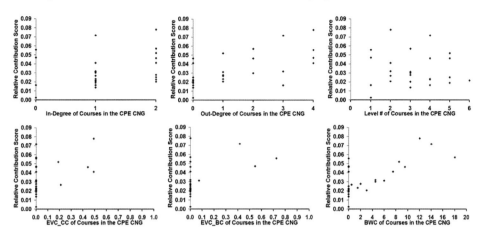

Figure 12. K Value vs. Sum of Squares of Errors (SSE) Scores: K-Means algorithm and elbow method

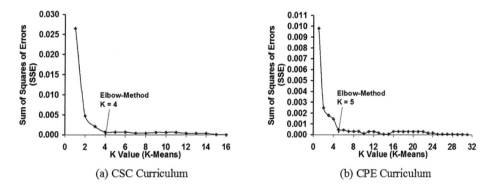

(a) CSC Curriculum   (b) CPE Curriculum

of a vertex has been modeled as the sum of the blocking factor and delay factor. The cruciality of the courses calculated with the above formulation has been observed to follow a power-law distribution (Slim et al., 2014a, 2014b): i.e., only a small percentage of the courses have been observed to be highly crucial for a curriculum. The complexity of a curriculum has been defined as the sum of the cruciality values of the courses that are part of the curriculum. Slim et al. (2014b) showed that the complexity of the curricula at two different institutions could be compared based on the cruciality scores of the courses that are part of the curricula. We contend that since degree and path length represent two different properties, the values for these two

Figure 13. Clustering of the courses with proximal relative contribution scores: K-Means algorithm

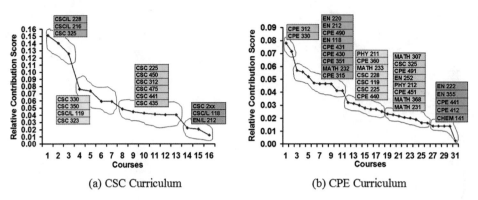

(a) CSC Curriculum   (b) CPE Curriculum

metrics should be individually normalized (as we do for the graph theoretic metrics considered in this chapter) and an appropriate weight could be also given to the metrics. In addition to the weakness associated with lack of normalization in the calculation of the cruciality score, another weakness of the above approach is that the complexity score for a curriculum (calculated as the sum of the cruciality scores) is also dependent on the number of courses whose cruciality scores are added up. We handle the above weaknesses in the calculation of the relative contribution scores of the courses in a curriculum by first normalizing the values for the individual graph theoretic metrics, then introducing weights for the metrics in the summation and finally by dividing the contribution scores of the courses by the sum of the contribution scores.

Aldrich (2014) used the in-degree, out-degree and betweenness centrality metrics to respectively identify information sources, hubs and bridges in a CNG. A significantly high correlation has been observed between the degree centrality metrics and betweenness centrality. In addition, it has been also shown by Aldrich (2014) that the various weakly connected components of a CNG could be identified and analyzed (for the centrality metrics) by treating it as an undirected graph.

Lightfood (2010) addressed the problem of identifying appropriate courses in the curriculum for enforcing coverage of fundamental and advanced topics, collecting assessment data and incorporating corrective action that emanate from assessment results. According to Lightfood (2010): the out-degree centrality metric has been used to locate courses that would be suitable to introduce topics and perform baseline assessment; the in-degree centrality is used to identify courses where exit assessment and higher-level learning activities should occur; courses with higher betweenness centrality and eigenvector centrality were considered to be suitable for assessment and topic reinforcement; courses with higher clustering coefficient (Newman, 2010) were considered appropriate to implement changes in the curriculum.

Komenda et al. (2015) model the medical curriculum as a similarity graph wherein the courses are the nodes and there is an edge between two courses if there is any overlap between the contents of these courses (determined based on the textual description of the courses) and the weight of the edge is assigned based on the cosine distance between the textual description of the courses (Tan et al., 2005). The authors employed various centrality measures and community detection algorithms (Newman, 2010) to determine outlier courses, courses that had significant overlap, courses that are within a well-knit community as well as to identify courses that belong to the most important parts of the curriculum. The analysis has been conducted on the basis of mapping the medical curriculum as an undirected graph and cannot be directly applied to DAGs.

Slim et al. (2014a, 2014b) propose to use a bipartite graph (Cormen et al., 2009) formulation (courses are one set of vertices and curricula are the other set of vertices; a course is linked to a curriculum if the course is part of the curriculum) to evaluate the cruciality of courses. A course that is part of several curricula has been proposed to be more crucial for the entire institution. As an extension of this work, Akbas et al. (2015) extract a directed graph of vertices and edges that is common in several curricula across the institution and apply graph theoretic algorithms and metrics on this intersection DAG to devise a degree plan (comprising of the common courses that are to be taken first) following which students can seamlessly transfer majors among related disciplines and graduate without any delay. Slim et al. (2014c) model CNGs as Markov networks (undirected graphs constructed probabilistically; Kindermann, 1980) and employ linear regression techniques (Marsland, 2009) to predict student grate point average (GPA) in their future semesters based on their performance in a single semester or a sequence of semesters earlier in the degree plan. Constantinov et al. (2015) extract a mapping of the skill set posted by alumni in their social and professional network (such as LinkedIn) to those that are covered in the various courses in the curriculum (to form a bipartite graph) and identify courses that significantly contribute to the attainment of skills for a successful career.

Our work differs from all of the above works in the following aspects: We have used topological sort as part of the formulation to rank the vertices in a DAG. We have also used the eigenvector centrality metric (typically used only for undirected graphs) for ranking the vertices by determining the metric on the cocitation and bibliographic coupling matrices. The proposed formulation serves as a comprehensive model for accommodating a suite of graph theoretic metrics and assigning appropriate weights to these metrics to ultimately quantify the relative contribution of the vertices (courses) in a DAG (CNG). We have also shown the applications of the proposed formulation to rank students based on a cumulative grade score and cumulative assessment score (that capture the performance of the students and assessment in the courses ranked on the basis of their relative contribution to the curriculum) as well as to cluster courses with comparable relative contribution scores.

6. CONCLUSION

Our contribution in this chapter is a formulation for quantifying the relative contribution (structurally) of the vertices in a directed acyclic graph: DAG (e.g., a curriculum network graph, CNG) using a suite of centrality metrics and the topological sort property that is specifically applicable for a DAG. We have illustrated the application of the proposed formulation on two real-world CNGs - Computer Science (CSC) and Computer Engineering (CPE) curricula at Jackson State University (JSU) to quantify the relative contribution of the courses in the graphs. We observe the betweenness centrality metric followed by the out-degree centrality metric to have a major influence in the ranking of courses based on the relative contribution scores. The eigenvector centrality-based cocitation coupling and bibliographic coupling values had the minimal impact in the magnitude of the relative contribution scores. We have also demonstrated the use of the relative contribution scores of the courses in a CNG to determine the cumulative grade score for a student (which could be used to rank students based on their performance in courses that are relatively more significant for a curriculum) as well as the cumulative assessment score for a curriculum (in the form of a weighted average assessment of the courses based on their relative contribution to the curriculum). Towards the end of the chapter, we have also shown the application of the proposed formulation to extract clusters (using the K-Means algorithm and the Elbow-method) of courses whose relative contribution scores are proximal enough to each other. We observe the number of clusters of courses with proximal relative contribution scores to be comparable for the two curricula even though the CPE curriculum had about twice the number of courses for the CSC curriculum.

7. FUTURE RESEARCH DIRECTIONS

The work presented in this chapter would serve as a model for analyzing any DAG-like real-world network and ranking the vertices on the basis of one or more graph theoretic metrics that are specifically suited for DAGs. As part of future work, we plan to implement algorithms for computing the Page Rank and the Authority scores (as part of the HITS algorithm) of the vertices in the curriculum network graph and compare the rankings (via Spearman's correlation coefficient) of the vertices based on the Page Rank scores, Authority scores and the relative contribution scores proposed in this chapter. We also propose to principal component analysis to minimize the number of features that are used in the computation of the relative contribution scores and assess the effectiveness of the approach.

REFERENCES

Akbas, M. I., Basavaraj, P., & Georgiopoulos, M. (2015). *Curriculum GPS: An Adaptive Curriculum Generation and Planning System.* Paper presented at the Interservice/Industry Training, Simulation, and Education Conference, Orlando, FL.

Aldrich, P. R. (2014). *The Curriculum Prerequisite Network*: *A Tool for Visualizing and Analyzing Academic Curricula.* arXiv: 1408.5340

Bonacich, P. (1987). Power and Centrality: A Family of Measures. *American Journal of Sociology*, 92(5), 1170–1182. doi:10.1086/228631

Brandes, U. (2001). A Faster Algorithm for Betweenness Centrality. *The Journal of Mathematical Sociology*, 25(2), 163–177. doi:10.1080/002225 0X.2001.9990249

Constantinov, C., Popescu, P. S., Poteras, C. M., & Mocanu, M. L. (2015). *Preliminary Results of a Curriculum Adjuster based on Professional Network Analysis*. Paper presented at the 19th International Conference on System Theory, Control and Computing, Cheile, Romania. 10.1109/ICSTCC.2015.7321402

Cormen, T. H., Leiserson, C. E., Rivest, R. L., & Stein, C. (2009). *Introduction to Algorithms* (3rd ed.). Cambridge, MA: MIT Press.

Gipp, B., & Beel, J. (2009). *Citation Proximity Analysis (CPA) - A New Approach for Identifying related Work based on Co-Citation Analysis*. Paper presented at the 12th International Conference on Scientometrics and Informetrics, Rio de Janeiro, Brazil.

Kindermann, R. (1980). *Markov Random Fields and their Applications* (1st ed.). Providence, RI: American Mathematical Society. doi:10.1090/conm/001

Komenda, M., Vita, M., Vaitsis, C., Schwarz, D., Pokorna, A., Zary, N., & Dusek, L. (2015). Curriculum Mapping with Academic Analytics in Medical and Healthcare Education. *PLoS One*, *10*(2), e0143748. doi:10.1371/journal.pone.0143748 PMID:26624281

Lay, D. C. (2011). *Linear Algebra and its Applications* (4th ed.). Upper Saddle River, NJ: Pearson Education.

Lightfood, J. M. (2010). A Graph-Theoretic Approach to Improved Curriculum Structure and Assessment Placement. *Communications of the IIMA*, *10*(2), 59–74.

Marsland, S. (2009). *Machine Learning: An Algorithmic Perspective* (1st ed.). Boca Raton, FL: Chapman and Hall/CRC Press.

Newman, M. (2010). *Networks: An Introduction* (1st ed.). Oxford, UK: Oxford University Press. doi:10.1093/acprof:oso/9780199206650.001.0001

Slim, A., Kozlick, J., Heileman, G. L., & Abdallah, C. T. (2014a). *The Complexity of University Curricula according to Course Cruciality*. Paper presented at the 8th International Conference on Complex, Intelligent and Software Intensive Systems, Birmingham, UK. 10.1109/CISIS.2014.34

Slim, A., Kozlick, J., Heileman, G. L., & Abdallah, C. T. (2014b). *Network Analysis of University Courses*. Paper presented at the 6th Annual Workshop on Simplifying Complex Networks for Practitioners, Seoul, South Korea. 10.1145/2567948.2579360

Slim, A., Kozlick, J., Heileman, G. L., & Abdallah, C. T. (2014c). *Employing Markov Networks on Curriculum Graphs to Predict Student Performance.* Paper presented at the 13th International Conference on Machine Learning and Applications, Detroit, MI. 10.1109/ICMLA.2014.74

Sugar, C. A., & James, G. M. (2003). Finding the Number of Clusters in a Data Set: An Information Theoretic Approach. *Journal of the American Statistical Association, 98,* 750–763. doi:10.1198/016214503000000666

Tan, P.-N., Steinbach, M., & Kumar, V. (2005). *Introduction to Data Mining* (1st ed.). Upper Saddle River, NJ: Pearson Education.

Zafarani, R., Abbasi, M. A., & Liu, H. (2014). *Social Media Mining: An Introduction* (1st ed.). Cambridge, UK: Cambridge University Press. doi:10.1017/CBO9781139088510

Zhao, D., & Strotmann, A. (2008). Evolution of Research Activities and Intellectual Influences in Information Science: Introducing Author Bibliographic-Coupling Analysis. *Journal of the American Society for Information Science and Technology, 59*(13), 2070–2086. doi:10.1002/asi.20910

Related Readings

To continue IGI Global's long-standing tradition of advancing innovation through emerging research, please find below a compiled list of recommended IGI Global book chapters and journal articles in the areas of heterogeneous computing, complex network analysis, and high performance computing. These related readings will provide additional information and guidance to further enrich your knowledge and assist you with your own research.

Acharjya, D. P., & Mary, A. G. (2014). Privacy Preservation in Information System. In B. Tripathy & D. Acharjya (Eds.), *Advances in Secure Computing, Internet Services, and Applications* (pp. 49–72). Hershey, PA: IGI Global. doi:10.4018/978-1-4666-4940-8.ch003

Adhikari, M., Das, A., & Mukherjee, A. (2016). Utility Computing and Its Utilization. In G. Deka, G. Siddesh, K. Srinivasa, & L. Patnaik (Eds.), *Emerging Research Surrounding Power Consumption and Performance Issues in Utility Computing* (pp. 1–21). Hershey, PA: IGI Global. doi:10.4018/978-1-4666-8853-7.ch001

Adhikari, M., & Kar, S. (2016). Advanced Topics GPU Programming and CUDA Architecture. In G. Deka, G. Siddesh, K. Srinivasa, & L. Patnaik (Eds.), *Emerging Research Surrounding Power Consumption and Performance Issues in Utility Computing* (pp. 175–203). Hershey, PA: IGI Global. doi:10.4018/978-1-4666-8853-7.ch008

Adhikari, M., & Roy, D. (2016). Green Computing. In G. Deka, G. Siddesh, K. Srinivasa, & L. Patnaik (Eds.), *Emerging Research Surrounding Power Consumption and Performance Issues in Utility Computing* (pp. 84–108). Hershey, PA: IGI Global. doi:10.4018/978-1-4666-8853-7.ch005

Related Readings

Ahmad, K., Kumar, G., Wahid, A., & Kirmani, M. M. (2016). Software Performance Estimate using Fuzzy Based Backpropagation Learning. In G. Deka, G. Siddesh, K. Srinivasa, & L. Patnaik (Eds.), *Emerging Research Surrounding Power Consumption and Performance Issues in Utility Computing* (pp. 320–344). Hershey, PA: IGI Global. doi:10.4018/978-1-4666-8853-7.ch016

Ahmed, M. S., Houser, J., Hoque, M. A., Raju, R., & Pfeiffer, P. (2017). Reducing Inter-Process Communication Overhead in Parallel Sparse Matrix-Matrix Multiplication. *International Journal of Grid and High Performance Computing*, *9*(3), 46–59. doi:10.4018/IJGHPC.2017070104

Akram, V. K., & Dagdeviren, O. (2016). On k-Connectivity Problems in Distributed Systems. In N. Meghanathan (Ed.), *Advanced Methods for Complex Network Analysis* (pp. 30–57). Hershey, PA: IGI Global. doi:10.4018/978-1-4666-9964-9.ch002

Alfredson, J., & Ohlander, U. (2015). Intelligent Fighter Pilot Support for Distributed Unmanned and Manned Decision Making. In K. Sarma, M. Sarma, & M. Sarma (Eds.), *Intelligent Applications for Heterogeneous System Modeling and Design* (pp. 1–22). Hershey, PA: IGI Global. doi:10.4018/978-1-4666-8493-5.ch001

Alling, A., Powers, N. R., & Soyata, T. (2016). Face Recognition: A Tutorial on Computational Aspects. In G. Deka, G. Siddesh, K. Srinivasa, & L. Patnaik (Eds.), *Emerging Research Surrounding Power Consumption and Performance Issues in Utility Computing* (pp. 405–425). Hershey, PA: IGI Global. doi:10.4018/978-1-4666-8853-7.ch020

Alsarhan, A., Abdallah, E. E., & Aljammal, A. H. (2017). Competitive Processors Allocation in 2D Mesh Connected Multicomputer Networks: A Dynamic Game Approach. *International Journal of Grid and High Performance Computing*, *9*(2), 53–69. doi:10.4018/IJGHPC.2017040104

Amitab, K., Kandar, D., & Maji, A. K. (2016). Speckle Noise Filtering Using Back-Propagation Multi-Layer Perceptron Network in Synthetic Aperture Radar Image. In P. Mallick (Ed.), *Research Advances in the Integration of Big Data and Smart Computing* (pp. 280–301). Hershey, PA: IGI Global. doi:10.4018/978-1-4666-8737-0.ch016

Aslanpour, M. S., & Dashti, S. E. (2017). Proactive Auto-Scaling Algorithm (PASA) for Cloud Application. *International Journal of Grid and High Performance Computing, 9*(3), 1–16. doi:10.4018/IJGHPC.2017070101

Balluff, S., Bendfeld, J., & Krauter, S. (2017). Meteorological Data Forecast using RNN. *International Journal of Grid and High Performance Computing, 9*(1), 61–74. doi:10.4018/IJGHPC.2017010106

Baragi, S., & Iyer, N. C. (2016). Face Recognition using Fast Fourier Transform. In P. Mallick (Ed.), *Research Advances in the Integration of Big Data and Smart Computing* (pp. 302–322). Hershey, PA: IGI Global. doi:10.4018/978-1-4666-8737-0.ch017

Benson, I., Kaplan, A., Flynn, J., & Katz, S. (2017). Fault-Tolerant and Deterministic Flight-Software System For a High Performance CubeSat. *International Journal of Grid and High Performance Computing, 9*(1), 92–104. doi:10.4018/IJGHPC.2017010108

Bhadoria, R. S. (2016). Performance of Enterprise Architecture in Utility Computing. In G. Deka, G. Siddesh, K. Srinivasa, & L. Patnaik (Eds.), *Emerging Research Surrounding Power Consumption and Performance Issues in Utility Computing* (pp. 44–68). Hershey, PA: IGI Global. doi:10.4018/978-1-4666-8853-7.ch003

Bhadoria, R. S., & Patil, C. (2016). Adaptive Mobile Architecture with Utility Computing. In G. Deka, G. Siddesh, K. Srinivasa, & L. Patnaik (Eds.), *Emerging Research Surrounding Power Consumption and Performance Issues in Utility Computing* (pp. 386–404). Hershey, PA: IGI Global. doi:10.4018/978-1-4666-8853-7.ch019

Bhargavi, K., & Babu, B. S. (2016). GPU Computation and Platforms. In G. Deka, G. Siddesh, K. Srinivasa, & L. Patnaik (Eds.), *Emerging Research Surrounding Power Consumption and Performance Issues in Utility Computing* (pp. 136–174). Hershey, PA: IGI Global. doi:10.4018/978-1-4666-8853-7.ch007

Bhat, C. G., & Kopparapu, S. K. (2017). Creating Sound Glyph Database for Video Subtitling. In M. S., & V. V. (Eds.), Multi-Core Computer Vision and Image Processing for Intelligent Applications (pp. 136-154). Hershey, PA: IGI Global. doi:10.4018/978-1-5225-0889-2.ch005

Bhoi, A. K., Sherpa, K. S., & Khandelwal, B. (2016). Baseline Drift Removal of ECG Signal: Comparative Analysis of Filtering Techniques. In P. Mallick (Ed.), *Research Advances in the Integration of Big Data and Smart Computing* (pp. 134–152). Hershey, PA: IGI Global. doi:10.4018/978-1-4666-8737-0.ch008

Bhura, M., Deshpande, P. H., & Chandrasekaran, K. (2016). CUDA or OpenCL: Which is Better? A Detailed Performance Analysis. In P. Mallick (Ed.), *Research Advances in the Integration of Big Data and Smart Computing* (pp. 267–279). Hershey, PA: IGI Global. doi:10.4018/978-1-4666-8737-0.ch015

Bisoy, S. K., & Pattnaik, P. K. (2016). Transmission Control Protocol for Mobile Ad Hoc Network. In P. Mallick (Ed.), *Research Advances in the Integration of Big Data and Smart Computing* (pp. 22–49). Hershey, PA: IGI Global. doi:10.4018/978-1-4666-8737-0.ch002

Borovikov, E., Vajda, S., Lingappa, G., & Bonifant, M. C. (2017). Parallel Computing in Face Image Retrieval: Practical Approach to the Real-World Image Search. In M. S., & V. V. (Eds.), Multi-Core Computer Vision and Image Processing for Intelligent Applications (pp. 155-189). Hershey, PA: IGI Global. doi:10.4018/978-1-5225-0889-2.ch006

Casillas, L., Daradoumis, T., & Caballe, S. (2016). A Network Analysis Method for Tailoring Academic Programs. In N. Meghanathan (Ed.), *Advanced Methods for Complex Network Analysis* (pp. 396–417). Hershey, PA: IGI Global. doi:10.4018/978-1-4666-9964-9.ch017

Chauhan, R., & Kaur, H. (2014). Predictive Analytics and Data Mining: A Framework for Optimizing Decisions with R Tool. In B. Tripathy & D. Acharjya (Eds.), *Advances in Secure Computing, Internet Services, and Applications* (pp. 73–88). Hershey, PA: IGI Global. doi:10.4018/978-1-4666-4940-8.ch004

Chen, G., Wang, E., Sun, X., & Lu, Y. (2016). An Intelligent Approval System for City Construction based on Cloud Computing and Big Data. *International Journal of Grid and High Performance Computing, 8*(3), 57–69. doi:10.4018/IJGHPC.2016070104

Chen, Z., Yang, S., Shang, Y., Liu, Y., Wang, F., Wang, L., & Fu, J. (2016). Fragment Re-Allocation Strategy Based on Hypergraph for NoSQL Database Systems. *International Journal of Grid and High Performance Computing, 8*(3), 1–23. doi:10.4018/IJGHPC.2016070101

Choudhury, A., Talukdar, A. K., & Sarma, K. K. (2015). A Review on Vision-Based Hand Gesture Recognition and Applications. In K. Sarma, M. Sarma, & M. Sarma (Eds.), *Intelligent Applications for Heterogeneous System Modeling and Design* (pp. 256–281). Hershey, PA: IGI Global. doi:10.4018/978-1-4666-8493-5.ch011

Coti, C. (2016). Fault Tolerance Techniques for Distributed, Parallel Applications. In Q. Hassan (Ed.), *Innovative Research and Applications in Next-Generation High Performance Computing* (pp. 221–252). Hershey, PA: IGI Global. doi:10.4018/978-1-5225-0287-6.ch009

Crespo, M. L., Cicuttin, A., Gazzano, J. D., & Rincon Calle, F. (2016). Reconfigurable Virtual Instrumentation Based on FPGA for Science and High-Education. In J. Gazzano, M. Crespo, A. Cicuttin, & F. Calle (Eds.), *Field-Programmable Gate Array (FPGA) Technologies for High Performance Instrumentation* (pp. 99–123). Hershey, PA: IGI Global. doi:10.4018/978-1-5225-0299-9.ch005

Daniel, D. K., & Bhandari, V. (2014). Neural Network Model to Estimate and Predict Cell Mass Concentration in Lipase Fermentation. In B. Tripathy & D. Acharjya (Eds.), *Advances in Secure Computing, Internet Services, and Applications* (pp. 303–316). Hershey, PA: IGI Global. doi:10.4018/978-1-4666-4940-8.ch015

Das, B., Sarma, M. P., & Sarma, K. K. (2015). Different Aspects of Interleaving Techniques in Wireless Communication. In K. Sarma, M. Sarma, & M. Sarma (Eds.), *Intelligent Applications for Heterogeneous System Modeling and Design* (pp. 335–374). Hershey, PA: IGI Global. doi:10.4018/978-1-4666-8493-5.ch015

Das, P. K. (2016). Comparative Study on XEN, KVM, VSphere, and Hyper-V. In G. Deka, G. Siddesh, K. Srinivasa, & L. Patnaik (Eds.), *Emerging Research Surrounding Power Consumption and Performance Issues in Utility Computing* (pp. 233–261). Hershey, PA: IGI Global. doi:10.4018/978-1-4666-8853-7.ch011

Das, P. K., & Deka, G. C. (2016). History and Evolution of GPU Architecture. In G. Deka, G. Siddesh, K. Srinivasa, & L. Patnaik (Eds.), *Emerging Research Surrounding Power Consumption and Performance Issues in Utility Computing* (pp. 109–135). Hershey, PA: IGI Global. doi:10.4018/978-1-4666-8853-7.ch006

Das, R., & Pradhan, M. K. (2014). Artificial Neural Network Modeling for Electrical Discharge Machining Parameters. In B. Tripathy & D. Acharjya (Eds.), *Advances in Secure Computing, Internet Services, and Applications* (pp. 281–302). Hershey, PA: IGI Global. doi:10.4018/978-1-4666-4940-8.ch014

Das, S., & Kalita, H. K. (2016). Advanced Dimensionality Reduction Method for Big Data. In P. Mallick (Ed.), *Research Advances in the Integration of Big Data and Smart Computing* (pp. 198–210). Hershey, PA: IGI Global. doi:10.4018/978-1-4666-8737-0.ch011

Das, S., & Kalita, H. K. (2016). Efficient Classification Rule Mining for Breast Cancer Detection. In P. Mallick (Ed.), *Research Advances in the Integration of Big Data and Smart Computing* (pp. 50–63). Hershey, PA: IGI Global. doi:10.4018/978-1-4666-8737-0.ch003

De Micco, L., & Larrondo, H. A. (2016). Methodology for FPGA Implementation of a Chaos-Based AWGN Generator. In J. Gazzano, M. Crespo, A. Cicuttin, & F. Calle (Eds.), *Field-Programmable Gate Array (FPGA) Technologies for High Performance Instrumentation* (pp. 43–58). Hershey, PA: IGI Global. doi:10.4018/978-1-5225-0299-9.ch003

de Souza, E. D., & Lima, E. J. II. (2017). Autonomic Computing in a Biomimetic Algorithm for Robots Dedicated to Rehabilitation of Ankle. *International Journal of Grid and High Performance Computing*, 9(1), 48–60. doi:10.4018/IJGHPC.2017010105

Deepika, R., Prasad, M. R., Chetana, S., & Manjunath, T. C. (2016). Adoption of Dual Iris and Periocular Recognition for Human Identification. In P. Mallick (Ed.), *Research Advances in the Integration of Big Data and Smart Computing* (pp. 250–266). Hershey, PA: IGI Global. doi:10.4018/978-1-4666-8737-0.ch014

Dey, P., & Roy, S. (2016). Social Network Analysis. In N. Meghanathan (Ed.), *Advanced Methods for Complex Network Analysis* (pp. 237–265). Hershey, PA: IGI Global. doi:10.4018/978-1-4666-9964-9.ch010

Don Clark, A. (2016). A Theoretic Representation of the Effects of Targeted Failures in HPC Systems. In Q. Hassan (Ed.), *Innovative Research and Applications in Next-Generation High Performance Computing* (pp. 253–276). Hershey, PA: IGI Global. doi:10.4018/978-1-5225-0287-6.ch010

Dutta, P., & Ojha, V. K. (2014). Conjugate Gradient Trained Neural Network for Intelligent Sensing of Manhole Gases to Avoid Human Fatality. In B. Tripathy & D. Acharjya (Eds.), *Advances in Secure Computing, Internet Services, and Applications* (pp. 257–280). Hershey, PA: IGI Global. doi:10.4018/978-1-4666-4940-8.ch013

Elkhodr, M., Shahrestani, S., & Cheung, H. (2016). Internet of Things Applications: Current and Future Development. In Q. Hassan (Ed.), *Innovative Research and Applications in Next-Generation High Performance Computing* (pp. 397–427). Hershey, PA: IGI Global. doi:10.4018/978-1-5225-0287-6.ch016

Elkhodr, M., Shahrestani, S., & Cheung, H. (2016). Wireless Enabling Technologies for the Internet of Things. In Q. Hassan (Ed.), *Innovative Research and Applications in Next-Generation High Performance Computing* (pp. 368–396). Hershey, PA: IGI Global. doi:10.4018/978-1-5225-0287-6.ch015

Elmisery, A. M., & Sertovic, M. (2017). Privacy Enhanced Cloud-Based Recommendation Service for Implicit Discovery of Relevant Support Groups in Healthcare Social Networks. *International Journal of Grid and High Performance Computing*, *9*(1), 75–91. doi:10.4018/IJGHPC.2017010107

Fazio, P., Tropea, M., Marano, S., & Curia, V. (2016). A Hybrid Complex Network Model for Wireless Sensor Networks and Performance Evaluation. In N. Meghanathan (Ed.), *Advanced Methods for Complex Network Analysis* (pp. 379–395). Hershey, PA: IGI Global. doi:10.4018/978-1-4666-9964-9.ch016

Fei, X., Li, K., Yang, W., & Li, K. (2016). CPU-GPU Computing: Overview, Optimization, and Applications. In Q. Hassan (Ed.), *Innovative Research and Applications in Next-Generation High Performance Computing* (pp. 159–193). Hershey, PA: IGI Global. doi:10.4018/978-1-5225-0287-6.ch007

Funes, M. A., Hadad, M. N., Donato, P. G., & Carrica, D. O. (2016). Optimization of Advanced Signal Processing Architectures for Detection of Signals Immersed in Noise. In J. Gazzano, M. Crespo, A. Cicuttin, & F. Calle (Eds.), *Field-Programmable Gate Array (FPGA) Technologies for High Performance Instrumentation* (pp. 171–212). Hershey, PA: IGI Global. doi:10.4018/978-1-5225-0299-9.ch008

Garcia-Robledo, A., Diaz-Perez, A., & Morales-Luna, G. (2016). Characterization and Coarsening of Autonomous System Networks: Measuring and Simplifying the Internet. In N. Meghanathan (Ed.), *Advanced Methods for Complex Network Analysis* (pp. 148–179). Hershey, PA: IGI Global. doi:10.4018/978-1-4666-9964-9.ch006

Garg, A., Biswas, A., & Biswas, B. (2016). Evolutionary Computation Techniques for Community Detection in Social Network Analysis. In N. Meghanathan (Ed.), *Advanced Methods for Complex Network Analysis* (pp. 266–284). Hershey, PA: IGI Global. doi:10.4018/978-1-4666-9964-9.ch011

Garg, P., & Gupta, A. (2016). Restoration Technique to Optimize Recovery Time for Efficient OSPF Network. In P. Mallick (Ed.), *Research Advances in the Integration of Big Data and Smart Computing* (pp. 64–88). Hershey, PA: IGI Global. doi:10.4018/978-1-4666-8737-0.ch004

Gazzano, J. D., Calle, F. R., Caba, J., de la Fuente, D., & Romero, J. B. (2016). Dynamic Reconfiguration for Internal Monitoring Services. In J. Gazzano, M. Crespo, A. Cicuttin, & F. Calle (Eds.), *Field-Programmable Gate Array (FPGA) Technologies for High Performance Instrumentation* (pp. 124–136). Hershey, PA: IGI Global. doi:10.4018/978-1-5225-0299-9.ch006

Geethanjali, P. (2014). Pattern Recognition and Robotics. In B. Tripathy & D. Acharjya (Eds.), *Advances in Secure Computing, Internet Services, and Applications* (pp. 35–48). Hershey, PA: IGI Global. doi:10.4018/978-1-4666-4940-8.ch002

Ghai, D., & Jain, N. (2016). Signal Processing: Iteration Bound and Loop Bound. In P. Mallick (Ed.), *Research Advances in the Integration of Big Data and Smart Computing* (pp. 153–177). Hershey, PA: IGI Global. doi:10.4018/978-1-4666-8737-0.ch009

Ghaiwat, S. N., & Arora, P. (2016). Cotton Leaf Disease Detection by Feature Extraction. In P. Mallick (Ed.), *Research Advances in the Integration of Big Data and Smart Computing* (pp. 89–104). Hershey, PA: IGI Global. doi:10.4018/978-1-4666-8737-0.ch005

Ghorpade-Aher, J., Pagare, R., Thengade, A., Ghorpade, S., & Kadam, M. (2016). Big Data: The Data Deluge. In P. Mallick (Ed.), *Research Advances in the Integration of Big Data and Smart Computing* (pp. 1–21). Hershey, PA: IGI Global. doi:10.4018/978-1-4666-8737-0.ch001

Gil-Costa, V., Molina, R. S., Petrino, R., Paez, C. F., Printista, A. M., & Gazzano, J. D. (2016). Hardware Acceleration of CBIR System with FPGA-Based Platform. In J. Gazzano, M. Crespo, A. Cicuttin, & F. Calle (Eds.), *Field-Programmable Gate Array (FPGA) Technologies for High Performance Instrumentation* (pp. 138–170). Hershey, PA: IGI Global. doi:10.4018/978-1-5225-0299-9.ch007

Goswami, S., Mehjabin, S., & Kashyap, P. A. (2015). Driverless Metro Train with Automatic Crowd Control System. In K. Sarma, M. Sarma, & M. Sarma (Eds.), *Intelligent Applications for Heterogeneous System Modeling and Design* (pp. 76–95). Hershey, PA: IGI Global. doi:10.4018/978-1-4666-8493-5.ch004

Guan, Q., DeBardeleben, N., Blanchard, S., Fu, S., Davis, C. H. IV, & Jones, W. M. (2016). Analyzing the Robustness of HPC Applications Using a Fine-Grained Soft Error Fault Injection Tool. In Q. Hassan (Ed.), *Innovative Research and Applications in Next-Generation High Performance Computing* (pp. 277–305). Hershey, PA: IGI Global. doi:10.4018/978-1-5225-0287-6.ch011

Guerrero, J. I., Monedero, Í., Biscarri, F., Biscarri, J., Millán, R., & León, C. (2014). Detection of Non-Technical Losses: The Project MIDAS. In B. Tripathy & D. Acharjya (Eds.), *Advances in Secure Computing, Internet Services, and Applications* (pp. 140–164). Hershey, PA: IGI Global. doi:10.4018/978-1-4666-4940-8.ch008

Habbal, A., Abdullah, S. A., Mkpojiogu, E. O., Hassan, S., & Benamar, N. (2017). Assessing Experimental Private Cloud Using Web of System Performance Model. *International Journal of Grid and High Performance Computing*, 9(2), 21–35. doi:10.4018/IJGHPC.2017040102

Habib, I., Islam, A., Chetia, S., & Saikia, S. J. (2015). A New Coding Scheme for Data Security in RF based Wireless Communication. In K. Sarma, M. Sarma, & M. Sarma (Eds.), *Intelligent Applications for Heterogeneous System Modeling and Design* (pp. 301–319). Hershey, PA: IGI Global. doi:10.4018/978-1-4666-8493-5.ch013

Hamilton, H., & Alasti, H. (2017). Controlled Intelligent Agents' Security Model for Multi-Tenant Cloud Computing Infrastructures. *International Journal of Grid and High Performance Computing*, 9(1), 1–13. doi:10.4018/IJGHPC.2017010101

Ileri, C. U., Ural, C. A., Dagdeviren, O., & Kavalci, V. (2016). On Vertex Cover Problems in Distributed Systems. In N. Meghanathan (Ed.), *Advanced Methods for Complex Network Analysis* (pp. 1–29). Hershey, PA: IGI Global. doi:10.4018/978-1-4666-9964-9.ch001

Ingale, A. G. (2014). Prediction of Structural and Functional Aspects of Protein: In-Silico Approach. In B. Tripathy & D. Acharjya (Eds.), *Advances in Secure Computing, Internet Services, and Applications* (pp. 317–333). Hershey, PA: IGI Global. doi:10.4018/978-1-4666-4940-8.ch016

Jadon, K. S., Mudgal, P., & Bhadoria, R. S. (2016). Optimization and Management of Resource in Utility Computing. In G. Deka, G. Siddesh, K. Srinivasa, & L. Patnaik (Eds.), *Emerging Research Surrounding Power Consumption and Performance Issues in Utility Computing* (pp. 22–43). Hershey, PA: IGI Global. doi:10.4018/978-1-4666-8853-7.ch002

K. G. S., G. M., S., Hiriyannaiah, S., Morappanavar, A., & Banerjee, A. (2016). A Novel Approach of Symmetric Key Cryptography using Genetic Algorithm Implemented on GPGPU. In G. Deka, G. Siddesh, K. Srinivasa, & L. Patnaik (Eds.), Emerging Research Surrounding Power Consumption and Performance Issues in Utility Computing (pp. 283-303). Hershey, PA: IGI Global. doi:10.4018/978-1-4666-8853-7.ch014

Kannan, R. (2014). Graphical Evaluation and Review Technique (GERT): The Panorama in the Computation and Visualization of Network-Based Project Management. In B. Tripathy & D. Acharjya (Eds.), *Advances in Secure Computing, Internet Services, and Applications* (pp. 165–179). Hershey, PA: IGI Global. doi:10.4018/978-1-4666-4940-8.ch009

Kasemsap, K. (2014). The Role of Knowledge Management on Job Satisfaction: A Systematic Framework. In B. Tripathy & D. Acharjya (Eds.), *Advances in Secure Computing, Internet Services, and Applications* (pp. 104–127). Hershey, PA: IGI Global. doi:10.4018/978-1-4666-4940-8.ch006

Khadtare, M. S. (2016). GPU Based Image Quality Assessment using Structural Similarity (SSIM) Index. In G. Deka, G. Siddesh, K. Srinivasa, & L. Patnaik (Eds.), *Emerging Research Surrounding Power Consumption and Performance Issues in Utility Computing* (pp. 276–282). Hershey, PA: IGI Global. doi:10.4018/978-1-4666-8853-7.ch013

Khan, A. U., & Khan, A. N. (2016). High Performance Computing on Mobile Devices. In Q. Hassan (Ed.), *Innovative Research and Applications in Next-Generation High Performance Computing* (pp. 334–348). Hershey, PA: IGI Global. doi:10.4018/978-1-5225-0287-6.ch013

Khan, M. S. (2016). A Study of Computer Virus Propagation on Scale Free Networks Using Differential Equations. In N. Meghanathan (Ed.), *Advanced Methods for Complex Network Analysis* (pp. 196–214). Hershey, PA: IGI Global. doi:10.4018/978-1-4666-9964-9.ch008

Khan, R. H. (2015). Utilizing UML, cTLA, and SRN: An Application to Distributed System Performance Modeling. In K. Sarma, M. Sarma, & M. Sarma (Eds.), *Intelligent Applications for Heterogeneous System Modeling and Design* (pp. 23–50). Hershey, PA: IGI Global. doi:10.4018/978-1-4666-8493-5.ch002

Konwar, P., & Bordoloi, H. (2015). An EOG Signal based Framework to Control a Wheel Chair. In K. Sarma, M. Sarma, & M. Sarma (Eds.), *Intelligent Applications for Heterogeneous System Modeling and Design* (pp. 51–75). Hershey, PA: IGI Global. doi:10.4018/978-1-4666-8493-5.ch003

Koppad, S. H., & Shwetha, T. M. (2016). Indic Language: Kannada to Braille Conversion Tool Using Client Server Architecture Model. In P. Mallick (Ed.), *Research Advances in the Integration of Big Data and Smart Computing* (pp. 120–133). Hershey, PA: IGI Global. doi:10.4018/978-1-4666-8737-0.ch007

Kumar, P. S., Pradhan, S. K., & Panda, S. (2016). The Pedagogy of English Teaching-Learning at Primary Level in Rural Government Schools: A Data Mining View. In P. Mallick (Ed.), *Research Advances in the Integration of Big Data and Smart Computing* (pp. 105–119). Hershey, PA: IGI Global. doi:10.4018/978-1-4666-8737-0.ch006

Kumar, S., Ranjan, P., Ramaswami, R., & Tripathy, M. R. (2017). Resource Efficient Clustering and Next Hop Knowledge Based Routing in Multiple Heterogeneous Wireless Sensor Networks. *International Journal of Grid and High Performance Computing*, 9(2), 1–20. doi:10.4018/IJGHPC.2017040101

Kunfang, S., & Lu, H. (2016). Efficient Querying Distributed Big-XML Data using MapReduce. *International Journal of Grid and High Performance Computing*, 8(3), 70–79. doi:10.4018/IJGHPC.2016070105

Li, Y., Zhai, J., & Li, K. (2016). Communication Analysis and Performance Prediction of Parallel Applications on Large-Scale Machines. In Q. Hassan (Ed.), *Innovative Research and Applications in Next-Generation High Performance Computing* (pp. 80–105). Hershey, PA: IGI Global. doi:10.4018/978-1-5225-0287-6.ch005

Lin, L., Li, S., Li, B., Zhan, J., & Zhao, Y. (2016). TVGuarder: A Trace-Enable Virtualization Protection Framework against Insider Threats for IaaS Environments. *International Journal of Grid and High Performance Computing*, *8*(4), 1–20. doi:10.4018/IJGHPC.2016100101

López, M. B. (2017). Mobile Platform Challenges in Interactive Computer Vision. In M. S., & V. V. (Eds.), Multi-Core Computer Vision and Image Processing for Intelligent Applications (pp. 47-73). Hershey, PA: IGI Global. doi:10.4018/978-1-5225-0889-2.ch002

Maarouf, A., El Qacimy, B., Marzouk, A., & Haqiq, A. (2017). Defining and Evaluating A Novel Penalty Model for Managing Violations in the Cloud Computing. *International Journal of Grid and High Performance Computing*, *9*(2), 36–52. doi:10.4018/IJGHPC.2017040103

Mahmoud, I. I. (2016). Implementation of Reactor Control Rod Position Sensing/Display Using a VLSI Chip. In J. Gazzano, M. Crespo, A. Cicuttin, & F. Calle (Eds.), *Field-Programmable Gate Array (FPGA) Technologies for High Performance Instrumentation* (pp. 1–16). Hershey, PA: IGI Global. doi:10.4018/978-1-5225-0299-9.ch001

Mahmoud, I. I., & El Tokhy, M. S. (2016). Development of Algorithms and Their Hardware Implementation for Gamma Radiation Spectrometry. In J. Gazzano, M. Crespo, A. Cicuttin, & F. Calle (Eds.), *Field-Programmable Gate Array (FPGA) Technologies for High Performance Instrumentation* (pp. 17–41). Hershey, PA: IGI Global. doi:10.4018/978-1-5225-0299-9.ch002

Mahmoud, I. I., Salama, M., & El Hamid, A. A. (2016). Hardware Implementation of a Genetic Algorithm for Motion Path Planning. In J. Gazzano, M. Crespo, A. Cicuttin, & F. Calle (Eds.), *Field-Programmable Gate Array (FPGA) Technologies for High Performance Instrumentation* (pp. 250–275). Hershey, PA: IGI Global. doi:10.4018/978-1-5225-0299-9.ch010

Maji, A. K., Rymbai, B., & Kandar, D. (2016). A Study on Different Facial Features Extraction Technique. In P. Mallick (Ed.), *Research Advances in the Integration of Big Data and Smart Computing* (pp. 224–249). Hershey, PA: IGI Global. doi:10.4018/978-1-4666-8737-0.ch013

Mallick, P. K., Mohanty, M. N., & Kumar, S. S. (2016). White Patch Detection in Brain MRI Image Using Evolutionary Clustering Algorithm. In P. Mallick (Ed.), *Research Advances in the Integration of Big Data and Smart Computing* (pp. 323–339). Hershey, PA: IGI Global. doi:10.4018/978-1-4666-8737-0.ch018

Mandal, B., Sarma, M. P., & Sarma, K. K. (2015). Design of a Power Aware Systolic Array based Support Vector Machine Classifier. In K. Sarma, M. Sarma, & M. Sarma (Eds.), *Intelligent Applications for Heterogeneous System Modeling and Design* (pp. 96–138). Hershey, PA: IGI Global. doi:10.4018/978-1-4666-8493-5.ch005

Manjaiah, D. H., & Payaswini, P. (2014). Design Issues of 4G-Network Mobility Management. In B. Tripathy & D. Acharjya (Eds.), *Advances in Secure Computing, Internet Services, and Applications* (pp. 210–238). Hershey, PA: IGI Global. doi:10.4018/978-1-4666-4940-8.ch011

Martinez-Gonzalez, R. F., Vazquez-Medina, R., Diaz-Mendez, J. A., & Lopez-Hernandez, J. (2016). FPGA Implementations for Chaotic Maps Using Fixed-Point and Floating-Point Representations. In J. Gazzano, M. Crespo, A. Cicuttin, & F. Calle (Eds.), *Field-Programmable Gate Array (FPGA) Technologies for High Performance Instrumentation* (pp. 59–97). Hershey, PA: IGI Global. doi:10.4018/978-1-5225-0299-9.ch004

Meddah, I. H., & Belkadi, K. (2017). Parallel Distributed Patterns Mining Using Hadoop MapReduce Framework. *International Journal of Grid and High Performance Computing, 9*(2), 70–85. doi:10.4018/IJGHPC.2017040105

Medhi, J. P. (2015). An Approach for Automatic Detection and Grading of Macular Edema. In K. Sarma, M. Sarma, & M. Sarma (Eds.), *Intelligent Applications for Heterogeneous System Modeling and Design* (pp. 204–231). Hershey, PA: IGI Global. doi:10.4018/978-1-4666-8493-5.ch009

Mishra, B. K., & Sahoo, A. K. (2016). Application of Big Data in Economic Policy. In P. Mallick (Ed.), *Research Advances in the Integration of Big Data and Smart Computing* (pp. 178–197). Hershey, PA: IGI Global. doi:10.4018/978-1-4666-8737-0.ch010

Mohan Khilar, P. (2014). Genetic Algorithms: Application to Fault Diagnosis in Distributed Embedded Systems. In B. Tripathy & D. Acharjya (Eds.), *Advances in Secure Computing, Internet Services, and Applications* (pp. 239–255). Hershey, PA: IGI Global. doi:10.4018/978-1-4666-4940-8.ch012

Mohanty, R. P., Turuk, A. K., & Sahoo, B. (2016). Designing of High Performance Multicore Processor with Improved Cache Configuration and Interconnect. In G. Deka, G. Siddesh, K. Srinivasa, & L. Patnaik (Eds.), *Emerging Research Surrounding Power Consumption and Performance Issues in Utility Computing* (pp. 204–219). Hershey, PA: IGI Global. doi:10.4018/978-1-4666-8853-7.ch009

Mohanty, S., Patra, P. K., & Mohapatra, S. (2016). Dynamic Task Assignment with Load Balancing in Cloud Platform. In G. Deka, G. Siddesh, K. Srinivasa, & L. Patnaik (Eds.), *Emerging Research Surrounding Power Consumption and Performance Issues in Utility Computing* (pp. 363–385). Hershey, PA: IGI Global. doi:10.4018/978-1-4666-8853-7.ch018

Mukherjee, A., Chatterjee, A., Das, D., & Naskar, M. K. (2016). Design of Structural Controllability for Complex Network Architecture. In N. Meghanathan (Ed.), *Advanced Methods for Complex Network Analysis* (pp. 98–124). Hershey, PA: IGI Global. doi:10.4018/978-1-4666-9964-9.ch004

Mukherjee, M. Kamarujjaman, & Maitra, M. (2016). Application of Biomedical Image Processing in Blood Cell Counting using Hough Transform. In N. Meghanathan (Ed.), Advanced Methods for Complex Network Analysis (pp. 359-378). Hershey, PA: IGI Global. doi:10.4018/978-1-4666-9964-9.ch015

Naseera, S. (2016). Dynamic Job Scheduling Strategy for Unreliable Nodes in a Volunteer Desktop Grid. *International Journal of Grid and High Performance Computing*, 8(4), 21–33. doi:10.4018/IJGHPC.2016100102

Netake, A., & Katti, P. K. (2016). HTLS Conductors: A Novel Aspect for Energy Conservation in Transmission System. In P. Mallick (Ed.), *Research Advances in the Integration of Big Data and Smart Computing* (pp. 211–223). Hershey, PA: IGI Global. doi:10.4018/978-1-4666-8737-0.ch012

Nirmala, S. R., & Sarma, P. (2015). A Computer Based System for ECG Arrhythmia Classification. In K. Sarma, M. Sarma, & M. Sarma (Eds.), *Intelligent Applications for Heterogeneous System Modeling and Design* (pp. 160–185). Hershey, PA: IGI Global. doi:10.4018/978-1-4666-8493-5.ch007

Nirmala, S. R., & Sharma, P. (2015). Computer Assisted Methods for Retinal Image Classification. In K. Sarma, M. Sarma, & M. Sarma (Eds.), *Intelligent Applications for Heterogeneous System Modeling and Design* (pp. 232–255). Hershey, PA: IGI Global. doi:10.4018/978-1-4666-8493-5.ch010

Omar, M., Ahmad, K., & Rizvi, M. (2016). Content Based Image Retrieval System. In G. Deka, G. Siddesh, K. Srinivasa, & L. Patnaik (Eds.), *Emerging Research Surrounding Power Consumption and Performance Issues in Utility Computing* (pp. 345–362). Hershey, PA: IGI Global. doi:10.4018/978-1-4666-8853-7.ch017

Panda, M., & Patra, M. R. (2014). Characterizing Intelligent Intrusion Detection and Prevention Systems Using Data Mining. In B. Tripathy & D. Acharjya (Eds.), *Advances in Secure Computing, Internet Services, and Applications* (pp. 89–102). Hershey, PA: IGI Global. doi:10.4018/978-1-4666-4940-8.ch005

Pang, X., Wan, B., Li, H., & Lin, W. (2016). MR-LDA: An Efficient Topic Model for Classification of Short Text in Big Social Data. *International Journal of Grid and High Performance Computing*, 8(4), 100–113. doi:10.4018/IJGHPC.2016100106

Perera, D. R., Mannathunga, K. S., Dharmasiri, R. A., Meegama, R. G., & Jayananda, K. (2016). Implementation of a Smart Sensor Node for Wireless Sensor Network Applications Using FPGAs. In J. Gazzano, M. Crespo, A. Cicuttin, & F. Calle (Eds.), *Field-Programmable Gate Array (FPGA) Technologies for High Performance Instrumentation* (pp. 213–249). Hershey, PA: IGI Global. doi:10.4018/978-1-5225-0299-9.ch009

Perez, H., Hernandez, B., Rudomin, I., & Ayguade, E. (2016). Task-Based Crowd Simulation for Heterogeneous Architectures. In Q. Hassan (Ed.), *Innovative Research and Applications in Next-Generation High Performance Computing* (pp. 194–219). Hershey, PA: IGI Global. doi:10.4018/978-1-5225-0287-6.ch008

Pourqasem, J., & Edalatpanah, S. (2016). Verification of Super-Peer Model for Query Processing in Peer-to-Peer Networks. In Q. Hassan (Ed.), *Innovative Research and Applications in Next-Generation High Performance Computing* (pp. 306–332). Hershey, PA: IGI Global. doi:10.4018/978-1-5225-0287-6.ch012

Pujari, M., & Kanawati, R. (2016). Link Prediction in Complex Networks. In N. Meghanathan (Ed.), *Advanced Methods for Complex Network Analysis* (pp. 58–97). Hershey, PA: IGI Global. doi:10.4018/978-1-4666-9964-9.ch003

Qian, H., Yong, W., Jia, L., & Mengfei, C. (2016). Publish/Subscribe and JXTA based Cloud Service Management with QoS. *International Journal of Grid and High Performance Computing*, *8*(3), 24–37. doi:10.4018/IJGHPC.2016070102

Raigoza, J., & Karande, V. (2017). A Study and Implementation of a Movie Recommendation System in a Cloud-based Environment. *International Journal of Grid and High Performance Computing*, *9*(1), 25–36. doi:10.4018/IJGHPC.2017010103

Ramalingam, V. V. S., M., Sugumaran, V., V., V., & Vadhanam, B. R. (2017). Controlling Prosthetic Limb Movements Using EEG Signals. In M. S., & V. V. (Eds.), Multi-Core Computer Vision and Image Processing for Intelligent Applications (pp. 211-233). Hershey, PA: IGI Global. doi:10.4018/978-1-5225-0889-2.ch008

Rawat, D. B., & Bhattacharya, S. (2016). Wireless Body Area Network for Healthcare Applications. In N. Meghanathan (Ed.), *Advanced Methods for Complex Network Analysis* (pp. 343–358). Hershey, PA: IGI Global. doi:10.4018/978-1-4666-9964-9.ch014

Rehman, M. H., Khan, A. U., & Batool, A. (2016). Big Data Analytics in Mobile and Cloud Computing Environments. In Q. Hassan (Ed.), *Innovative Research and Applications in Next-Generation High Performance Computing* (pp. 349–367). Hershey, PA: IGI Global. doi:10.4018/978-1-5225-0287-6.ch014

Rico-Diaz, A. J., Rodriguez, A., Puertas, J., & Bermudez, M. (2017). Fish Monitoring, Sizing, and Detection Using Stereovision, Laser Technology, and Computer Vision. In M. S., & V. V. (Eds.), Multi-Core Computer Vision and Image Processing for Intelligent Applications (pp. 190-210). Hershey, PA: IGI Global. doi:10.4018/978-1-5225-0889-2.ch007

Rodriguez, A., Rico-Diaz, A. J., Rabuñal, J. R., & Gestal, M. (2017). Fish Tracking with Computer Vision Techniques: An Application to Vertical Slot Fishways. In M. S., & V. V. (Eds.), Multi-Core Computer Vision and Image Processing for Intelligent Applications (pp. 74-104). Hershey, PA: IGI Global. doi:10.4018/978-1-5225-0889-2.ch003

S., J. R., & Omman, B. (2017). A Technical Assessment on License Plate Detection System. In M. S., & V. V. (Eds.), *Multi-Core Computer Vision and Image Processing for Intelligent Applications* (pp. 234-258). Hershey, PA: IGI Global. doi:10.4018/978-1-5225-0889-2.ch009

Saadat, N., & Rahmani, A. M. (2016). A Two-Level Fuzzy Value-Based Replica Replacement Algorithm in Data Grids. *International Journal of Grid and High Performance Computing*, 8(4), 78–99. doi:10.4018/IJGHPC.2016100105

Sah, P., & Sarma, K. K. (2015). Bloodless Technique to Detect Diabetes using Soft Computational Tool. In K. Sarma, M. Sarma, & M. Sarma (Eds.), *Intelligent Applications for Heterogeneous System Modeling and Design* (pp. 139–158). Hershey, PA: IGI Global. doi:10.4018/978-1-4666-8493-5.ch006

Sahoo, B., Jena, S. K., & Mahapatra, S. (2014). Heuristic Resource Allocation Algorithms for Dynamic Load Balancing in Heterogeneous Distributed Computing System. In B. Tripathy & D. Acharjya (Eds.), *Advances in Secure Computing, Internet Services, and Applications* (pp. 181–209). Hershey, PA: IGI Global. doi:10.4018/978-1-4666-4940-8.ch010

Sarma, M., & Sarma, K. K. (2015). Acoustic Modeling of Speech Signal using Artificial Neural Network: A Review of Techniques and Current Trends. In K. Sarma, M. Sarma, & M. Sarma (Eds.), *Intelligent Applications for Heterogeneous System Modeling and Design* (pp. 282–299). Hershey, PA: IGI Global. doi:10.4018/978-1-4666-8493-5.ch012

Shahid, A., Arif, S., Qadri, M. Y., & Munawar, S. (2016). Power Optimization Using Clock Gating and Power Gating: A Review. In Q. Hassan (Ed.), *Innovative Research and Applications in Next-Generation High Performance Computing* (pp. 1–20). Hershey, PA: IGI Global. doi:10.4018/978-1-5225-0287-6.ch001

Shahid, A., Khalid, B., Qadri, M. Y., Qadri, N. N., & Ahmed, J. (2016). Design Space Exploration Using Cycle Accurate Simulator. In Q. Hassan (Ed.), *Innovative Research and Applications in Next-Generation High Performance Computing* (pp. 66–79). Hershey, PA: IGI Global. doi:10.4018/978-1-5225-0287-6.ch004

Shahid, A., Murad, M., Qadri, M. Y., Qadri, N. N., & Ahmed, J. (2016). Hardware Transactional Memories: A Survey. In Q. Hassan (Ed.), *Innovative Research and Applications in Next-Generation High Performance Computing* (pp. 47–65). Hershey, PA: IGI Global. doi:10.4018/978-1-5225-0287-6.ch003

Sharma, O., & Saini, H. (2017). SLA and Performance Efficient Heuristics for Virtual Machines Placement in Cloud Data Centers. *International Journal of Grid and High Performance Computing, 9*(3), 17–33. doi:10.4018/IJGHPC.2017070102

Sheikh, A. (2017). Utilizing an Augmented Reality System to Address Phantom Limb Syndrome in a Cloud-Based Environment. *International Journal of Grid and High Performance Computing, 9*(1), 14–24. doi:10.4018/IJGHPC.2017010102

Shojafar, M., Cordeschi, N., & Baccarelli, E. (2016). Resource Scheduling for Energy-Aware Reconfigurable Internet Data Centers. In Q. Hassan (Ed.), *Innovative Research and Applications in Next-Generation High Performance Computing* (pp. 21–46). Hershey, PA: IGI Global. doi:10.4018/978-1-5225-0287-6.ch002

Singh, S., & Gond, S. (2016). Green Computing and Its Impact. In G. Deka, G. Siddesh, K. Srinivasa, & L. Patnaik (Eds.), *Emerging Research Surrounding Power Consumption and Performance Issues in Utility Computing* (pp. 69–83). Hershey, PA: IGI Global. doi:10.4018/978-1-4666-8853-7.ch004

Sirisha, D., & Vijayakumari, G. (2017). Towards Efficient Bounds on Completion Time and Resource Provisioning for Scheduling Workflows on Heterogeneous Processing Systems. *International Journal of Grid and High Performance Computing, 9*(3), 60–82. doi:10.4018/IJGHPC.2017070105

Sk, K., Mukherjee, M., & Maitra, M. (2017). FPGA-Based Re-Configurable Architecture for Window-Based Image Processing. In M. S., & V. V. (Eds.), *Multi-Core Computer Vision and Image Processing for Intelligent Applications* (pp. 1-46). Hershey, PA: IGI Global. doi:10.4018/978-1-5225-0889-2.ch001

Skanderova, L., & Zelinka, I. (2016). Differential Evolution Dynamic Analysis in the Form of Complex Networks. In N. Meghanathan (Ed.), *Advanced Methods for Complex Network Analysis* (pp. 285–318). Hershey, PA: IGI Global. doi:10.4018/978-1-4666-9964-9.ch012

Sreekumar,, & Patel, G. (2014). Assessment of Technical Efficiency of Indian B-Schools: A Comparison between the Cross-Sectional and Time-Series Analysis. In B. Tripathy, & D. Acharjya (Eds.), *Advances in Secure Computing, Internet Services, and Applications* (pp. 128-139). Hershey, PA: IGI Global. doi:10.4018/978-1-4666-4940-8.ch007

Srinivasa, K. G., Hegde, G., Sideesh, G. M., & Hiriyannaiah, S. (2016). A Viability Analysis of an Economical Private Cloud Storage Solution Powered by Raspberry Pi in the NSA Era: A Survey and Analysis of Cost and Security. In G. Deka, G. Siddesh, K. Srinivasa, & L. Patnaik (Eds.), *Emerging Research Surrounding Power Consumption and Performance Issues in Utility Computing* (pp. 220–232). Hershey, PA: IGI Global. doi:10.4018/978-1-4666-8853-7.ch010

Srinivasa, K. G., Siddesh, G. M., Hiriyannaiah, S., Mishra, K., Prajeeth, C. S., & Talha, A. M. (2016). GPU Implementation of Friend Recommendation System using CUDA for Social Networking Services. In G. Deka, G. Siddesh, K. Srinivasa, & L. Patnaik (Eds.), *Emerging Research Surrounding Power Consumption and Performance Issues in Utility Computing* (pp. 304–319). Hershey, PA: IGI Global. doi:10.4018/978-1-4666-8853-7.ch015

Swargiary, D., Paul, J., Amin, R., & Bordoloi, H. (2015). Eye Ball Detection Using Labview and Application for Design of Obstacle Detector. In K. Sarma, M. Sarma, & M. Sarma (Eds.), *Intelligent Applications for Heterogeneous System Modeling and Design* (pp. 186–203). Hershey, PA: IGI Global. doi:10.4018/978-1-4666-8493-5.ch008

Swarnkar, M., & Bhadoria, R. S. (2016). Security Aspects in Utility Computing. In G. Deka, G. Siddesh, K. Srinivasa, & L. Patnaik (Eds.), *Emerging Research Surrounding Power Consumption and Performance Issues in Utility Computing* (pp. 262–275). Hershey, PA: IGI Global. doi:10.4018/978-1-4666-8853-7.ch012

Tchendji, V. K., Myoupo, J. F., & Dequen, G. (2016). High Performance CGM-based Parallel Algorithms for the Optimal Binary Search Tree Problem. *International Journal of Grid and High Performance Computing, 8*(4), 55–77. doi:10.4018/IJGHPC.2016100104

Tian, J., & Zhang, H. (2016). A Credible Cloud Service Model based on Behavior Graphs and Tripartite Decision-Making Mechanism. *International Journal of Grid and High Performance Computing, 8*(3), 38–56. doi:10.4018/IJGHPC.2016070103

Tiru, B. (2015). Exploiting Power Line for Communication Purpose: Features and Prospects of Power Line Communication. In K. Sarma, M. Sarma, & M. Sarma (Eds.), *Intelligent Applications for Heterogeneous System Modeling and Design* (pp. 320–334). Hershey, PA: IGI Global. doi:10.4018/978-1-4666-8493-5.ch014

Tripathy, B. K. (2014). Multi-Granular Computing through Rough Sets. In B. Tripathy & D. Acharjya (Eds.), *Advances in Secure Computing, Internet Services, and Applications* (pp. 1–34). Hershey, PA: IGI Global. doi:10.4018/978-1-4666-4940-8.ch001

Vadhanam, B. R. S., M., Sugumaran, V., V., V., & Ramalingam, V. V. (2017). Computer Vision Based Classification on Commercial Videos. In M. S., & V. V. (Eds.), Multi-Core Computer Vision and Image Processing for Intelligent Applications (pp. 105-135). Hershey, PA: IGI Global. doi:10.4018/978-1-5225-0889-2.ch004

Valero-Lara, P., Paz-Gallardo, A., Foster, E. L., Prieto-Matías, M., Pinelli, A., & Jansson, J. (2016). Multicore and Manycore: Hybrid Computing Architectures and Applications. In Q. Hassan (Ed.), *Innovative Research and Applications in Next-Generation High Performance Computing* (pp. 107–158). Hershey, PA: IGI Global. doi:10.4018/978-1-5225-0287-6.ch006

Winkler, M. (2016). Triadic Substructures in Complex Networks. In N. Meghanathan (Ed.), *Advanced Methods for Complex Network Analysis* (pp. 125–147). Hershey, PA: IGI Global. doi:10.4018/978-1-4666-9964-9.ch005

Xu, H., Rong, H., Mao, R., Chen, G., & Shan, Z. (2016). Hilbert Index-based Outlier Detection Algorithm in Metric Space. *International Journal of Grid and High Performance Computing, 8*(4), 34–54. doi:10.4018/IJGHPC.2016100103

Xu, R., & Faragó, A. (2016). Connectivity and Structure in Large Networks. In N. Meghanathan (Ed.), *Advanced Methods for Complex Network Analysis* (pp. 180–195). Hershey, PA: IGI Global. doi:10.4018/978-1-4666-9964-9.ch007

Youssef, B., Midkiff, S. F., & Rizk, M. R. (2016). SNAM: A Heterogeneous Complex Networks Generation Model. In N. Meghanathan (Ed.), *Advanced Methods for Complex Network Analysis* (pp. 215–236). Hershey, PA: IGI Global. doi:10.4018/978-1-4666-9964-9.ch009

Zahera, H. M., & El-Sisi, A. B. (2017). Accelerating Training Process in Logistic Regression Model using OpenCL Framework. *International Journal of Grid and High Performance Computing, 9*(3), 34–45. doi:10.4018/IJGHPC.2017070103

Zelinka, I. (2016). On Mutual Relations amongst Evolutionary Algorithm Dynamics and Its Hidden Complex Network Structures: An Overview and Recent Advances. In N. Meghanathan (Ed.), *Advanced Methods for Complex Network Analysis* (pp. 319–342). Hershey, PA: IGI Global. doi:10.4018/978-1-4666-9964-9.ch013

Ziesche, S., & Yampolskiy, R. V. (2017). High Performance Computing of Possible Minds. *International Journal of Grid and High Performance Computing, 9*(1), 37–47. doi:10.4018/IJGHPC.2017010104

About the Author

Natarajan Meghanathan is a tenured Full Professor of Computer Science at Jackson State University, Jackson, MS. He graduated with a Ph.D. in Computer Science from The University of Texas at Dallas in May 2005. Dr. Meghanathan has published more than 175 peer-reviewed articles (more than half of them being journal publications). He has also received federal education and research grants from the U. S. National Science Foundation, Army Research Lab and Air Force Research Lab. Dr. Meghanathan has been serving in the editorial board of several international journals and in the Technical Program Committees and Organization Committees of several international conferences. His research interests are Wireless Ad hoc Networks and Sensor Networks, Graph Theory and Network Science, Cyber Security, Machine Learning, Bioinformatics and Computational Biology. For more information, visit http://www.jsums.edu/nmeghanathan.

Index

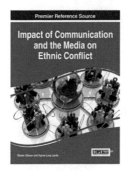

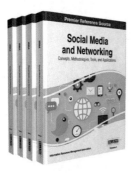
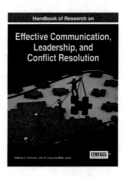

Stay Current on the Latest Emerging Research Developments

Become an IGI Global Reviewer for Authored Book Projects

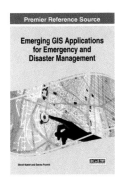

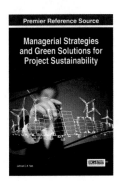

The overall success of an authored book project is dependent on quality and timely reviews.

In this competitive age of scholarly publishing, constructive and timely feedback significantly decreases the turnaround time of manuscripts from submission to acceptance, allowing the publication and discovery of progressive research at a much more expeditious rate. Several IGI Global authored book projects are currently seeking highly qualified experts in the field to fill vacancies on their respective editorial review boards:

Applications may be sent to:
development@igi-global.com

Applicants must have a doctorate (or an equivalent degree) as well as publishing and reviewing experience. Reviewers are asked to write reviews in a timely, collegial, and constructive manner. All reviewers will begin their role on an ad-hoc basis for a period of one year, and upon successful completion of this term can be considered for full editorial review board status, with the potential for a subsequent promotion to Associate Editor.

If you have a colleague that may be interested in this opportunity, we encourage you to share this information with them.

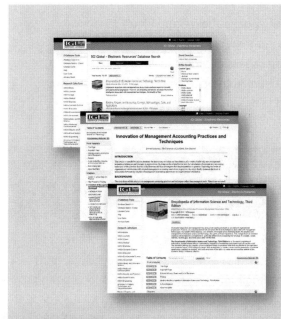